Spiritual Letters

Titles in the *New Ark Library*

Spiritual Letters

John Chapman

Capy 2

Sheed and Ward
London

Copyright © 1935 by the Trustees of Downside Abbey. First published 1935; this edition 1976, reprinted 1983. ISBN 0 7220 7671 1. All rights reserved. *Nihil obstat* Stephen Marron, Censor. *Imprimatur* William Lee, Clifton, 8 January 1935. Printed in Great Britain for Sheed & Ward Ltd, 2 Creechurch Lane, London EC3A 5AQ by Biddles Ltd, Guildford, Surrey.

PREFACE TO THE FIRST EDITION

THE late Abbot Chapman was best known to the outside world through his writings in connection with Biblical and Patristic Studies, which placed him in the front rank of modern critical scholars both in England and on the Continent. To his personal friends, however, and especially to his brethren in the Religious State, this side of his life and work was only one facet of a character whose versatility and brilliance would have sufficed to win him fame in many different spheres of learning; for his knowledge of classical literature, philosophy, Church history and Art was such that, had he chosen to specialize in them, he might have ranked as high in these branches of study as in Scripture or Patrology.

In the life of a monk, however, such external work must always be a secondary thing, his main pre-occupation being the direct service of God, by self-abnegation and by prayer, both liturgical and private. Only the time left over from priestly and monastic duties can be given to those activities of which the outside world sees most, and by which it estimates the " usefulness " of monasticism; for, with magnificent arrogance, the world values monastic institutions for the service rendered by them to itself, ignoring that rendered directly to God !

From the monk's point of view the exact opposite is the case, and such, of course, was Abbot Chapman's attitude. Consequently, while he gladly placed his great learning at the disposal of all who sought his aid, he never hesitated to put such work on one side or leave it unfinished, when called upon to preach Retreats, hear

Confessions, attend a Sick-call, or do any of the multifarious duties to which a Regular, no less than a Secular Priest is liable.

Though one of the least sentimental of men, to whom any suggestion of a *cher maître* attitude was most repugnant, Abbot Chapman possessed great gifts of sympathy and understanding. With these were united kindness, thought for others, and a generosity of soul which made him simply unable to resist any appeal for help, no matter whence it came. As a young monk, at Maredsous, he had been a pupil of Dom Columba Marmion, probably the most famous Retreat-giver of modern times, and within a few years of his ordination in 1895 he found himself called upon to give Retreats, his audiences being most frequently Clergy or Religious. In this, as in all his work, he was above all things methodical, and he therefore worked out a definite scheme or theory as a basis for his discourses. This scheme he never departed from, though its treatment was modified to suit different audiences, so that he used to say he had only *one* Retreat, and in consequence would not go a second time to a convent or seminary where he had already been. But his teaching was so striking, and the method of its presentation so original, that a Retreat from him not unfrequently gave a fresh start to some of those who heard him, and led them to re-shape their inner life anew on the experience of that one week.

In this way his reputation as a guide in things spiritual spread widely, and a steady stream of letters came to him asking for advice and help. Such letters he never failed to answer with his own hand, the replies being often many pages in length ; and after his death it seemed to me that a collection of these, if it could be got together, would form the best memorial to him, and especially to that side of his life and work which he himself would have ranked highest, albeit so little known to the outside world. In the last few years of his life, when I acted as his Secretary, he used not unfrequently to read portions of such letters to me before despatching them, to make sure that his meaning was clear. In this way I learned the names of a number of his correspondents, and in answer to my appeal many of these have allowed me to include his letters to them in the present collection. For obvious reasons I have omitted their names and any personal details which might reveal their identity,[1] but I wish to put on record here my deep sense of gratitude to those whose generous co-operation has thus made possible the achievement of my plan.

There must, no doubt, be a number of others who received letters of this kind from Abbot Chapman, and if this volume comes into the hands of any of these, I would beg to be allowed to see such letters and to incorporate them in a later edition of the work, should this be called for.

As the collection gradually came together, the letters fell naturally into two main classes, viz. those to persons living in the world, and those to Religious and Priests. I have adopted this division therefore, grouping the letters to each correspondent in chronological order, the various groups being arranged according to the date of the first letter in each series ; so that the development of Abbot Chapman's views and those of his correspondent might appear so far as possible. One series, however, written to a friend of special intimacy, is so exceptional that I have kept it apart from the rest in Part III. This group of letters covers a period of more than twelve years, from the time when its recipient was a young Scholastic

---

[1] One exception to this rule was unavoidable, viz. the letters written in 1930 to the Editor of *The Dublin Review*. As these could not be printed without shewing to whom they were written, Mr. Algar Thorold has kindly allowed me to let his name appear.

until after his ordination to the priesthood. It differs from the rest, moreover, in one important respect, viz. that while it took its origin like the rest in an appeal for help and guidance, the position of master and disciple is largely modified, if not actually reversed in the later letters, when Abbot Chapman writes to his correspondent as to one whose knowledge and experience in matters spiritual equal, if they do not surpass, his own.

To prevent possible misunderstanding on the part of readers who never knew Abbot Chapman personally, it may be well to mention some traits of his character which come out in the letters. Throughout his life a sense of humour, fantastic and peculiarly his own, flickered over and illuminated all he said and did, even when—as here —he was desperately in earnest. Like St. Teresa or Blessed Thomas More, to both of whom he had a great devotion, Abbot Chapman thought that a man's religion was likely to be all the more sincere if he was able to make jokes about it ; and such flashes of wit will be found not unfrequently in the letters, helping to light up the deepest subjects and give point to his wisdom. To argue from these that the writer is dealing with serious matters in a flippant way, would be to do him a grave injustice.

He possessed, too, an exceptional clearness of mind coupled with a very rapid power of reasoning. This enabled him to detect at once any fallacy in a logical process, and to put his finger on the point where the argument went astray ; with the result that he was some-times impatient with those whose process of thought moved so much more slowly, or who got be-fogged in trying to reach their conclusions. In such cases the tempta-tion to startle his hearers with exaggeration or deliberate over-statement sometimes proved irresistible ; with the result that he had subsequently to explain some passage which had been taken too literally or even misunderstood.

It must be remembered also that the letters here printed were written straight off, *currente calamo*, with nothing like a rough draft or preparatory plan to guide him. This fact, the truth of which I can personally vouch for, makes their logical sequence and wonderful clearness the more remarkable, for very few men can see a subject as a whole, and divide it in their mind into heads and subheads, in the way Abbot Chapman habitually did, without first working it out on paper. Very many of the letters, too, were written during the years when he was most deeply immersed in higher studies or in the practical details of ruling a large community, so that the time for writing them was snatched from other occupations, and the actual composition was subject to the constant interruptions which a Religious Superior has to suffer with patience and forbearance.

It is probably needless to mention that the letters were meant only for the benefit of the actual correspondents to whom they were written, no idea that they would be made public ever entering the Abbot's mind. But this fact adds not a little to their charm and interest as a revelation of his character, and of those qualities of mind and heart which led so many—friends and strangers alike—to turn to him for help and guidance. It also explains why, when writing to a correspondent who could be trusted to understand him rightly, he is occasionally less exact in his use of theological terms than he would have been in writing for publication.

In one case Abbot Chapman—contrary to his usual rule—had one of his letters copied before it was despatched. This is Letter No. XLIII " To an Augustinian Canoness ", in which he deals at considerable length with the subject of Contemplative Prayer. This letter was written during his year at Caldey Island, as Superior of the Benedictine community which had recently been reconciled to the

Catholic Church; and, when it was completed, he read it to one of his subjects to make sure that the whole was clear. The young monk begged to be allowed to make a copy of the letter for his own use, and this was subsequently shewn to others of the Caldey *familia*. Finding that what he had written seemed to be of use to a considerable number, Abbot Chapman revised the whole and allowed it to appear in *Pax*, the Caldey periodical. The number of *Pax* which contained it was speedily sold out, and the article was then reprinted as a leaflet, entitled "*Contemplative Prayer*, a few simple rules."[1] In this form it has been re-issued several times. As the leaflet is referred to in a number of the Letters, I have reprinted it as Appendix I to this volume, together with a Note containing some criticisms of it, which are replied to in Letter XXII.

In a number of the Letters Abbot Chapman deals with the subject of Mysticism, in which he was deeply interested. As, however, these references are largely tentative suggestions or discussions of difficult details, they leave the subject somewhat ' in the air '. I have therefore reprinted, as Appendix II, an article entitled " What *is* Mysticism ? " which was published by him in the *Downside Review* for January, 1928, so as to show his considered opinion on the whole subject. It should be added that the Notes to this Appendix are Abbot Chapman's own, those in other parts of the volume being by myself.

When preparing the book for publication, my original intention was to include in it a number of Abbot Chapman's other writings on things spiritual, especially his *Retreat*, with the idea that these should fill in the gaps inevitable to a collection of Letters, which cannot possess the homogeneity of a finished work, or give a complete view of the way in which the writer surveyed the spiritual life as a whole. It soon became clear, however, that such

[1] Copies of this leaflet, 3d. post free, may be obtained from the Editor.

a collection would be too large for a single volume, so as the Letters were ready for printing I decided to issue these first, leaving the other writings to be published later.

To supply some background for the Letters, therefore, and give them more connection, I have prefixed to these a short Memoir of Abbot Chapman; giving in Part I of this a brief outline of his life and active work, with some indication in Part II of what may be called the angle of vision from which he surveyed the spiritual horizon of life. In this way, it is hoped, those readers who never met him may be enabled to form some idea of his vivid personality, and of the very varied achievement of his well-filled life.

It is proposed shortly to issue a companion volume to the present one, which shall contain his *Retreat*, with a number of his other writings on things spiritual. When this is done, his teaching will appear as a consistent whole, in a way which cannot be expected of a work like the present, the contents of which were called forth by the needs of a number of different souls, most of whom already knew his general line of doctrine, and were trying to follow it out in practice.

When that is published, I hope to complete the Biography of him of which a considerable portion is already written. For this there exists a quantity of material of exceptional interest, which will make it possible to produce a portrait of him and an account of his work that shall be more worthy of his stature than the slight sketch prefixed to the present volume.

Downside Abbey, G. ROGER HUDLESTON.
November 7, 1934.

CONTENTS

Part III

LETTERS TO A JESUIT

Appendix I

Appendix II

SUPPLEMENT

A MEMOIR OF ABBOT CHAPMAN

A MEMOIR OF ABBOT CHAPMAN

BY

DOM ROGER HUDLESTON, O.S.B.

I

HENRY PALMER CHAPMAN, in religion Dom John, O.S.B., was the son of the Ven. F. R. Chapman, Archdeacon of Sudbury and Canon of Ely, and his wife, Mary Frances Bedford. He was born at Ashfield, Suffolk, on April 25, 1865, being the youngest of the family and the only boy. Put to join the lessons given to his sisters, while still almost a baby, he at once gave proof of exceptional intelligence and an astonishing memory; growing up practically bilingual, for he could not remember a time when he did not speak French almost as easily as English. As a child his delicacy of constitution occasioned anxiety, but in spite of this he was sent for a time to Dr. Hawtrey's famous Preparatory School, where he carried off practically every prize !

His father had intended that, on leaving Hawtrey's, the boy should go to Eton, but his health forbade this. Instead he remained at home from the age of fourteen, working with tutors for a few hours every day, and filling in the rest of his time by omnivorous reading, in which Art history and criticism, Architecture, Literature, and Poetry figured largely; varied by occasional dashes into Egyptology, Hebrew, Music and Sketching, with many hours of novel-reading, English, French, German, and Italian. It was, as he himself described it, "a curious

I

preparation for life ", and it left its mark upon him to the end, thanks to his amazing memory. But he lost the one great advantage of a public-school education; viz. that process of erosion, whereby the too protuberant features of a boy's character are ground down by rubbing shoulders with some hundreds of other boys. Had he gone through the mill at Eton, Dom John would probably have emerged no less brilliant or original, but more tolerant of stupidity, more patient with those who could not keep pace with his rapidity of thought and argument, and without the tendency to overstress some notes of his personality, which jarred at times, and led some to judge him unfairly. His health improved steadily during this period, however, and, while never a strong man, he developed a physique which was equal to the exacting demands he made upon it by his life of unceasing work as monk and student.

At Michaelmas 1883 he entered at Christ Church, Oxford, but did not go into residence until the following January. A photograph taken at this date shows him as a decidedly handsome young man, with a heavy dark moustache, who evidently took considerable pains over his toilet; a conclusion borne out by a contemporary, who writes of him :—

One remembers him endowed with social gifts which made him acceptable and welcome among men of quite different types. Highly strung, vivacious, overflowing with humour, brilliant in conversation, he was never the creature of moods; his self-control and his will being even then far more disciplined than we thought. There was much about him in his Oxford days which would have made those whose knowledge of him was only superficial smile at the thought of his ever becoming a monk. Extremely well dressed, because it never occurred to him that you could get your clothes from any but one particular London tailor, or your boots from anyone but Peal, or wear any coat in winter except a fur one. It never occurred to him that you could play on anything but a grand piano; so a grand piano was in his rooms and in his lodgings.

That he did a considerable amount of work during his years at Oxford is proved by the fact of his taking a first in Greats; though he personally declared his success to be " more due to cleverness in essay-writing and a very quick concentration of thought, added to a real love of philosophy, than to any accurate stores of learning ".

After taking his degree, in the summer of 1887, he stayed up at Oxford for another year reading Theology, in which he took a third. But the year was an important once, since in it he decided finally to take Orders in the Church of England.

Archdeacon Chapman's father had been a partner in the firm of Herries, Farquhar and Chapman, Bankers, of St. James's Street, and the original plan for Dom John had been that, on going down from Oxford, he should obtain a post in the Treasury Office, which his family influence would secure for him, or possibly a berth in the Diplomatic Service. But in 1885 the death of his mother —to whom he had been devotedly attached—turned his thoughts in more serious directions; and the influence of some Oxford friends, notably that of his tutor (the late R. L. Ottley, subsequently Regius Professor of Pastoral Theology at Oxford), had decided him.

In July 1888 he went to Cuddesdon, the Theological College near Oxford, of which Ottley was now Vice-Principal—a fact which no doubt influenced his choice— and remained there a year. He already possessed a knowledge of Catholic Theology far beyond that of the average Church of England clergyman; for, in a letter of this date, he mentions " St. Thomas, Scotus, St. Bonaventure, Vasquez, Soto, Suarez ", among the authors he has " read and analysed ". The chief effect of his time at Cuddesdon, therefore, was on the spiritual side, and he began there that inner life, with its habits of prayer and regularity, which, humanly speaking, led him to the cloister, and made him essentially a contemplative, despite his diverse interests and varied activities.

In June 1889, having accepted the offer of a curacy at the parish of St. Pancras, London, he was ordained deacon at St. Paul's by Bishop Temple, and entered at once on his duties, under the Rev. H. L. Paget (subsequently Bishop of Chester), who was then Vicar of St. Pancras. Despite some misgivings as to his fitness for parish work, his strong sense of duty made him throw all his energies into it; but it proved disappointing and distasteful. The parish contained a large proportion of mean streets; the houses being let out in tenements, whose occupants changed too often to permit any real influence being brought to bear upon them. " I found the smells and the filth of the overcrowded houses appalling," he wrote; and, like many over-sensitive men, he worried constantly about the conditions under which his people lived, forgetting that they were so accustomed thereto as to be almost unconscious of what, to him, were so many petty horrors.

More serious grounds for worry were not long in appearing, for Dom John, whose reading had embraced many works of history as well as of theology, found himself involved in ever deepening difficulties as to the position of the Church of England, and the validity of High Church pretensions; of which his keenly logical mind and robust common sense—while they made it easy for him to grasp and accept the entire system of Catholic theology—became increasingly suspicious. As a preliminary to ordination he had, of course, to swear to the

XXXIX Articles, but he disliked doing so intensely, writing a day or two later: "I confess that I have still qualms of conscience, and that never in my life have I committed any action which made me feel so uncomfortable."

He seems to have been assured that work in a parish would allay his doubts by creating new interests. But long before the year he had to serve as a deacon was completed, he had become too uncertain of his position to proceed to priest's orders, and he felt obliged to tell his vicar that he thought he ought not to continue working at St. Pancras. On the latter's suggestion he spent a short holiday at Oxford; but long hours of study at the Bodleian and the Pusey House, aided by conferences with Dr. Gore and the learned Canon Bright of Christ Church, both of whom were old friends of his, brought no restoration of confidence in the Anglican position, but rather confirmed the Catholic view. Then came Trinity Sunday with the reminder that he ought properly to have been ordained priest on that day, had not his difficulties made this impossible; and a little later he left the parish for good.

Just at this date it chanced that Archdeacon Chapman had taken a lease of Hengrave Hall, Suffolk, and there Dom John spent the next few months. The beautiful old Tudor house—the seat of the Gage family, which had always remained Catholic—contained a library of Catholic books as well as a private chapel; the tenants, however, being precluded from holding services in the latter. Long hours of reading in the one and of prayer in the other brought no final decision, and eventually Dom John decided to go and spend some time quite alone, in a place where he knew nobody, and so would be free from the silent influences of home and family, which held his heart too firmly to allow his brain fair play.

In November 1890, therefore, he betook himself to Dovercourt, near Harwich, a little seaside resort quite destitute of visitors so late in the season, and there, in complete solitude, the last round of his spiritual conflict was fought. In a letter written from there to one of his greatest friends and confidants, he wrote:

"Please pray for me, as my difficulties are a real terror and agony. I am in a great strait. People talk lightly about 'secession' as the 'easy path'. If only they knew what it feels like ! And I have known it for six months almost unbearably. So pray for me— not that my path may be made easy, but that it may be plain, and that I may have the grace to walk in it by the light of the Lord."

Ten days were passed at Dovercourt in a solitude and silence that were all but absolute ; the sequel can be told in his own words:

"He had completed an intellectual and spiritual self-examination, and he could see only one course open to him. He might go on for ever reading, without getting any clearer. He had long had no belief in the Church of England. On the other hand, he saw a Church, one, historical, uninterrupted in her succession, unfaltering in her witness to truth, the Mother of the martyrs and the saints, outnumbering still all the many sects which had gone out from her. There was only one road to certainty, to intellectual satisfaction. He felt no attraction, only fear at the darkness before him. He saw the pain to his father, the division from friends, the complete change like death that threatened him. But he determined to act calmly and coldly, according to the dictates of reason, and with the help that he could count upon from prayer.

" One day more was spent in writing a few letters, the chief of which was to his father. He said that he had decided to go to London, and ask for instruction at the Oratory. He knew no priest personally. He added a list of books he had read—to show, he said, that he could not possibly have neglected any serious argument on either side. Another day passed in an attempt at some spiritual exercise. Next day he went, at last, to London."

On December 7, 1890, he was reconciled to the Catholic Church at the Oratory, by Father Kenelm Digby Best, who remained always one of his greatest friends.

No one who has not actually gone through the experience, can appreciate fully the mental suffering involved in such a severance from all that has hitherto been nearest and dearest in life, or tell the veritable agony which it entails on the soul which thus leaves everything for conscience' sake. Beside the anxiety of a leap into the unknown, and those lingering fears of Catholicism as a system which a Protestant upbringing bites into the soul as acid bites an etching into the copper, there is the cruel pain of knowing that the action, which seems an overpowering duty to him who does it, must cause the keenest suffering and bitterest disappointment to those whom, most of all, he hates to wound ; with the realization that what costs the convert so dear must seem, to those he leaves, a piece of wanton folly or infatuation, almost akin to madness.

Only too often the strain is so great that those relations of love and friendship, which promised to be eternal, snap beneath the severity of the test. It speaks eloquently for both sides when, as in Dom John's case, the old affectionate relations survive between the one who has " gone over to Rome " and so large a number of those he leaves behind him when he comes to the parting of the ways.

Among the friends Dom John had made at Cuddesdon there were two—R. P. Camm and L. B. Lasseter—who, like himself, had caught " Roman fever " but had made their submission more speedily. To both of them he wrote, at once, the news of his reception, and both replied begging him to go and see them; Brother Bede Camm from the Abbey of Maredsous, where he was now a Benedictine Novice, Mr. Lasseter from Rome, where he was completing his studies for the priesthood.

Dom John accepted both invitations, going to Maredsous for Christmas, and staying nearly three weeks there before going on to Rome, which he reached about the middle of January 1891. Soon afterwards he writes to a friend in England :

" You must pray for me, please, as I have a great deal to decide. I hope to know clearly what is God's will concerning me before I go back—whether I shall be a Benedictine or an Oratorian or what—or whether a Trappist, or a Jesuit, in or out of disguise ! However, if I pray a great deal, I am quite sure God will lead me. I am intensely happy, as you may suppose."

Three months later the decision was made, and after assisting at Lasseter's ordination on Holy Saturday, he returned to England ; spending a few days at Maredsous *en route*, before entering the Jesuit Noviciate at Manresa House, Roehampton, at the end of April 1891. Eight months there made it clear both to the Novice-Master and to himself that his vocation was not to the Society of Jesus. In December, therefore, he left Manresa, having first—on the advice of his Jesuit Directors—applied to the Abbot of Maredsous for admission to the Noviciate there. His petition being granted, the second Noviciate proved successful, and he took his simple vows a year later, on March 25, 1893; was ordained priest by special dispensation at Whitsuntide 1895, and solemnly professed at Erdington in October of that year.

The Priory of St. Thomas of Canterbury, at Erdington, was a foundation made by Benedictine monks of the Congregation of Beuron in the year 1876, at what was then a little village four miles out of Birmingham; but in the nineteen years which had elapsed only a single English subject had joined the community before the arrival of Dom Bede Camm and Dom John Chapman in 1895. In August 1896 Erdington was raised to the rank of an Abbey, and Abbot de Hemptinne of Maredsous—whom Pope Leo XIII had now appointed Abbot Primate of the Benedictine Order—endeavoured to secure the nomination of Dom John as its first Abbot, despite the very short time he had spent in the monastic state. The right of appointment, however, rested with Dom Placid Wolter, the Arch-abbot of Beuron, since Erdington had been founded by that Abbey; but the influence of Abbot de Hemptinne, who had formerly been Prior of Erdington and so possessed an intimate knowledge of the place and its needs, naturally carried great weight with him. For nearly three years the matter lay in abeyance, until at length Don Ansgar Höckelmann, a monk of Beuron who had lived for some time at Erdington, was appointed in July 1899. It was natural, no doubt, for a German Arch-abbot to appoint a German monk as Abbot of a monastery founded from Germany, with a community predominantly German; but in view of later developments the decision was unfortunate. The history both of Erdington and of Downside would have been different if the advice of Abbot de Hemptinne had been followed.

In his various offices—Sub-prior, Novice-Master and Prior—Dom John threw himself into the work of the place, striving especially to build up a community of English monks, who in time might replace those borrowed from various houses of the Beuron Congregation on the Continent. The time left free from conventual and official duties, he devoted to writing, and his numerous articles in the *Revue Bénédictine*, the *Journal of Theological Studies*, etc., dealing with knotty points of Patrology or early Church history, soon gained him a recognized position in the front rank of patristic scholars, both in England and abroad.

His reputation as an authority in such studies brought him a large correspondence, which made heavy inroads upon his time; for he never failed to reply to such letters, often writing at great length to correspondents unknown to him personally, who perhaps failed to realize the labour and research that were needed to answer their questions. He looked on such work as the way in which he could best serve the Catholic cause, and never grudged the time given to it, least of all when the appeal came from one in authority, as it did when Bishop Ilsley of Birmingham begged him to "write a popular pamphlet" in answer to Bishop Gore's book *The Roman Catholic Claims*; a cheap edition of which had been issued on the occasion of the latter's translation to the new Anglican See of Birmingham.

In this instance the labour was enormous, since it involved checking references by the hundred, examining passage after passage from the early Fathers, to see that the extracts were not used unfairly when divorced from their context, etc. The "popular pamphlet" thus grew into a highly technical work of some 80,000 words, the whole being completed in a bare three months ! As a reply to Dr. Gore it was overwhelming, but the publication had the unfortunate result of labelling Dom John as a controversialist in the eyes of the public, and it was a lifelong source of chagrin to him that his other far more important writings never corrected the impression thus established. He had hoped before his death to reissue a number of his most important articles, revised and corrected in the light of subsequent study, but apart from one volume, *Studies in the Early Papacy*, issued by Messrs. Sheed and Ward in 1928, nothing of the kind was achieved, and the vast extent of his learning can only be realized by those who will go to the labour of disinterring his work from the various learned periodicals wherein it lies entombed.

It was during the Erdington period, also, that he published his two most important books, viz. *John the Presbyter* and *Notes on the Early History of the Vulgate Gospels*, both issued by the Oxford Press in the year 1908. The former attacked, and one may say disposed of, the theory propounded by Professor Harnack and other critics, that the Fourth Gospel was written, not by the Apostle St. John, but by a certain " John the Presbyter " mentioned by Papias. It is a good example of his critical methods and especially of the use of sheer common sense in dealing with too ingenious theories, which was a feature of all his work. The latter book had an effect on his subsequent career, since it was primarily responsible for his being sent to Rome to work on the Commission for the Revision of the Vulgate, which occupied him for several years after the war.

Although he had lived in England since 1895, Dom John remained a monk of Maredsous, being only " lent " to Erdington by Abbot de Hemptinne. The latter had always cherished the idea of making another Foundation in England, if possible at Oxford, a scheme which had the enthusiastic support of Dom John. Nothing was done, however, and the idea had almost faded, when in 1909 Abbot de Hemptinne was succeeded as Abbot of Maredsous by an Irishman, Dom Columba Marmion. The unusual circumstance of a British subject being Abbot of the Belgian monastery not unnaturally revived the hopes of the English monks at Erdington, and the project of a new Foundation was taken up with energy by Dom John and others. Abbot Marmion, always more enthusiastic than practical, gave it his blessing, and a devout English layman, who had a scheme for establishing a Catholic village as a " dormitory " for Catholics working in London, volunteered to supply a site if the new Abbey would plant itself at an appropriate locality. It must be owned that the Abbot of Erdington threw cold water on the scheme, but as the new monastery was to be an offshoot of Maredsous, he could do no more than indicate the objections to it ; and these were thought to be counterbalanced by the support which it was felt could be relied upon from Abbot de Hemptinne, who was still Abbot Primate, though he had resigned his post as Superior of Maredsous.

For months letters passed between the various parties interested, and in 1911 Dom John and others inspected place after place, in search of a suitable property, with a house that could serve as a nucleus for the future Abbey. Eventually a place was actually chosen, near Dorking, the purchase price was agreed upon, the devout layman was ready to co-operate, and it only remained to secure official approval by the General Chapter of the Beuron Congregation, which discussed the proposal early in the year 1912. What precisely were the reasons governing its decision was not divulged, though it can hardly have ignored the danger to Erdington of a rival Beuronese monastery established in a position so far superior to that which had now become a suburb of Birmingham. But the result was an absolute veto of the scheme by authority, and a few weeks later Dom John was recalled to Maredsous by Abbot Marmion; he had been at Erdington almost seventeen years, the last seven of them as Claustral Prior.

He now spent nine months or so at Maredsous, or in giving retreats to various convents, planning to do some important literary work in the immediate future; but Providence had other designs for him. In February 1913 he learned of his appointment to the Commission for the Revision of the Vulgate, with the corollary that he would henceforth reside in Rome for the greater part of the year. But almost at once came the conversion of the Caldey Benedictines, and he was ordered instead to go to Caldey, as Superior, for a year at least; while Abbot Carlyle was doing his Noviciate at Maredsous. The appointment was one of no little difficulty and required all the tact and consideration Dom John possessed; since it laid on him the whole responsibility of forming the Anglican community into a Catholic one, and of substituting traditional Benedictine ideas and methods for those which had grown up and become habitual in the community during the years of its development in the Church of England. The number of *Pax* for January 1934 bears eloquent witness to his success in the duty imposed upon him, saying: " No one else could have discharged this very delicate task as he did."

His time at Caldey ended just as the world plunged into war in August 1914. There could be no question of a return to Maredsous, from which a number of the younger monks had fled to England, to be received for some months at Downside. There Dom John joined them, acting as their Professor of Theology until early in 1915, when they moved to Ireland and he was left free to take a commission as Chaplain to the Forces. He at once offered himself to the War Office, and after the usual delays was gazetted Chaplain and instructed to proceed to Salisbury Plain to join the —th Brigade of "Kitchener's Army". The brigade in question had completed its training and was waiting for a supply of rifles and machine-guns to enable it to take the field. But the delay of a couple of months or so proved an advantage to Dom John, since it gave him time to learn the ways of the Army, and get accustomed to a Chaplain's work before going to France. At last the long-awaited rifles arrived, and later still the machine-guns. A course of musketry practice was hurried through, and at the end of July 1915 the brigade arrived in France.

Dom John was now past fifty years old, and had never been a robust man, but he went through with the job he had undertaken, sharing the dangers and hardships of life in the trenches with the 12th King's Liverpools, to which he was attached. The autumn of 1915 was wretchedly wet, and the mud and misery of trench life under the conditions then prevailing will never be forgotten by those who endured them; but in his letters he made light of the whole. In September he injured one of his knees, and this, though fortunately it did not prevent him from riding as he went about his work, made the difficulties greater than before. He carried on, however, until mid-November, when the M.O. ordered him to hospital, in the hope that a week or two of rest would cure the trouble. Instead of this, it was found necessary to invalid him home, and he remained in hospital until Christmas Eve. After a short leave he was stationed at Boyton Camp, Wilts, for several months, and then returned to France until, at the end of 1917, he was transferred to Switzerland, where a Chaplain with the gift of tongues was urgently needed for the camps of interned prisoners, who were drawn from various nations and languages. Here he remained until the Armistice.

On demobilization, in 1919, Dom John at last took up his residence in Rome, at San Calisto, and began to work on the Vulgate Commission under Cardinal Gasquet, who had secured his appointment thereto in 1913; devoting to this practically all his time and energy until the end of 1922. He was already a recognized authority on the subject, and the large collection of photographs, collations of MSS., etc., already in the hands of the Commission enabled him to bring his knowledge to a very high degree of perfection.

Although Cardinal Gasquet was President of the Commission for the Revision of the Vulgate, he left the decision on points of textual criticism to his two chief assistants, since he was not himself an expert on this highly technical subject. Unfortunately, these two authorities did not see eye to eye on a fundamental issue; viz. the best method to adopt in deciding upon the text, where the MSS. gave variant readings. In spite of prolonged discussion no agreement had been arrived at when, in the end of 1922, the newly elected Abbot of Downside, Dom Leander Ramsay, asked that Dom John might return to Downside—to which Abbey he had been affiliated in 1919—to take up the post of Claustral Prior. After some hesitation Cardinal Gasquet agreed to release him, and on Christmas Eve he was installed in his new office.

With the return to Downside in December 1922 Dom John's life enters upon its last phase. The post of Claustral Prior gave scope for the use of his learning, which ranged over an extraordinary variety of subjects, for he was always ready to help any who came to consult him, whether in theology, philosophy, classics, art or music. He would be found in the School at one time, giving a class in religious instruction to the senior boys, or playing for the youthful musicians a programme of Chopin—which he still executed with great artistry, though perhaps a less skilful technique than in earlier years—at another time, in the monastery teaching scripture or theology or philosophy to the younger monks.

Despite all this, and the constant interruptions to which a prior is always subject, he found time to write a number of articles, many reviews of books, and in particular his last published volume, the brilliant, if sometimes too ingenious, study, *St. Benedict and the Sixth Century*, which appeared in 1929.

It did not take long for the resident *familia* at Downside to appreciate his greatness both of mind and heart, and he soon became the confidant and adviser of many in things spiritual and temporal alike. Consequently, when Abbot Ramsay died in March 1929, the community gave Dom John a supreme proof of their regard by choosing him for Abbot; a wonderful evidence of the position he had won among them since—almost a complete stranger —he had petitioned for affiliation to the Abbey, less than ten years before.

Plans for a permanent library and an additional wing to the monastery were the first things to occupy his mind. These he insisted on working out in detail himself, declaring—with characteristic exaggeration—that he had drawn many more plans in his life than any professional architect ! But he allowed Sir Giles Scott a free hand in designing a new science block, which was added to the school within a year of his election ; and the same artist was left untrammelled in designing the beautiful tomb over the grave of Cardinal Gasquet in the Abbey Church. The new choir-stalls, however, which are a replica of those at Chester, indicate Abbot Chapman's personal preference for purely imitative work—typical of the " Gothic Revival "—which he had acquired in his mid-Victorian youth, and retained, unaltered, to the end.

To supply the much-needed accommodation in the monastery, he had a wing of temporary cells erected on the west side of the cloister garth, and this—by the irony of fate—remains his sole addition to the monastery, since later developments led him to abandon the scheme he had elaborated so carefully for a library and permanent wing.

The plans for these had been approved and the site actually pegged out for digging the foundations when, in January 1932, he received private information that Milton Abbey, Dorset, was for sale. The news interested him enormously, since Milton was the only pre-Reformation Abbey not in ruins, which was in private hands and capable of reacquisition by the monks who had built it. Adjoining the beautiful Abbey Church was a great house, incorporating part of the former monastery, while, close at hand, was a Norman chapel, said to stand on the site of one built by Athelstane after the battle of Brunanburgh.

The offer had obvious attractions. First of all, it would secure the restoration of an ancient Benedictine Abbey to its original purpose ; secondly, it would permit a " swarm " of monks being sent out as the nucleus of a new foundation which, in time, would become an independent monastery ; thirdly, it would solve the much-discussed question of the Downside Junior School, by supplying new quarters for it, in a new environment, a point strongly recommended by modern educational opinion. Moreover, these three very desirable ends would be attained at smaller cost than the proposed additions at Downside.

There was, indeed, one obstacle to be surmounted ; viz. the fact that a former owner had given the vicar and parishioners of Milton Abbas the right to hold services in the Abbey, with an option—which still had several years to run—of taking it over as their parish church.

But the vendor, it was stated, had arranged, at his own cost, to recompense the vicar and parishioners for the surrender of their rights, and his offer had been accepted by them. In his enthusiasm, Abbot Chapman made light of this difficulty, but from the first there were not wanting those who regarded it as insurmountable. In the end this view proved the right one. Downside withdrew from the field, and Milton Abbey passed into the ownership of the Ecclesiastical Commissioners.

The failure of his scheme was an acute disappointment to the Abbot, but he had become more convinced than ever that Downside ought to make a new foundation and move the Junior School to it; so the autumn and winter of 1932–33 saw him scouring the southern half of England in search of a property suited for this purpose. More than two hundred places were offered to him. Twenty-nine of these he inspected in person, and in two cases negotiations were carried almost to completion, only to break down when apparently on the eve of success. At length, in June 1933, his purpose was achieved by the purchase of the late Lord Cowdray's place at Worth, in Sussex.

Except for occasional attacks of asthma, Abbot Chapman kept his usual good health and tireless energy undiminished until the autumn of 1932, when he had an attack of influenza, insisted on getting up and resuming work before he should have done so, and caught a second bout of it. This pulled him down greatly, but he declined to abandon his house-hunting expeditions, though it was clear to those who accompanied him that the effort involved was becoming almost beyond his strength. Early in 1933 he made the long journey to Whitehaven, arrived there very unwell, and went to bed at once with a third attack of influenza, but again insisted on resuming work far too soon.

Though now obviously a sick man, he made light of his condition, only agreeing to go away for a fortnight on the Italian lakes with his sister and brother-in-law; and during this absence the negotiations for the purchase of Worth were completed. He returned for the Chapter meeting which approved the purchase and new foundation there, and at once set to work upon plans for adding a wing to the house. These he completed by the beginning of July, in spite of increasing weakness, but the effort was almost more than he could manage, and at last—when too late—he surrendered to the doctors, undergoing treatment for some weeks in a London nursing-home.

The next four months witnessed a steady decline in strength, as his illness gained upon him in spite of rest and change of scene. In October he returned to the same nursing-home for further treatment, but his strength was now unequal to the strain, and the doctors gave warning that the end was at hand. On November 6 he received the Last Sacraments while fully conscious, and sank quietly out of life twenty-four hours later. It was a strange feature of his illness that he had no pain at all throughout, only a steady increase of weakness until he died.

II

In the Preface to this volume reference has been made to Abbot Chapman's fame as a Retreat-giver, but for which it is probable that few of the letters here published would ever have been written, since many of his correspondents met him first in that capacity. His success in this sphere of work, however, was not due to oratorical skill or to charm of speech. Its source lay far deeper than such accidental features, though his remarkable clarity of exposition and originality of illustration certainly helped to hold the attention of his hearers.

I have mentioned how weak health caused the precocious boy, endowed by nature with exceptional intelligence, to be educated at home during the most impressionable years of his youth, and the long hours of solitary work and reading developed in him, at an exceptionally early age, the habit of thinking things out for himself. Consequently, when he went up to Oxford and studied philosophy for " Greats ", the need for a satisfying, logical theory of life, based upon first principles of unquestionable veracity, was felt by him with an urgency that is comparatively rare among Englishmen, who as a race are only too ready to let their mental processes remain arrested, and to be satisfied with a state of suspense which would be intolerable, say, to a Frenchman, with his characteristic clarity of mind and thought.

It was the failure to arrive at such a logical basis in regard to religion that led him out of Anglicanism into the Catholic Church. He had hoped that the lack of this, which had troubled him so much as an undergraduate, would be satisfied during his years of training at Cuddesdon, but this was far from being the case. As he wrote during his last term there:—

" He was quite aware that he had not yet solved the problems which had placed themselves in his path. He had not even a working theory of the Church, and he felt very vague about a Rule of Faith. But he was not so much distressed as simply disappointed. He perceived that those around him had even less of foundation than he himself had, and he was in hopes that the question would gradually answer itself. Perhaps he had been premature and over-selfconfident in expecting to solve such fundamental difficulties at once.

" Yet it was a disappointment. The High Church views which he had embraced had seemed to take him by the hand and lead him into a pleasant garden of devotion, rich with the blossoms and fruit that ancient and mediæval sanctity had brought forth. Therein he had found satisfying and solid food for sanctification and had seemed to see vistas opening out before him of self-renouncing perfection and of union with God. He had confidently expected that the same school of teaching, which appeared to do so much for his soul, would equally convince his reason, and at once supply him with an intellectual explanation of life, and satisfy the yearnings of a rational nature for system, logic and consistency. At the least, he had supposed that he should find at Cuddesdon a body of teaching, distinct, certain, accepted and proved to the hilt, about the Rule of Faith, the nature of Authority and such matters. He had found in reality, not only that the students cared for none of these things—which was hardly surprising —but that their instructors had only tentative views to offer."

It was not only clear dogmatic teaching, to satisfy his intellect, that he wanted, a set of definite principles was equally necessary to discipline the soul, to rule the will, control the emotions and direct conduct; and he realised that without this his spiritual life could never achieve any real and permanent success. As he wrote a little later:—

"Devotion, if it is to be reasonable, must be founded on what you believe, else it is only sentiment. When one has to teach and preach, one finds that one must have a stock of definite views—at least I have found it so. I know lots of men who talk any amount of vague piety, without knowing what they mean themselves, and certainly no one else knows. Not merely devotional feelings must be taken into account, but what can in practice be taught to others; and something more, Truth."

After his conversion he found what he needed in the study of Catholic theology, Dogmatic, Moral and Ascetic; the principles of which—he insisted—must be applied by the well-disposed soul in a business-like fashion, so as to avoid waste of time and energy. Further, each individual soul would require special attention and treatment, so that it might avoid practices which—however excellent in themselves, or however profitable they might be for others, or might have been for itself at an earlier period—were not only unprofitable for it here and now, but might perhaps be positively harmful. But how was the soul to decide such matters? The answer came quickly, once he was inside the fold of the Church, as he wrote some three months after his reception.

"I am very happy to be able to begin again as a little child. One gradually gets to know how ignorant one is in spiritual things. I have been my own Director, and that is very hard, though for an Anglican it is a necessity, since variety of faith prevents one's trusting anyone ; and also no one has the necessary training and experience of a Catholic Director.

" A place of supernatural holiness, like Maredsous, with its system and its helps and adjustments, is a wonderful revelation. There are no hot-house growths (like dear Cuddesdon), no imprudences, but real knowledge. With the Jesuits it will be the same, only more so. All those virtues of supernatural humility and interior mortification, those habits of the Presence of God and of Union with Christ at all times, which one has admired in the Saints, are *taught* to Religious, as if they were children at school, *and they learn them*. There are different systems of training, of course, and nothing could be more opposed than the Benedictine and Jesuit methods, for instance ; but they are for different vocations of different temperaments, and different work. *Omnis spiritus laudet Dominum.*"

No one, however, was stronger than Abbot Chapman in condemnation of over-direction. The real purpose of direction, he insisted, was to keep the soul humble, and prevent it from trusting to its unaided judgement, or putting too much confidence in its own lights. He was fully alive to the dangers to which an imprudent Director could expose his penitents, realising how disastrous it was if—as sometimes happened—direction should degenerate into an orgy of self-analysis or over-introspection. A good Director, he held, must be a nurse, no more. He should confine himself to the task of teaching his penitent how to walk alone and unaided. That done, he should be ready to retire into the background ; only emerging on rare occasions when unusual circumstances or some particular crisis called for his assistance. Directors of this kind would be no danger to simplicity or humility, while an over-dogmatic or too eager Director, giving unsuitable or unnecessary advice with relish and impressiveness, would harm both his penitent and himself.

The spiritual life is nourished—to speak of natural means only—chiefly by prayer and by reading, and on these Abbot Chapman had clear views. With regard to books, he insisted on two definite principles; *first*, that one should read only what appealed to one, and *secondly*, that different books were necessary at different times in the soul's progress. On the second of these points, it may be of interest to note the stages in his own case. In his Anglican days he relied most on *The Imitation of Christ*, which he called "that most wonderful of all human books", Book II, Chapter 8, *De familiari amicitia Jesu*, being his favourite portion of the work.

In a letter written on June 12, 1895, four days after his Ordination as a Priest, he mentions as the books most dear to him at that date, St. Francis de Sales, *On the Love of God*, the *Spiritual Combat* of Scupoli, especially the little book, *Of inward peace*, at the end of this, and the section on *L'Abandon* in Mgr. Gay's *Les Vertues Chretiennes*. Later on he came to value most highly the writings of St. Teresa, and later still those of St. John of the Cross, while in the last decade or so of his life he obtained more help from Père de Caussade, S.J., and especially from his Letters, than from any writer since St. Francis de Sales. Two others whom he loved and quoted frequently were Blosius, and the Jesuit Père Grou, whose *Maximes Spirituelles* was the only book besides his Breviary which he took with him to the nursing-home where he died.

The letters here printed are concerned especially with prayer. Here he was on ground peculiarly his own.

" He knew more about Prayer than anyone I have ever met," wrote one whose own writings on the subject are famous ; and this would be confirmed by all who have had first-hand experience of his dealings with souls.

His two favourite maxims on the subject were these :—

First, " Pray as you can, and don't try to pray as you can't ! " and secondly, " The less you pray, the worse it goes."

Put very briefly his argument would be as follows. Our Faith is the most precious gift we have, because it leads us to a supernatural form of life. If our Faith is to be made vivid, it must be by meditation. We are told that " Faith cometh by hearing ", and we believe what God tells us through His messengers. But we have to do more than hear it, merely. Meditation is meant to make our Faith real to us, so that we shall realise in our lives what we know and believe. So long as we can meditate in our prayer, we must ; but what happens when we can't ?

At the outset of their spiritual life people can't speak to God or realise what He is. He is distant from them. Then He seems to come nearer, and they can speak to Him, and their prayer tends to become more affective. Before long, all their prayer becomes affective, all colloquy ; what Fr. Baker calls " the Prayer of forced acts of the Will ". Later still this too goes, and they pass into the prayer of aspirations. This happens with most Religious, and with practically all those in the more contemplative orders.

" I don't think," he wrote, " that Father Baker means that one kind of prayer grows into another, though one may read it so. I think there is a definite break. Meditation stops, and contemplation begins. This is described with the greatest care by St. John of the Cross, the greater part of whose writings were written for beginners. I know it is not generally held that St. John of the Cross wrote for beginners, most people nowadays would say just the contrary. So I was delighted to read in an old Italian book—written by a Carmelite and almost contemporary with St. Teresa and St. John of the Cross[1]—that ' Our Mother Teresa wrote for the advanced, and our Father Fra John of the Cross for beginners'. This is the early Carmelite tradition."

As a part of this process, he held, souls must expect to go into and through what St. John of the Cross calls the " Night of the Senses " and the " Night of the Spirit ", each of these having an active and a passive side. " The Active Night is what *we* do; our acts of mortification, etc. The Passive Night is what God does to us; taking away all that keeps us from Him." Thus the Night of the Senses is the purgation of the lower part of the soul— the bodily senses, imagination and emotions. The Night of the Spirit is the purgation of the higher part of the soul —the intellect and the will. When the soul has passed through both these Nights, it is ready for the completest union with God which is possible in this world.

In order to test his theory, Abbot Chapman interrogated a large number of Religious, both monks and enclosed nuns. His conclusion was that nearly all such go into the Night of the Senses. The first symptom of this is their inability to " meditate " in mental prayer. The second is that no consolation is derived from mental prayer any longer, yet all the time the soul craves for God. This, he maintained, *is* the " Night of the Senses ", because all sensible love and satisfaction in the spiritual life has gone. Meditation has done its work. It has led the soul to God, and the soul now wants merely to be with Him, not to think about Him—not even about His Passion—but to

[1] Joseph de Jesus-Maria. See Letter xc, and note to same, p. 265.

think of Him as present here and now. The lower nature has been filled with the thought of God. Meditation has prepared the way for God to come, and He has come. He has taken possession of the will, and the soul no longer wants sensible pleasure. But this is a different life from what we have been accustomed to, and therefore it is uncomfortable, and its prayer feels to the soul as if it was simply waste of time. "There are two states in which the soul can be ; consolation and aridity. To say ' O God, I love Thee so much ', is the prayer of consolation ; but what is *our* love, it is so miserable and unworthy. To say ' O God, I love Thee so little ! ' is the prayer of aridity. Let us be satisfied with either ; whatever God gives is best. But if we are to choose, I should say perhaps that the last is the better. Aridity is fervour, and if God wants it, it is best for us ; besides it keeps us humble."

So we simply have to do our best to pray in the way God wishes us to pray, not to ask for feelings of consolation, or for this or that or the other ; but to unite our wills to God's will, and wish for whatever He wishes to give us, and will to be whatever He wills us to be. "My God, I only want Thee ! "

In practice, therefore, he maintained, the soul has most need of Hope ; for Hope is, in a sense, more necessary for it than any other virtue. Not, of course, Hope in the ordinary sense, as meaning, "I hope, but I am not sure" ; but Hope in the theological sense of looking forward with absolute confidence, in the expectation that God will give us everything which is necessary to bring us to the end He has in view for us. "We are saved by Hope,"[1] says St. Paul. How ? Because Hope brings us through all trials and difficulties to our last end, thus securing the grace of final perseverance. Or in other words, because Hope gives us confidence in God.

[1] Romans viii. 24.

27

Hope has two parts :—(1) Courage, or high aims, and (2) Perseverance.

High aims make us resolve to attempt something difficult ; great things are not accomplished by accident, we must aim at them. We aim at being Saints. Not, as Aristotle said, because it is worthy of us, but because we know God wants it. This is really a part of humility, because we confide in God to help us. It is the courageous souls who attain, who think nothing too hard, too difficult. It is easy to *say* in our prayer that our aim is to give as God has given, i.e. to give up our wills absolutely to Him, to love Him as much as possible ; but it requires great courage to keep this up in our lives, all day and every day, and not to give way to discouragement when we see how miserably we fall short of this in practice, how great a difference there is between what we are in prayer and out of it !

Perseverance comes in here, we get nothing without perseverance, and this requires concentrated effort. Here again God treats different souls differently. Some seem to get immense graces, and become spiritual giants at once, some go crawling along so slowly that there seems to be no visible progress. But if we never know when we are beaten, we shall go on, and get through difficulties. We *must* persevere, even if we have to go on fighting against the devil, or the weaknesses of our fallen nature all through our lives.

Confidence in God is therefore the essential part of Hope. In worldly matters self-confidence carries us a long way, but in spiritual matters we can do nothing without God. Our confidence in God is absolutely justified, because we know that God *can* help us and that He *will*. God is essentially goodness, and this goodness takes the form of mercy to us sinners, to us who have no right to it. God wants us to go to heaven, therefore He draws us by His grace, and is always drawing us. Our confidence consists in saying to Him: "Draw us, we will run after Thee."

Consequently we must have confidence in God's actions, i.e. in His way of treating us. We get trials and troubles, and we think that some of them are not good for us. But God knows best. He knows what we do not know, i.e. what He means to make of us; and so He will work at us in His own way. We don't understand what He is doing to us, so confidence in Him is necessary. It is very like Humility, which means that we put no confidence in self, but unlimited confidence in God. "I am nothing, I can do nothing, but God can do all in me."

To see how important Hope is, let us look at its contrary, despair, or at the half-way house, discouragement. This keeps us back and prevents our going faster. Père de Caussade wrote *L'Abandon à la Providence Divine* for some holy nuns, who were in the Night of the Spirit and in great desolation, fearing they would be lost. So our Holy Father St. Benedict tells us, in the last of his *Instruments of good works*, 'Never to despair of the mercy of God'.

In practice then, Hope, with its components Courage and Perseverance, comes back to *l'abandon à Dieu*. Abbot Chapman had held and taught this doctrine for many years, but the writings of Père de Caussade, which he met with only in the last decade of his life, did not merely confirm his doctrine, but carried it a step further.

The development peculiar to de Caussade consists in this: that, while every soul which is really trying to live an interior life endeavours to do God's holy will always, everywhere and in all things, de Caussade insists that it best achieves its end, *not* by anxious search after God's 'signified will' (*voluntas signi*), not by deliberate acts of resignation to his 'will of good pleasure' (*voluntas bene-placiti*), but by simply receiving what comes to it, moment by moment, and abandoning itself thereto ; accepting and *willing* everything *because* it comes as God's will for that soul *hic et nunc*, in this actual moment of time, which is the only moment in the soul's control. This view of the present as literally a 'revelation' or unveiling of God's will for me at the precise instant in which I have to do that will, de Caussade calls 'the Sacrament of the present moment'—an illuminating phrase which, by its startling originality, brings home the value of his teaching that God reveals His will to us under the outward and visible circumstances of our lives, in much the same way as He imparts His graces to us under the tangible symbols of His sacraments.

De Caussade's doctrine and method—at once so simple and so complete—became therefore Abbot Chapman's ruling principle in the last years of his life. He never tired of inculcating it upon others, holding that this '*abandon*' to God's will was essentially *active*, since by it the soul did not merely resign itself to and accept whatever came to it, but *willed* this, and so participated actively in what God was doing in its regard at every moment.

On the last day of his life, when administering the last Sacraments to him, I ventured to remind him how he had always insisted upon this as essentially the right attitude for a Christian soul, and that at the hour of death it must apply without qualification.

" Yes," he said at length, after a long silence. " That is true, quite true. If God sees best for me to die, what in the world should one wish to live for ? "

G. R. H.

Part I

LETTERS TO LAY FOLK

LETTERS TO LAY FOLK

I: TO ONE LIVING IN THE WORLD.

The Abbey,
Isle of Caldey,
June 30, 1914. *nr. Tenby.*

My dear . . . .

I expect the interior peace you would like to have is not attainable under the circumstances. But there is another interior peace, which consists in simply willing what God wills, even though it seems to be just the unpleasant distraction and exteriorizing which one supposes to be bad for one. The only thing is to accept all the circumstances of one's life, and all the effect they seem to produce upon one, and use them as means of annihilating one's own will, cheerfully and willingly. There is no other recipe for prayer, I think.

Ever yours affec.,
fr. JOHN CHAPMAN, O.S.B.

II: TO THE SAME.

30th General Hospital,
Aug. 29, 1916. *No.* 4 *A.P.O., B.E.F.*

My dear . . . .

Though I cannot give you absolute "direction", I can tell you my views, which I hold rather strongly.

I do not think that at the present day it is possible to follow the mediaeval rule that every idea of entering

33

religious life should be followed up, and that the question needs no discussion, because it is obviously the desire of something better.

On the contrary, I hold that the rule to be followed is this : " I am not meant to be a religious, unless God *forces* me into it ". In other words, if a man feels " I *must* ", then it is a true vocation, and not otherwise.[1]

A mere wish is not sufficient. The mere feeling that it is a higher life will not carry a man through the noviciate. Not even an intellectual conviction, resting on well-reasoned premises :—the life is suitable to me, and I am meant for the life—, will be sufficiently strong as a motive. The number of novices who leave before many months are up, is large. Unfortunately there are even some who leave after their simple vows.

As to the desire of time for prayer, and separation from the world, you would probably be disappointed in almost any community. And then you would regret having entered, and would wonder if you had mistaken your vocation.

It seems to me that it is the right thing for a " director " to discourage people who think they have a vocation. If it is real, it will vanquish all obstacles, and will stand out, not as a mere invitation, but as a categorical imperative. Unless it takes that form in your case, I think you should simply dismiss it from your mind, not as a temptation, but as a waste of strength. There are many people who waste their energy in imagining they are meant to be religious, and (alas !) they " try their vocation " again and again. They do no good and get no good.

On the other hand, do not be afraid of " spiritual pride ". The religious state is a state of humility. If God *should* mercifully call you to the safer path, thank Him for preserving you from dangers which others can tackle. Especially if you want to pray well, you must

[1] For explanation of this passage see p. 38, par. 2.

34

feel yourself absolutely unworthy, weak, useless. And prayer will teach you humility. (I hope you have read *The Cloud of Unknowing*.) I think spiritual pride is not dangerous to anyone who tries seriously to serve God; the great danger is usually *despondency* (though this arises from a kind of pride :—wounded pride), because one is not better.

Again, if you are drawn to contemplative prayer, you are also drawn to a passive form of spirituality, in which God does all, while we wait and wonder. Consequently, give yourself to prayer, when you can, and trust in God that He will lead you, without your choosing your path. Mr. Asquith is an excellent model (not for Cabinet Ministers), but for contemplatives : wait for pressure from without ; do not act unless you must ; let the *Daily Mail* take the initiative.

Be sure that if you give yourself up blindly to God's Will, all will come right, though it may seem all wrong. Do not worry, but be confident. If you cannot pray in the least, and only waste time, and moon, and wander, still hold on ; on no account ever make a violent decision.

These are my views. I am not infallible. But I think they are reasonable, and work well in practice. Pray for me,

Ever yours in Dn̄o,

H. JOHN CHAPMAN, O.S.B., C.F.

III: TO THE SAME.

30th *General Hospital*,
No. 4 *A.P.O., B.E.F.*

Sept. 11, 1916.

My dear . . . .

From your letter, I certainly gather that you have no religious vocation. But it is extremely difficult to give any advice as to the details of your life ; it is so much a question of circumstances.

35

I don't see any reason for fearing spiritual pride. You must go in the way in which God leads you; it is a very ordinary way, and you will find yourself continually humiliated in it, especially by feeling that you are entirely unsuccessful in prayer. But don't give it up.

Of course you can meditate—anybody can. Only you can do it with a pencil in your hand, or a pipe. It is not prayer, though it is useful, and even necessary. Spiritual reading or study of theology, if made devoutly, is most fruitful meditation.

I think you will find that the more time you can reasonably give to being alone with God, the easier it becomes to enjoy it (I don't mean pleasure, but the feeling that it is worth doing—that you are not simply lazy and wasting time). The test is not whether you feel anything at the time, but whether *afterwards* you feel (quite illogically) better, and more determined to serve God. The one thing you should gain by quiet prayer (just remaining with God, and making a number of aspirations to keep your imagination from wandering) is to feel the rest of the day that you want God's Will and nothing else.

Now, though this induces a certain *passivity in the spiritual life*, on account of which it seems that we make no effort, but God does everything, it ought not to produce passivity in other things. You should be as energetic, or more energetic, in all you do.

If God was leading you to religious life, it would be quite reasonable to say " *à quoi bon ?* " of poetry or theology, or of money-making or your daily business. But if you must remain " in the world " (as seems clear), then you must say " All these things are nothing in themselves, and in the light of eternity they are nothings; but in so far as they are activities which I can offer to God, they may be of great value ". So you can write and study, and work, and try to get on, with fervour and anxiety,

36

protesting to God that you do each thing, not for its own sake, but because it is doing His Will. If you have to make more money in order to marry, then that is God's Will also.

On the other hand, contemplative life is not compatible with too much rushing about, activity of mind in many spheres, worry, worldliness. It is easier in country than in town, and so forth.

But I think your temperament is probably an indolent one; you are not *naturally* given to self-confidence, or push, or enthusiasms. Do not confuse natural tendencies with the spiritual passivity to which you are drawn. They look very much alike. Yet contemplation often urges people to the most violent activity for God's sake (though they always find time for prayer, all the same).

I am inclined to suppose that you ought to fight against being dreamy and taking life too easily. I am sure it is always right to throw oneself, heart and soul, into everything one does.

But I quite agree that you should not *unnecessarily* increase work, or (still more) social " duties ". It is all a question of details, of common sense applied to the little things of life. You must necessarily judge for yourself about every point, as it arises; with the general principles : not to go in for too much distraction, amusement, self-indulgence, on the one hand; not to go in for any extraordinary actions or abstentions, on the other; but to live in such a way that no one will call you unsociable, or strangely retired, or idle, or dissipated, or a man of pleasure ! It is a question of moderation.

(Another important principle is this : do not be *anxious or worried about small decisions*, e.g. " Shall I, or shall I not, accept this invitation ? " Decide what you think reasonable, and don't go back over it (e.g. " If I had stayed at home, I should have done some prayer or spiritual reading ").

37

Remember that the proper result of contemplative prayer is *simplicity* in the whole life; so that a contemplative is always doing the same thing all day and all night. He is praying, or having breakfast, or talking, or working, or amusing himself; but he is principally conscious that he is *doing God's Will;* the different external activities seem to him a sort of varied outcome of one continuous internal intention (as if in a long walk: one goes up hill and down, in rain or sun or wind, but the act of walking remains the same all the time, the same movement of the legs, but sometimes easy, sometimes hard, sometimes pleasant, sometimes unpleasant).

As to a joint religious life of husband and wife, that must depend (like all extraordinary resolutions) on a *very* decided call from God to *both* parties, and it must be *very* plain and certain. Just as it is a mistake to waste time over decisions about small matters, so it is important to be very careful about big matters. And very strong reasons indeed are always needed for anything which is unusual. If both found it easy and delightful, and longed for it, and hated the idea of anything else, that would be a strong reason. But it would never do for either to be persuaded into it, or to take the decision from a mere sense of duty, where there is no duty.

Ever yours in Dn̄o,

H. JOHN CHAPMAN, O.S.B., C.F.

IV: TO THE SAME.

Monday, Jan. 28, 1917.   *30th General Hospital,*
      No. 4 *A.P.O., B.E.F.*

My dear . . . .

As far as your question is concerned, I must say that I have never been able to understand why some authors lay so much stress upon preparation,[1] meaning some formal preparation.

It seems to me that common sense teaches us that, when a man is distracted, a certain amount of preparation is needed before he is in the right frame of mind to pray. But, on the contrary, when his life is one of quiet and recollection, he more often comes to his prayer as to a relief, as though a spring were released.

I mean that there are two extreme classes: on the one hand, those whose daily life absorbs their interests, so that it is difficult for them to turn to God, and they are obliged to use considerable efforts to obtain "introversion"; whereas the opposite class are naturally turned towards God, and need effort to set them at other work, all (or much of) which they are able to do in some kind of recollection.

Between the extreme classes are the numerous people who wobble to and fro. Sometimes they need some preparation and effort (sometimes more, sometimes less), while at other times prayer is easy and begins at once.

When no preparation is needed, it is *absurd* as well as useless. If you can begin prayer straight off, begin it straight off. Why waste time on inferior acts, to prepare for what is ready at hand?

I have put off studying Dame Gertrude More; but I imagine she is very good. There are bits in Fr. Baker's life of her which one feels doubtful about. I am very fond of the "*Cloud*".

Of course meditation on our Lord's life leaves you cold. To read or think on the subject *out*side *prayer time* is very profitable, but you can't combine it with prayer, I think. I should advise you simply to *despise* temptations against the Faith, and not take them seriously. Those "flashes" mean nothing at all, as you have rightly per-

---

[1] i.e. preparation of meditation or mental prayer.

39

ceived. All you say seems perfectly normal, and what one would expect you to say.

The cold here is appalling ! We have had a week of blue skies, and many degrees of frost. I do not like living in tents like Abraham, Isaac and Jacob.

Ever yours in D̄n̄o,

H. JOHN CHAPMAN, O.S.B., C.F.

V : TO THE SAME.

No. 30 *General Hospital,*

Calais.

July 17, 1917.

My dear . . . .

I don't feel inclined to answer any of your suggestive remarks and questions about spiritual matters ; the environment here is not suitable !

No doubt a layman may suck much good out of the Rule of St. Benedict. The question of Third Orders is a difficult one. As at first started by St. Francis, and imitated by other orders, there was much prayer and fasting involved—even in wearing the Brown Scapular. Leo XIII, himself a Franciscan oblate, abolished all that was difficult, so that any good layman might easily join. Consequently the feeling of being almost a religious tended to disappear. But many religious of St. Francis and St. Dominic (nuns, at least) are Third Order, and with vows. The *Tor de Specchi* nuns at Rome are oblates of St. Benedict without vows, as founded by St. Frances of Rome. So there are *grades* in the Third Order. And so there is no reason why a member of the ordinary Third Order should not keep considerably more observance, and be half-way, as it were, between the third-order communities and the simply lay Associates. But it would be a good thing to have two rules,—one as at present, another stricter, for the few.

40

As to "True Devotion", I should not venture to "approve it" (which would be ridiculous presumption), or to disparage it (which would be scandalous). It is recommended by saints, and found most valuable by saintly people. But it seems only to suit some people, and I wrote to D. that it seems to be a sort of vocation.

There are people who go in for "devotions", and others who (being less imaginative and less sentimental) want *unity*. This unity is rarely arrived at, I imagine, except by contemplative prayer, which gives it at once. I take it that the "True Devotion" belongs to the second class, though it may be imitated by the first class. I can think of one case in which the unification by contemplation takes this form—a lay person, whose contemplative prayer is *all* at the feet of our Lady, and inseparable from this method—and outside prayer time is the same.

Benedictines, on the other hand, seem to be quite in the opposite direction. I am rather struck by the very moderate place taken by our B. Lady in monastic minds (of course I mean "amount of space occupied", not "moderately high place").

Theoretically, St. Alphonsus's doctrine that all grace ever comes by Mary, as it originally came by her, seems to me quite true.

Ever yours affecly,

H. JOHN CHAPMAN, O.S.B.

VI: TO THE SAME.

Hotel Rosat,
Chateau d'Oex,
Switzerland.

Feb. 16, 1918.

My dear . . . .

I expect that writing at length about your spiritual difficulties may, of itself, have made you understand them better, and it has probably already done you good.

I understand that while you were full of temporal troubles you were at peace internally. Now, on the contrary, you are better in health, and temporal matters are going well, whereas you feel " depression and anxiety ", together with " bewilderment ".

The obvious fact is, that a man of prayer has to bear with equal patience temporal and spiritual difficulties. To bear sickness, pain, poverty, is a simple matter ; I mean that it may be very hard, and need great heroism, but it is simple, straightforward and obvious, and therefore easy (in one sense). Just as it is easy to walk twenty miles, but difficult to drive a motor twenty miles, though the former is far more tiring.

So it is less painful (sometimes) to bear spiritual discomfort, but it is much more difficult to do,—or rather, more difficult to know how—because it is not simple, straightforward and obvious. But when once you know how, it is quite simple ; just as a chauffeur, who drives daily, does it automatically and unconsciously.

Now the way is this :—accept with simplicity, or (better) take and seize with both hands, whatever feelings God sends you.

How is it possible to be anxious, worried, self-conscious, bewildered, " with simplicity " ?

The answer is " *abandon* "—which is a French word (" *une âme abandonnée* " always sounds to me like " an abandoned character ").

The point is that all anxiety, worry, etc., has its seat in the lower (not the lowest) part of the soul—in the imagination and emotions, or even in the intellect ; but above this (or below it, if you like) is the " apex " or " ground " of the soul, wherein prayer takes place, and union with God. Simplicity consists in keeping the whole soul subject to this ground (*fundus*) or apex; and this sovereign point (or hidden ground—whichever metaphor you like) must be continually united to God's Will.

If the soul turns to prayer, it *feels* the division: there is (1) worry and anxiety and trouble and bewilderment, and there is (2) also an unfelt, yet real, acquiescence in being anxious, troubled and bewildered, and a consciousness that the *real* self is at peace, while the anxiety and worry is unreal. It is like a peaceful lake, whose surface reflects all sorts of changes, because it is calm. If you were not seeking God, you would not feel this spiritual worry and bewilderment. Therefore, the very fact that you do feel it, should help to make you feel at peace.

There are two kinds of peace.

A. One kind is merely tepidity—the exact meaning of which is self-satisfaction:—" Thou sayest that thou art rich ", etc.

B. The other kind is based upon dissatisfaction:—" I have nothing; I am useless; I am simply a lump of wretchedness ". This is a kind of worry—anxiety—but is *the only way* of having peace with God.

Always remember that fervour is the contrary of lukewarmness, and therefore it always means (for us poor sinners) *a profound dissatisfaction with our own state.* When you become a saint, you will believe yourself to be the *greatest* of sinners—that is real fervour, when combined with the determination still to go on fighting.

But peace with God is the paradoxical result of this state of mind. Only it is not a peace which is *felt* (emotionally, sensibly), but supersensible. If you try to translate it into language, you may find yourself saying something like this :—" What *does* it all matter? What does it matter whether I enjoy Mass, or feel distracted or annoyed? What do my feelings matter? I came here for God, not

43

for myself. What do *I* matter? Only God matters. The whole world doesn't matter. Glory to God, that is the whole of everything".

And you look down at your soul, with a sort of amused pity, as a little wriggling worm, that won't keep still.

I wonder now whether any of this will help you? I am trying to show how it is as easy to bear spiritual trials as temporal ones with straightforward simplicity. I expect you practise all this, without knowing that you practise it.

That you imagine you are slack, is, of course, a sign of fervour.

You say "this feeling of being in the dark and pushed along I know not where, is very trying after a while". Only because you expected something else! On the contrary, there ought to be nothing more (supersensibly) satisfactory than to be pushed along, you know not where. "Choose Thou my path; I do not ask to see the distant scene." And again, you say :—"The prevailing feeling is one of preparation, and I haven't the least idea how to prepare". Preparation for heaven, not for anything else. "How to prepare"—only God knows that, and He works, we leave Him to work.

You are the block, God is the sculptor; you cannot know what He is hitting you for, and you *never will* in this life. All you want is patience, trust, confidence, and He does it all. It is very simple—simplicity itself.

One thing more : definite prayer of petition. We can't act much—we let God act. But we can pray—continually, and before everything we do. Then we shall have the same confidence expressed in the ordinary part of our soul that is subsensibly dominating the apex (or ground). Besides, we shall get what we ask, as a general rule.

"Would give anything for definite leading" : why, God is leading you. "Some sort of vocation to prayer"—of

44

course you have. Let it be a prayer of simplicity, of *"simple remise à Dieu"*—simply giving yourself wholeheartedly into His hands, to worry, and be troubled and bewildered, etc.

But you will want some *time* for this prayer of contemplation—just as you can manage—and a real retreat once a year (not listening to sermons in great numbers, or making elaborate meditations, but staying alone with God, distracted or not, as He pleases) ; after a time alone, all goes on oiled wheels for a time.

Ever yours sincerely,

H. John Chapman, O.S.B., C.F.

VII: TO THE SAME.

Downside Abbey,
Stratton-on-the-Fosse,
Nr. Bath.

Aug. 23, 1922.

My dear . . . .

The great difficulty is to be sufficiently " recollected ". This comes best after a retreat ; otherwise it may (or may not) come after a couple of hours' attempt at prayer. But a multiplicity of business and worries makes one so materialistic and distracted that it seems *impossible* to concentrate on the one thing needful. But distraction—and the feeling that " nothing happens "—is no proof whatever that one ought not to be using " simple " prayer. It only proves that one ought to use it more.

I take it that, if you pray, you can probably pray in no other way. I do not dogmatize, for, as you say, I do not know you well enough. But your continued attraction towards this kind of prayer decidedly confirms my original opinion that it is your way to God.

It is absolutely *easy*, if only you realise that it is a prayer of the *will*, not of the intellect, or the imagination, or of the emotions. For it follows that *thinking* about all sorts of other things doesn't matter, provided it is quite involuntary; and *feeling* nothing at all doesn't matter either. If you have passed a given time in continual distraction and discomfort, you will have made a *fruitful* prayer, provided you come away from it discontented with yourself.

St. John of the Cross explains: *tepidity* is satisfaction with your own state; *fervour* is dissatisfaction (active) therewith.

It is not necessary to "want God and want nothing else". You have only to "want to want God, and want to want nothing else". Few get beyond this really! But God is loving, and takes not only the will for the deed, but the will to will, or the wish to will.

Consequently I can't help advising you to pray. (The longer one prays, the better it goes.) But when it goes badly, it goes well; for it becomes a continued humiliation: "Oh my God, you see I can't pray, I can't even desire, I can't keep my attention, etc." The great thing is union with God's Will; hence one can pass the time in accepting one's own baseness and incapacity. "*Domine, non est exaltatum cor meum, neque elati sunt oculi mei*"; my soul is as a weaned child. "This is all you can expect of me, and I don't ask for one crumb of comfort more—only not to sin."

It is a dry land where no water is; and *consequently* "*sicut desiderat cervus, etc.*" Only the desire is a *will*, not an emotion.

All depends on whether you have the courage for so dry a prayer. And yet it has a supra-sensible consolation.

It is one long act of love—not of my love to God, but of His to me. It is always going on—but in prayer you put yourself into it by an act of faith.

What I am writing about is a prayer of "beginners". I know nothing about any other. There is nothing high about it. It is for those who have got beyond the stage where they want to *think about* our Lord as absent. They [the last named] have not really begun, although that is (from another point of view) a good beginning and carries people a long way.

I hope this answers your question sufficiently. Take what time you can. And pray in this way when you hear Mass. And it will be going all right, if it feels all wrong !

Pray for me.
Ever yours in D n̄o,
H. JOHN CHAPMAN.

VIII: TO THE SAME.

Downside Abbey,
Stratton-on-the-Fosse,
Jan. 16, 1923.   *Nr. Bath.*

My dear . . . .

A propos of your remarks—in the 17th–18th centuries most pious souls seem to have gone through a period in which they felt sure that God had reprobated them (for example, the nuns to whom Père de Caussade wrote his wonderful letters). This doesn't seem to happen nowadays.

But the *corresponding trial* of our contemporaries seems to be the *feeling of not having any faith* ; not temptations against any particular article (usually), but a mere feeling that religion is not true. It is an admirable purgative, just as the 18th cent. one was ; it takes all pleasure out of spiritual exercises, and strips the soul naked. It is very unpleasant. But the " Night of the Spirit " is not pleasant in any of its many forms. The only remedy is to *despise* the whole thing, and pay no attention to it— except (of course) to assure our Lord that one is ready to suffer from it as long as He wishes, which seems an absurd paradox to say to a Person one doesn't believe in ! But then, that is the trial. Faith is really particularly strong all the time.

Ever yours affecly,

H. John Chapman.

IX: TO THE SAME.

Downside Abbey,
Stratton-on-the-Fosse,
Nr. Bath.

(*Early in* 1923)

My dear . . . .

I only admit that society is " pagan " in the sense that it doesn't think much about religion—only the pagan did, and made religion enter into everything. But the Western world is thoroughly permeated by Christian ethics and Christian ideals still. As for those who want to live a purer life, there are monasteries to flee to, and (for women) enclosed orders.

But we will talk when you come.

Ever yours in D$\overline{no}$,

H. John Chapman.

X: TO THE SAME.

Downside Abbey,
Stratton-on-the-Fosse,
Nr. Bath.

March 2, 1923.

My dear . . . .

I have not seen Kidd's *History of the Church*. Part of Duchesne's and part of Batiffol's series have been translated into English, and so for the early centuries Catholics are well provided. And I fancy that Funk's Manual for the whole history is also translated ; it is of course first rate.

48

Everyone knows that Gwatkin, though learned, wrote directly *against* the High Church view, as represented by Bright. The latter was very good on doctrine, but not up to date, esp. in German books; Gwatkin was more up to date, but nothing like so completely as Batiffol or Duchesne. I think you would find that both these Frenchmen are more used in England than the two English writers. Bigg's book was meritorious, but not up to the best. I was once offered about £500 for a history of the first four centuries, but had no time! I daresay it would have been poor; and I don't think it was wanted.

I, personally, think it is right that dogma should have the first place in the seminary curriculum. The better a man knows his dogmatic theology, the better he ought to preach. And I don't believe in its being taught *too* historically; that (I think) should come partly under Eccl. History. But I suppose you are right, that history gets neglected. Probably the reason is that an attempt is made to cover the *whole* history of the Church. I think one period, or two periods, should be gone into properly, and only the swiftest outline should be given of the rest.

Forty or fifty years ago, Hurter's Theology was much in use; it is very anti-scholastic, and makes the proofs from Scripture and the Fathers the principal part—and Hurter knew the Fathers. But I prefer the scholastic way, when you have no time for both.

As the Western world is Christian in a general sort of way, but no more, I don't see that proofs from Scripture or the Fathers, or History, or anything, matter so much as *doctrine pure and simple*, made reasonable and correlated and united by good theologians.[1]

---

[1] By this the writer does not mean, of course, that proofs from Scripture, the Fathers or History are not important in themselves. He is insisting that, when dealing with those who, while they claim to be Christians do not accept the full Catholic teaching, the first essential is to give them a clear statement of Catholic doctrine, so as to show its reasonableness, logical sequence and

I don't think (as I wrote before) that I should call the world pagan. Only in relation to the theory of Christian monogamy does it seem to be relapsing towards paganism. But it is still an *enormous* distance from the unmoral point of view of the chastest of ancient Romans.

As to " direction ", I think most people at the present day want very little of it. The good director is like a nurse who teaches children how to walk alone.

The description you give of your spiritual state is very vivid, and I know it well enough by experience. It seems to me a very good state ; but all good states may become better. The discomfort in it is lessened by more quiet, or more time for prayer, alone with God. But when this is not possible, there is all the same the consciousness (as you say) " of the existence of God and His claim on me ". And that is enough to make sins and imperfections felt most startlingly as discomforts ; it makes the conscience very much awake ; indeed, it may make it too sensitive. All the feeling of discomfort and dissatisfaction with oneself should be turned (as far as possible) into a habitual practice of humbling oneself before God—as a useless servant, a prodigal son, a mere nothingness—, but at the same time, a practice of absolute resignation to and union with God's Will that we should be what we are (apart from any *wholly* wilful sins) and of absolute confidence in Him, because He made us what we are, and put us where we are, simply out of love.

There is no reason why the Presence of God (whether merely *known*, or felt) should be " pleasurable ". But it ought to have its effect in keeping us close to His Will, as the only thing that matters.

---

completeness ; since, before proving the Catholic position by means of authority (such as Scripture, the Fathers, etc.), the enquirer should be led to admit that the Church's position is logically sound and her doctrinal system complete and reasonable. See also *supra* Letter ix, p. 48.

It is very difficult to write to the point about what is in itself so vague, though you have painted it clearly.

Perhaps what you mean by "escaping" is somewhat parallel to what I feel, as though one didn't belong to this world at all, and that one is obliged to act a part in a very odd comedy, where one does it (and it is a very odd part) seriously, and yet half-laughing at it all, at the bottom of one's heart, and one feels it has no importance except that it is God's Will. My habitual feeling is that the world is so extremely odd, and everything in it so surprising. Why *should* there be green grass and liquid water, and why *have* I got hands and feet?

Ever yours affecly,

H. JOHN CHAPMAN.

XI: TO THE SAME.

Downside Abbey,
Stratton-on-the-Fosse,
Nr. Bath.

Jan. 20, 1925.

My dear . . . .

I think you are quite right not to try meditation. No doubt meditation as a mental exercise would be possible—in this sense it always is. But do not trouble—simply pray. All that you say shows that your *imagination* is not of any use to you religiously. You like a crib or a picture simply as a focus; that is, not to help your imagination by exciting it, but on the contrary to still it.

I should not worry about *how* to say the Rosary. The easiest thing is to have some *simple* thought in connection with each mystery; e.g. the first mystery: that our Lady simply gives herself up to God; or the last mystery: just Heaven; and so forth. If you try to make a mental picture ("composition of place") you will waste energy, and get no good.

As to your uselessness, that is a good feeling. We *cannot be useful to God!* He can do without us perfectly well. But if He chooses to use us, it is a great honour. Only we do not generally know that He is using us.

The only thing that matters is *now.* I mean that we have to be exactly in God's Will—united actively and passively with what He has arranged for us to be and to do, so that at every moment we are quite simply in touch with God, because we are wishing to do what He wants of us, and to be as we find He wishes us to be. There is no other perfection than this. To-morrow and yesterday are quite of secondary importance.

Ever yours affecly,

H. JOHN CHAPMAN.

XII: TO THE SAME.

Downside Abbey,
Stratton-on-the-Fosse,
Nr. Bath.

April 11, 1927.

My dear . . . .

As to advice, I can only tell you what I think.

I recommend you prayer, because it is good for every-body, and our Lord tells us to pray. As to method, do what you can do, and what suits you. It seems obvious that most spiritual reading and meditation fails to help you; and the simplest kind of prayer is the best. So use that.

But prayer, in the sense of union with God, is the most crucifying thing there is. One must do it for God's sake; but one will not get any satisfaction out of it, in the sense of feeling "I am good at prayer", "I have an infallible method". That would be disastrous, since what we want to learn is precisely our own weakness, powerlessness, unworthiness. Nor ought one to expect " a sense of the reality of the supernatural " of which you speak. And one should wish for no prayer, except precisely the prayer that God gives us—probably very distracted and unsatisfactory in every way !

On the other hand, the only way to pray is to pray; and the way to pray well is to pray much. If one has no time for this, then one must at least pray regularly. But the less one prays, the worse it goes. And if circumstances do not permit even regularity, then one must put up with the fact that when one does try to pray, one can't pray—and our prayer will probably consist of telling this to God.

As to beginning afresh, or where you left off, I don't think you have any choice ! You simply have to begin wherever you find yourself. Make any acts you want to make and feel you ought to make ; but do not force yourself into *feelings* of any kind.

You say very naturally that you do not know what to do if you have a quarter of an hour alone in Church. Yes, I suspect the only thing to do is to shut out the Church and everything else, and just give yourself to God and beg Him to have mercy on you, and offer Him all your distractions.

As to religious matters being " confused and overwhelming ", I daresay they may remain so—in a sense—, but if you get the right simple relation to God by prayer, you have got into the centre of the wheel, where the revolving does not matter. We can't get rid of the worries of this world, or of the questionings of the intellect ; but we can laugh at and despise them so far as they are worries.

Ever yours affecly,

H. John Chapman.

XIII: TO THE SAME.

The Worcestershire Brine Baths Hotel,

Monday, July 13, [1927?] *Droitwich.*

My dear . . . .

I don't wonder that you can't pray. What you mean is that you can't *think* when you pray. Have the *right intention,* and then it is prayer. But you need not understand what you mean, or think about it. Distractions do not interfere with prayer when they are involuntary. If we prayed simply because we wanted the " consolations of religion ", this state of things would be very disappointing. But if we only pray in order to give ourselves to God, then the prayer that we *can* do, whatever it is (doubtless it is not the very best we can do, but in general it is the only *kind* we can do), is what God wants, though it is far from being what *we* want. Only we must try to want what God wants, and only that. Don't worry.

Ever yours affecly,

H. JOHN CHAPMAN.

XIV: TO THE SAME.

Downside Abbey,
Stratton-on-the-Fosse,

Oct. 19, 1927. *Nr. Bath.*

My dear . . . .

One would so much like to " report progress ", to feel one is doing something. Only one can't—one wouldn't ! If you *could* do it, you *should* do it ! Only to try it when one can't succeed only makes things much worse.

The other way is what St. Francis de Sales and St. Ignatius call " indifference ", and others call " *abandon* ".

And this *is* doing something, and something very hard. Only it is usually humbling, rather than " consoling ".

Of course quiet is necessary for peace. But if God does not wish us to have peace, we must be satisfied with confusion, and that *is* peace, of an elusive kind.

Diligentibus Deum omnia cooperantur in bonum. Every circumstance of our life is a means of getting to heaven, and a part of God's Providence ; so that at every moment we are in touch with God. So we need not see Him, as we feel His hand in every outward thing and in every inward non-wilful feeling—and even in our will as well, when it is good. Only this is a truth to be acted upon rather than meditated upon.

You will see that the little book (*Contemplative Prayer*)[1] is very cheap and common, and very small print, though readable. I purposely made no change in it (though it might easily be improved) so that it should not be regarded as a treatise or my " last word " on a subject on which I would on no account dogmatise !

Ever yours affecly,

H. JOHN CHAPMAN.

XV: TO THE SAME.

Downside Abbey,
Stratton-on-the-Fosse,
Nr. Bath.

Feb. 26, 1930.

My dear . . . .

I dislike Bremond's " pure prayer " theories, and still more his idea that " prayer " is " habitual grace ". This seems to be nonsense. Prayer (even " habitual prayer ") is an *act* not a *habit*. The habit which produces the prayer is not the essence of the prayer. The essence of electric

---

[1] See *infra*. Appendix I, p. 287.

55

light is not electricity, but light. I think Bremond philosophically hopeless, and he ought never to have tried his hand at it. But his acumen and psychology and power of expression are marvellous.

These are all my own views, for the moment, but I don't pretend to have *studied* all these matters.

What a pity that Père de Caussade did not write a formal treatise on *abandon*. Certainly P. Ramière has arranged it very well. The account of the many editions in the *Revue d'Ascétique et Mystique* (which Thorold has sent me) shows that some editions only gave half. Gabalda has sold 75,000 copies !

Written in haste.

Ever yours affecly,

H. JOHN CHAPMAN.

XVI: TO THE SAME.

Downside Abbey,
Stratton-on-the-Fosse,
Nr. Bath.

Jan. 26, 1931.

My dear . . . .

M. has been putting to me the same difficulty as you have done. I replied that I was glad to say I had often the same difficulty myself ! One says, " this *abandon*, and this formless prayer, are for advanced souls, whereas I am a pig ". Of course we can't be saints without feeling we are pigs.

My answer to her seems to have satisfied her :—" *Can* you do anything else ? *Can* you choose your path, your prayer, your method or want of method ? " *Solvitur ambulando.* There is no real difficulty, except our inveterate habit of the " *retour sur soi-même* ". Live for God and one's neighbour, and don't let's look into our heart, which St. James says is "desperately wicked". St. Peter did not say, "It is only to advanced souls that I recommend (πᾶσαν τὴν μέριμναν ὑμῶν ἐπιρρίψαντες ἐπ' αὐτὸν) to throw away all your worry upon Him, for He takes care for you, since He does not take care for beginners". We are not meant to ask ourselves whether we are beginners or "advanced", or to find out.

I hold to my view that we ought to try to do what we can, and not what we can't. Also that we should stick to the spiritual books which suit us, not to those which give us no help.

Ever yours affecly,

H. JOHN CHAPMAN.

XVII: TO A LITERARY MAN.

Downside Abbey,
Michaelmas, 1920. *Near Bath.*

My dear . . . .

I dislike giving advice, and besides I haven't much to go on in what you say. So the best thing is to explain the theory, which is based (I hope correctly) on St. John of the Cross.

1. The reason why Meditation is impossible is that, when one takes to prayer, the intellect is occupied in doing something else; viz. contemplating. But this Contemplation is so obscure that it is unperceived. It is subconscious, like the circulation of the blood, but quite as real. It is deep down at the root of the intellect, and, in unimaginative and unemotional people, has absolutely *no effect* on the imagination and emotions. In imaginative and emotional people it *does* "translate" itself into "phantasmata", and the imagination (and emotions) may be full of joy, etc. (prayer of quiet, union, etc.) or of visions and locutions, etc.

2. But the higher *will* does follow the higher intellect; therefore the effect of the subconscious (or rather " superconscious ") contemplation *is felt in the will*, though not in the imagination and emotions. To exercise these latter is to impede or stop the prayer. But *they must have something to do*. When the will fixes itself on God, and leaves the imagination entirely to itself, the latter flies off into any absurdity. Provided these imaginations are not *wilful* they don't matter in the least. But if the will has to run after them, to bring them back, it has to detach itself from God to do so; and besides we often find the imaginations interesting, and dwell upon them willingly and wilfully, or half-wilfully.

3. So, to keep the imagination quiet, the best thing is *to keep it in tune with the will* and higher intellect, by very simple " acts ". The mere *imagined words* give the imagination food; by sticking to them (the same act or many, as you like) the imagination may even get lazy, or almost mesmerised (for a short time usually). But, generally, one has to go on keeping it quiet, running after it, and bringing it back. But there is the curious feeling that *these imaginations are not you*—they are mechanical, like those in a dream. You leave them as nearly uncontrolled as possible, in order to have the will fixed on nothing in particular—which is God, of course.

4. Consequently, the symptoms of ordinary contemplative prayer are :—

(*a*) A distinct perception of what the imagination is doing, viz. making very peaceful acts; which continually tend to run off into good thoughts, or worldly thoughts, or anything, and have to be very gently brought back.

(*b*) A confused perception of what the acts mean. If you try to *understand them*, you are detaching your *intellect* from God. You have a general consciousness that you are expressing the want of God, or praise, or adoration, or simply the giving of self. It really doesn't matter what the words mean. It is the *imagined sounds* which fill the imagination, and (I suppose) other filmy images connected with them. That is why very expressive words are best ; either expressive in sense (as " O God, I want Thee, and nothing but Thee "), or by beauty of sound (say, some verse of the Psalms, " *Exultabunt labia mea cum cantavero Tibi, et anima mea quam redemisti* " is an excellent ' tag '), because there is association of ideas between such sounds and the almost imperceptible clinging of the will to God.

(c) There is a very pure and indefinite and complete conviction that God is everything, and that nothing else is worth having. This is the clinging of the will, or intention. It is obviously an act of love ; but it doesn't feel like it, because it isn't *felt* at all.

(d) In the intellect there is *no perception at all*, if the prayer is pure. One might call it an act of ignorance, or a sensation of idiocy ! But this is only by reflection ; you ask yourself :—" What on earth do I mean by saying I want God and nothing else ? " and the only answer is :—" I don't mean anything." " What do I mean by God ? " " I have no idea."[1]

[1] This passage must, of course, be understood in accordance with the teaching of Catholic theologians, many of whom speak in similar terms of the way in which the soul, in contemplation, is dazed or blinded by the divine light. The sense of intellectual helplessness, here described, is recognised by St. John of the Cross as a special feature of contemplative prayer, and he deals with it at some length (v. *Ascent of Mount Carmel*, xiii–xv ; *The Living Flame of Love*, Stanza III, Section 34 *et seq.; Dark Night of the Soul*, Bk. I, Ch. ix, Section 7 *et seq.*). A vivid description of this state, clearly based upon personal experience, is given by the Benedictine, Abbot Blosius :—" When the soul hath thus entered into the vast solitude of the Godhead, it happily loseth itself. Enlightened by the splendour of this bright cloud, in its excess of knowledge it becometh without knowledge, and is established in what may be called a kind of wise ignorance. In this state, although it knoweth not what God is, to whom it is united in love, although it seeth not God as He is in his glory, nevertheless it learneth by experimental knowledge that He infinitely surpasseth

That is all the description I can give of contemplative prayer in its lowest terms. But metaphor is perhaps clearer. One can give any number of analogical descriptions, e.g. :—

1. I am in our Lord's arms; so close to His Heart that I cannot see His Face.

2. I am in a dark room; saying words—which mean nothing—to some one who is not there.

3. I am occupied in simply *giving* myself to God; "*oraison de simple remise.*" I always add :—"*c'est dans cette remise qu'on trouve la voiture qui nous méne au ciel! On ne va plus à pied.*"

4. It is the prayer of *stripping*; in which all our natural powers are useless, all pleasure is renounced, and we remain naked before God. *Ego sum mendicus et pauper, Dominus sollicitus est mei.*

It follows (if what I have said is right) that this is *not* a " prayer of aspirations ", a " prayer of acts ", or " affective prayer ". The " aspirations ", " acts ", " affections " are merely a sop to Cerberus; merely crumbs thrown to the imagination. They are not the prayer.

Nor are any *affections*, which come in the prayer, the prayer. They are concomitants (impurities, St. John of the Cross would say) which make it more human and consoling—and consequently less " stripping ". If you put together the four symptoms (*a, b, c, d*) you will see that the outcome is a *quantity of tepid acts, with a buzzing or fog underneath,* and continual distraction, more or less worrying. It is like a lot of harmonies on a pedal point, or (say) like a note on the organ ciphering, so that every-

---

all things that can be known by the senses, and whatever can be written, spoken or conceived by the mind of man. Now doth it understand how far better it is to go forth into God without any image in the mind, than to contemplate Him in the noblest and most divine images and likenesses." (*Speculum Spirituale* XI, i. 2, translated by Fr. B. Wilberforce, O.P.)

thing which is played, however beautiful, sounds hideous, and you can only pay attention to the ciphering note which spoils all the rest. Only, in our case, the note which spoils all the rest and makes the beautiful " acts " unmeaning and dry, is *not* heard, and yet is the only thing worth hearing.

What Père Poulain calls the " ligature " (he explains it wrongly) is simply the fact that one can't (easily) put one's mind to two things at once. When the intellect is occupied with God, it can't think out a subject and meditate. When the will is fixed on God, it can't run about after other things; e.g. you know what it is to try and say the *Pater noster* slowly and devoutly, with the result that you can't imagine what it means. I think most people know this. Another example is to read a difficult book, while you are half-listening to other people talking to each other. You read the words again and again, and then read them half aloud, and they convey no meaning. In the case of the " Our Father ", if it is no conscious distraction that prevents your understanding the words, it is the ' ligature '; viz. the more devout you try to be, the more meaningless the words seem, because you are simply driving your intellect more and more wholly into the imperceptible contemplation.

That this is so, is shown by the way it goes further, when the state of prayer makes it impossible to read a book, or (yet further) to pronounce the words of the Office. It makes contemplatives into idiots for the moment, upon occasions. It is just the same in effect as the ordinary absence of mind, which we suffer from concentration on one thought. Only, in the case of the ' ligature ', the thought happens to be (more or less) imperceptible.

Practical result. I should prefer a bare and dry prayer, to an explosion followed by a short intoxication; because the second seems to be self-made, and therefore less pure. But I don't dogmatise.

What matters is the result. *The after effects of good prayer are more definite than the prayer itself;* I mean a determination to follow God's Will, and to care for nothing else, without any reason to be given for the determination.

I rarely write letters. But, when I do, they frequently turn out to be very long indeed.

It is a long time since I read Ribot "On Attention," and I don't remember what he says about St. Teresa.

From what you say, I conclude that you are bound to use Contemplative prayer. I have been reading (for the first time) some of *Père de Caussade's l'Abandon à la Providence divine.* It is extraordinarily good. But, like St. John of the Cross, it makes one realise that a simple *remise à Dieu* is not so simple. It is as easy as jumping into a fire, which you had not seen, and has the same effect. It burns your clothes first, then your flesh, and then your bones. It is a fearful thing to fall into the hands of the Living God. But He is Infinite Wisdom and Infinite Love all the same. It is quite a question whether the broad way is any more comfortable than the narrow one.

Ever yours in D\overline{no},

H. JOHN CHAPMAN, O.S.B.

I don't remember, but I think it probable that I have merely repeated in this letter what I said in the leaflet![1]

P.S. It is possible that all this description of a dry prayer in a fog may seem rather austere. But I hardly think you will suppose this. For, to beginners, it leaves (afterwards) the world just as it was before, just as beautiful and attractive—only as dust and ashes (" *ut*

[1] *Contemplative Prayer—v.* Appendix I, p. 287.

stercora" as St. Paul has it) *in comparison* with the Infinite or Divine Darkness. It follows that there must be (and there certainly is) in this prayer a transcendental, super-sensual satisfaction of most extraordinary power, since it has this effect.

In the *pure* form there is no enjoyment—often continual worry—and yet, somehow or other, it is satisfying, *and one wants nothing else.* The whole thing is perfectly inexplicable.

But then, if it was explicable, it couldn't be a contact with the Infinite !

XVIII: TO THE SAME.

Ash Wednesday, 1921
Palazzo S. Calisto, Roma (14).

My dear . . . .

The common teaching used to be that Holy Communion was a sort of reward : daily Communion was reserved for those who had " no attachment for venial sin,"—and even then they were told to omit their Communion once a week as a sign of humility. Nuns used to deprive girls in their schools of so many Communions as a punishment. I remember a lay-brother telling me his Confessor had reduced the number of his Communions, because he had committed a grave sin (or the Confessor thought he had).

Pius X absolutely condemned all this quite usual doctrine, and his decisions are fully authoritative, and in Religious communities they have to be read publicly every year.

A. He insists that the conditions for frequent and daily Communion are the same as for any one Communion :— viz. two only, (1) a right intention (this is necessary for the validity of any Sacrament) ; (2) a state of grace. Consequently children are *strictly bound* to receive it, directly they arrive at the age of reason, and first Communion cannot be deferred until they understand fully what it means. It is sufficient that they understand it is a religious rite, giving grace, and not an ordinary meal.

B. It is not a reward, but a means of grace for sinners. If one Communion gives so much grace, given certain dispositions, we shall get twice as much by two Communions with equal dispositions. " The more perfect our dispositions, the more grace we get ", was the old Jansenistic idea—it is absolutely true—but the conclusion drawn was entirely false, " therefore let us take weeks or months of preparation, so as to get all the grace we can." This is obviously rubbish.

If Holy Communion gives grace, it will help me to make a better one next time. If I want to make a good communion at Easter, and prepare myself all through Lent, if I try all possible spiritual exercises, it will be absurd to omit the best of them—viz. daily Communion—all through Lent !

C. Consequently Pius X officially recommends *daily Holy Communion* to all the faithful, without exception. Very many religious Orders only allowed about four times a week to those who were not Priests, (most Benedictines !). Scarcely any Confessor allowed more than six times a week. People were afraid of asking for more, for fear of seeming to lack humility. Now children are trained to daily Communion, (as Don Bosco had already started doing many years before), and *everyone* is recommended to go to Holy Communion as often as they can ; *not because they are good*, but because they *ought to be better*.

D. The Church explains to us quite simply the proper preparation :—

(1) Before the Mass the Priest says the *Confiteor*, and it is said in the name of the people before Holy Communion is given.

(2) Then, *immediately* before receiving, the Priest has to say *Domine, non sum dignus*, and he has to say it in the name of the people before he communicates them. That is to say, the one preparation is NOT *the judgement of our confessor that we are good people* (that was the old view), but *our own recognition that we are bad*. We come to the Physician because we are sickly. We come for strength because our Wills are wobbly. If we were sure we had " no affection to venial sins ", we might, perhaps, do without daily Communion !

This long explanation, of what you doubtless knew already, is simply to show that I have no right to give any answer to your question except to tell you that our Lord instituted Holy Communion in order that we should take advantage of it, and that the oftener we do so the better. No Confessor has any right to say anything else. The old idea of " limiting the number of Communions " has gone for ever. The " Director's " business is to urge everyone to frequent and daily Communion. Nor can one even recommend to " omit one day a week out of humility "; for the extra Communion ought to give more humility than the omission could do.

As to being " worthy " of receiving, no Angel is, nor was our Blessed Lady. Our preparation consists in saying : " I am *not* worthy."

I quite agree with the criticism that my little paper on Prayer is " not Christian ". Prayer is not particularly Christian, in itself. It is Christian to pray to Christ, or our Lady, or to end our prayers *per Jesum Christum Dominum nostrum*. The latter is assumed. But the *Pater noster* is not " Christian " except in the sense that it is

" the Lord's Prayer "—it is Natural Religion in its highest form. I used to dislike St. John of the Cross, because I said he wasn't Christian ! I called him " Buddhist "— " Sufi " would have been as good—for you find mystics in all monotheistic religions. But contemplative prayer makes people good Catholics.

Yours ever in D$\overline{no}$,

H. JOHN CHAPMAN, O.S.B.

N.B. Pius X. says it is *quite right* for people to ask their confessors about frequent communion. But this is evidently because (1) there may be practical reasons making it more perfect to abstain,—because of other duties. (2) There are people who wish to show off their clothes or their piety, and some may need to be humbled by their " director "—and so forth. (The Pope took care to safe-guard the right of the Confessor as a judge, while instructing him as to what he has to say, and what principles are right, and what are wrong.) (3) It gives the Confessor the chance of finding out that people don't go often enough, and of urging them to more.

XIX: TO THE SAME.

Palazzo S. Calisto,
Dec. 1, 1922.   *Roma* (14).

My dear . . . .

Without having read Roja's book, one cannot tell exactly why it was condemned. Probably it contained exaggerated views about passivity,—not praying for anything definite. Besides, the ' Interior Silence ' might have played into the hands of the Quietists, without being in itself objected to.

But, anyhow, there is no reason to suppose that the account of the prayer of Silence *as paraphrased by Father*

66

Baker would have been condemned; else Father Baker would deserve to be condemned.

Anyhow, the *preparation* (which is the principal point for you, I gather) could not have been condemned, since it is rather anti-quietistic, and consists of perfectly definite Acts. I gather that you find this preparation useful, as tending to produce greater quiet afterwards. The one thing that prayer can be judged by is its *fruit*. As you say it has all the right effects, it must surely be a good prayer. So I should say, " Go on with it ", and be grateful to God for having shown you a method which just suits you.

I don't much like the expression, " Interior Silence ", as it suggests that people arrive at a real silence, without any acts; but Father Baker carefully points out that to ' listen ' is an act, and, as being merely an attitude, does not imply anything heard. But I think ' quiet ', ' peace ', are better words than ' silence '. Probably the author started from the idea of not using words (imagined words); but it is possible to have ' acts ' without words, though they are more imperceptible.

I am reading Abbot Butler's *Western Mysticism*, which came out a week ago; I had read most of it in MS. I like his views. But I am inclined to think he takes the ' illuminative way ' to be the whole of ' Mystical Theology '. It seems to be doubtful whether St. Augustine or St. Gregory, or even St. Bernard, ever reached the " Unitive Way ". This does not (in my view) detract from their sanctity.

What you say about Holy Communion seems all right. I think, if you try to make a ' formal thanksgiving ', you will only produce ' dryness ' and distractions.

Ever yours in D$\overline{no}$,

H. JOHN CHAPMAN.

Downside Abbey,
Nr. Bath.

Jan. 26, 1925.

My dear . . . .

(*a*) " Acquired " Contemplation and " infused " often mean the same as " active " and " passive ". My *own* opinion is that the distinction is not very fruitful, being a case of *degree* not of kind.

St. John of the Cross, I can swear, would not admit the distinction at all. He most certainly regards *all* contemplation (as he uses the word) as being infused. When meditation ceases, this cessation is *caused* by the obscure and unperceived contemplation which has already been infused. I think it safest to follow this author, who had great experience, chiefly of nuns. But he was evidently a contemplative himself. I am inclined to think that some parts of his works are founded on his personal experiences, though so much is academic.

But those very frequent authors who teach " prayer of acts ", must distinguish between " active " and " passive ", or " acquired " and " infused ". Father Augustine Baker has three stages (after meditation) :—(1) Acts (" forced acts "), (2) Aspirations, (3) Passive Unions. I have no objection to this classification, except that it is empirical, not scientific ; just as I have no objection to classifying cats as (1) white, (2) black, (3) tabby, etc ; (Note : in the dark all cats are black).

But St. John of the Cross would certainly say that " acts " and even " aspirations " are merely superficial phenomena. When the infused contemplation is so *weak,* or so much *obscured* by distractions, or so *pure* as to be imperceptible, the lower part of the soul will be making " acts " or " aspirations " (as the case may be). The " forced acts " are to keep the attention ; the " aspirations " (which come of themselves) are not the cause but the result of the attention. But the " contemplation " is something apart from either ; and if it is not really underneath them, then these acts and aspirations are merely the result of meditation and are in the purgative way, and there is no contemplation at all.

(*b*) Dominicans always appeal to the " gifts of the Holy Ghost ", so I will take (*c*) first.

(*c*) Contemplation and Grace. Up to St. Thomas's time " grace " was used vaguely, as by St. Paul and St. Augustine, and only later was the great distinction made of :

(1) *Actual* grace,—assistance given by God, either *supernatural* in itself (internal), or *natural* in essence, but supernatural in intention (e.g. to be born of Christian parents, to hear a sermon, etc.).

(2) *Habitual,* or sanctifying grace.

St. Thomas never distinguishes the one from the other. Yet they are totally different, and not connected : e.g. Habitual grace can be increased or diminished, but never lost (i.e. is never wanting). One may have more habitual grace now than yesterday, but less actual. Habitual grace is a created participation of God's Nature. Actual grace is only an assistance given by God ; the highest kinds being illuminations of the intellect and strengthenings of the will.

(*b*) (once more). Hence part of St. Thomas's doctrine of the " gifts ". Isaias (Hebrew) mentions *six* Spirits as descending on the Messias. The Septuagint (which is full of doublets, dittographs, glosses, interpolations) gives seven. So does the Old Latin. *And so does the Vulgate.* But whether St. Jerome gave seven, I do not know ; it is likely the seventh came into the MSS. from the Old Latin. But I know nothing of the MSS. of Isaias, and I forget what St. Jerome says in his commentary.

Anyhow, the Latin Church—long before St. Thomas —was accustomed to enumerate these seven Spirits (a poetical enumeration) and to speak of them as "*The seven gifts*", given not only to Christ, but to all Christians.

Now, when St. Thomas describes the *infused virtues*, he has to acknowledge that they only give the *potentia* and not the *act* of doing the supernatural acts of those virtues : e.g. without the *infused virtue* of Faith we cannot possibly make an act of Faith. But even this *virtue* is not like an acquired (natural) virtue, it does not give the *facility;* we need an actual assistance also, [and this actual assistance, accompanied by a *virtus transiens*, would enable us to make an act of Faith without having the habit (i.e. the *virtus* in the full sense)]. This would be, by the moderns, called "actual grace", but St. Thomas puts it down to the seven gifts.

Consequently, a Christian doing a good act, when in a state of grace, is raised to the higher power by the virtue, and then the act proceeds from the virtue by means of the *donum*. You will find all this in the *Summa;* but not in the theologians.

But St. Thomas considers that the *dona* in their higher form give *more* than the infused virtues. Especially *sapientia* and *intellectus* give something higher than faith,—a (dark) knowledge. He is not quite consistent about the functions of each gift : he has three slightly differing views—the earliest in the "Sentences", another in the *Summa*, and a slightly different explanation further on in the *Summa*.

Thus the Dominicans are quite correct in saying that St. Thomas attributed mystical Theology and mystical Contemplation to the *dona*, (especially *sapientia* and *intellectus*, though, as I said, he varies slightly in the distinction between these two).

But this is no more than to say that they are *gifts of God*—of the Holy Ghost,—actual graces. So that I find fault with those Dominicans who think they have explained the whole of "Mysticism" by saying that it is one (or two) of the gifts of the Holy Ghost, in one of their highest ways of working. In reality they have *explained* nothing at all.

All Christian mystics regard their experiences as supernatural, and call them " *graces* ", gifts of God, and in particular of the Holy Ghost. But this does not tell us *what* they are, whether they are *ordinary* or *extraordinary*, merited or freely given, etc. So that it is a harmless doctrine, but unfruitful.

On the whole, *all* the theologians, Jesuits and Dominicans, are inclined to look upon " Mysticism " as some freak on God's part ; the Jesuits (like Suarez) making it miraculous, the Dominicans regarding it as a *special* gift of the Holy Ghost, not ordinary.

I am not disposed to agree altogether. I hold it probable that a natural psychological preparation (so unusual as to be rather *praeter*-natural) is found in certain persons, upon which God works ; for, according to St. Thomas, God works in accordance with our nature. The door to the unseen is connatural to *natura integra* (Adam), but filled up with lumber by original sin. But, in some souls, there is a little light shining through, and if they blow out or shade their terrene candles and lamps, they begin to perceive this light. Once they use it, God can increase it, and communicate with them in this new and higher way.

Thus (1) the *door* is a part of the perfection of human nature ; (2) the blocking of it is from the imperfection of our nature (but some people's nature is more perfect than other's, as all admit :—some having more powerful wills, some being taller, some having only one leg, etc.) ; (3) the light through the door is supernatural, and all communication through it is from God—therefore a grace, a gift, and from the Holy Ghost.

But some people have a crack, and reflections from this light come into the lumber of their minds. They do not

71

look through the crack, nor get any communication with God, yet they get an impression of a higher light somewhere, a reality outside this "cosy little universe" in which they are shut up. These are the Nature-mystics, like Tennyson and Wordsworth, or the children of whom Wordsworth wrote, who so often have impressions of eternity and that imperial Palace whence they came.

The more people are immersed in the business or the pleasures of this world, the more the door is blocked with lumber. The more imagination, the less possibility of perceiving the spiritual light; hence the Irish are almost never mystics.

But actually to look at the crack or through it, means looking at God; and only the pure in heart can do this.

But the light is often an ultra-violet ray, which warms —or burns—but is invisible. Hence *obscure* contemplation. The Will feels the warmth but sees no light, and imagines the warmth comes from the "acts" it is making—its own efforts. But this warmth ceases dead, the moment a wilful imperfection stops the light out, or turns the eye from it.

At this point St. Thomas disagrees with St. John of the Cross. St. Thomas says that *love* is often greater than *knowledge*. St. John admits this, so far as words go, but he holds that increase of love follows increase of *unconscious knowledge*. I daresay, if they could talk it over, St. Thomas would hardly say that he was speaking of conscious knowledge, and had no wish to deny the "ray of darkness" of the Areopagite.

Of course I hold that a mystical temperament is very rare. But the "ultra-violet" rays may come to any pious person who practises detachment. Or perhaps they are "infra-red" rays, which I imagine are the hottest. They certainly cause great dryness.

Ever yours affecty,

H. John Chapman.

72

Downside Abbey,
Bath.

Jan. 4, 1926.

My dear . . . .

As to what I said:—"It is generally easiest to pray before the Blessed Sacrament," I can't see any harm in it. I know so little about the subject, and other people can help one so little, that it is difficult to say anything.

But it seems to me that, for beginners, the great difficulty is with distractions. The imagination (and also the lower appetites) have to be kept quiet, but they cannot be stopped. So that it is, on the one hand, useful to have certain words to repeat, which keep the imagination occupied (it is like throwing a bone to a dog, to keep him quiet while he gnaws it) and, on the other hand, to be in a *place* which is quieting, hallowing, restful.

Many people can only find this in Church; and many nuns (for example) find that kneeling before the Blessed Sacrament helps them to recollection (partly by habit), and to put away merely worldly preoccupations. I really believe it *is* a help to most people, especially women. Of course *the dark* is a most suitable environment; but then it is difficult to obtain in the morning.

Mr. Watkin says:—"And the object of contemplative prayer is not the Humanity, but the transcendent, unimaginable Godhead." *Distinguo. Ut cognitum, Nego, Ut incognitum, Concedo.*

Hence to *think* about the transcendence and unimaginability of God is just as little a part of contemplation as to *think* about the Sacred Humanity. But the former might easily be mere philosophy, while the latter is religion.

If people *think* about the Blessed Sacrament instead of

contemplating, they will be doing an excellent religious act. If they *can* do it, I should presume they would be wasting their time in trying to ' contemplate ', because, if people can contemplate, they *can't* think; hence the presence of the Blessed Sacrament will not distract them, but may help them to quiet and recollection.

I never meant to recommend any particular place; only to say that most people found this the most convenient, tranquil and reposeful place.

Many people find their own room distracting, even though they shut their eyes; because they know, too well, all the calls of business and interest that are close by. But it is good to accustom oneself to be recollected in one's own room.

I am not speaking of " born mystics ", nor of beginners who are recollected anywhere, nor of " advanced souls " who can be recollected in the midst of business; but of the ordinary person who at once *wants* to pray and *wants* to think of other things, and has many distracting interests and duties and pleasures. Environment is, to these folk, an important condition—sometimes acting as a " suggestion " very strongly—don't you think so ?

I am sure that beginners arrive at Contemplation *through* the Dark night of the senses, *after* meditating on our Lord's Humanity. Whereas I have little evidence to the effect that meditation on the attributes of God (for instance) is useful, except in the sense that any Theology is useful. I know plenty of writers, not always modern, who think that meditation on our Lord's Humanity leads up to meditation on the Divinity; and I think there is just this much of truth in it, that in the " Night of the senses " *for a short time* people take pleasure in thinking about the Divine attributes. Otherwise, I should imagine such philosophical contemplation to be of little use towards real Contemplation.

74

But, of course, I know that I ought not to put forward my views. I only do so tentatively.

Ever yours affectly,

H. JOHN CHAPMAN.

XXII: TO THE SAME.

Downside Abbey,
Nr. Bath.

Feb. 7, 1928.

My dear . . . .

The 'note' is interesting as formulating clearly the objections I have always felt myself ![1] I do not think my paper deserved any commendation, except as a candid description written straight off (14? years ago).

The chief defence is in No. 12. I have *always* said that I cannot admit *any other* criterion of prayer than its effects.

It is a practical matter. To *wish* for graces seems to me a poor reason for praying. But if people find that an idiotic kind of prayer actually corrects their faults, and an earlier practice of intellectual considerations had little effect, then they ought to prefer the latter to the former! Not that they can choose between them. For if they can do the latter, they can't do the former, and ought not to try.

Supposing there is auto-suggestion,—why not? If it actually strengthens the will, I should say " persevere in it, and don't worry about the nick-name ".

On the other hand, I should deny that the 'acts' have any 'suggestion' in them ; on the contrary they are

---

[1] The reference is to some criticisms of the paper, *Contemplative Prayer*, which had been sent to the recipient of this letter, who had forwarded them to Abbot Chapman. I have printed these as an *addendum* to the paper itself in Appendix I of this volume, so that the reader may know the points dealt with in this letter.

' suggested '. I should further deny that they are automatically or sub-consciously suggested,—what comes automatically is the distractions of the imagination. The ' acts ' are merely to prevent these, and they are kept up by an act of the will, though with very little effort.

It is a very interesting fact that mystics and contemplatives are from the beginning inclined, perhaps forced, to distinguish the different faculties in themselves.

A psychologist will talk as if our imagination was our intellect, and as if our emotions were our will. But any contemplative will be like St. Teresa, and know perfectly well that there are complete and full distinctions between the upper part and the lower part of the soul :—

Intellect	Will
Imagination Senses }	{ Emotions Pains

(Four valves of the soul, like four valves of the heart!)

I think the conclusion is obvious: the essence of 'Mysticism' is the use of *pure intellect* without images, and *pure will* without emotions. The images and emotions cease to be ' *me* ' : they are ' peripheral ' (I hate jargon), and they are like my clothes, not like my heart. Most people think the clothes are the man (or the woman).

Hence in ' contemplation ', the intellect is facing a blank, and the will follows it. Consequently the imagination and feeling wander into distractions (as when one is half awake). The ' acts ' are just to give them some matter to work upon.

Supposing that our soul is simply like that of animals —that we have no free-will but only feelings, that we have no intellect but only successions of images—then

76

this practice of auto-suggestion will be quite meaningless :
but then it ought also to be useless, and it isn't.

Second defence : from authority.

St. John of the Cross teaches it, and had considerable
experience of its good effect. So had de Caussade, a great
director of nuns.

Third defence.

The ' ligature ' (that is the beginning of ligature) which
makes it *impossible* to meditate in time of prayer, begins,
of course, while people are *trying* to meditate.

The advice I give is to renounce trying to do the
impossible, and to take to the only kind of prayer which
is possible. So it is evident that the advice does not cause
the ligature, which *happens* in most pious people, and
they never cease to try and meditate. All their efforts
are against it.

When, on the contrary, they find somebody who tells
them to give up these vain efforts, and merely ' give themselves to God ', the ' ligature ' is not thereby intensified.
On the contrary I believe it gradually weakens. This
seems to be all in favour of *my* explanation, and against
what psychologists would say.

My explanation will shortly appear, shortly described,
in the *Downside Review.*[1]   I have written it wholly for
theologians. It is quite incomplete. I could have written
it in vague, philosophical, misty jargon, for modern readers.
But I want to 'apologise' first to theologians!

You see, I don't think either the act or the faculty of
contemplation is *supernatural*,—only unusual, ' preternatural '. But it is a vehicle of grace, just as the rest of
the soul is. As God can help us through the emotions

[1] This article, entitled *What* is *Mysticism,* will be found reprinted as
Appendix II of this volume, p. 297.

77

and imagination, and by the intellect and will, so He can help us through this *fundus*, or *apex animae*, which I take to be the ' pure ' use of the intellect, contemplating truth.

Ever yours affectly,

H. JOHN CHAPMAN.

P.S. I forgot. I meant to say this. I take it that this kind of prayer *may* seem at first (I don't know, but it seems possible) to decrease devotion to our Lord's Humanity. But I have never found any reason for thinking it does so eventually. I believe exactly the contrary.

The interpolations in St. John of the Cross, to the effect that the thought of our Lord's Human Nature could never be a distraction used to worry me, until I found that they were not in the best originals. For :—

(1) to *think* deliberately about anything during prayer is obviously a distraction, as it takes the will off its object.

(2) It is also obviously impossible to beginners in contemplation, because the only reason or justification for contemplative prayer is that they *can't* meditate.

Hence St. John of the Cross could not have inserted rubbish, and he didn't.

Outside prayer, meditation (thinking out a subject, as for a sermon) is just as easy as before. Only it is not done ' prayerfully '.

There is no reason why the ' acts ' should not be addressed to our Lord *as* Man ; or to our Lady, as in a case I know.

But what matters is always the effect of prayer. The *Night of the Senses* took away all sensible sweetness, or satisfaction of the intellect, in meditating on our Lord's Life and Passion. The regret of this is a stronger act of love than before ; and this act of *wish to love* must go

78

on increasing, or I should say at once the prayer is bad. But whether there is any emotional feeling outside prayer depends on the character of the person in question. But I am sure good prayer *must* increase tenderness (so to speak) and appreciation, in a momentary look, without long consideration. And I am sure there is an ' irradiation ' from prayer on ordinary knowledge, making it broader and more comprehensive.

Last P.S. Of course I really know nothing about it all.

XXIII: TO ALGAR THOROLD, ESQ.

Editor of *The Dublin Review*.

Downside Abbey,
Bath.

Sept. 24, 1930.

My dear Thorold,

I am sorry you don't like it.[1] I thought the contrast of Balduke made de Caussade's teaching clear. I thought I said something nice about Balduke, but I *do* think he is all wrong in theory.

As to St. John of the Cross, he has an Active Night of the senses, and an Active Night of the spirit (in the " Ascent of Mount Carmel "), which explain what *we* ought to try and do *ourselves*. It is negative—mortification, stripping—and is a *condition*, but not a *cause* of union with God. He makes no definite promises as to a result.

He *also* gives a Passive Night of the senses and a Passive Night of the spirit (in the " Dark Night of the Soul "). This is what *God* does, and it will produce the effect God wishes, provided the soul does not resist. (The soul's correspondence, or non-resistance is the ' active night '.)

[1] The reference is to an article entitled *J. P. de Caussade* (which appeared in *The Dublin Review*, for January, 1931).

Now Balduke clearly has only the 'active night' as the cause, and the 'passive night' as the effect. To make a *schema* :—

	Balduke	St. John of the Cross
Active night (mortification)	cause	condition (almost a *sine qua non*)
Passive night (God's action)	effect ⎫	cause
Divine union	effect ⎭	effect

This is very rough, and gives what I think they mean, though not what they say. Some idiot (I learn from *La Vie Spirituelle*) has lately declared that St. John of the Cross puts the Active Nights *first in time*, and makes them *followed by* the Passive Nights!

Of course there are not *four* nights, but *two !* The active and passive are two sides of the same phenomenon. If I push a Bath chair, the same phenomenon (motion) is active in me, and passive in the chair. But if the chair was alive and had a will, it would react by either resisting or abandoning itself. The active night is a voluntary stripping and abandonment, and (so far) co-operation. The passive night is God's far more effective action in stripping and scrubbing.

Balduke definitely promises that those who follow his prescription will attain the desired result. And he aims, like Evagrius, at ʼ$\alpha\pi\alpha\theta\epsilon\acute{\iota}\alpha$.[1] I like Evagrius, and have never given up the idea of writing a book upon him. But Balduke ought to have known better. Arintero lately wrote that all mystical graces *cadunt sub merito*. They are the measure of sanctity, and are obtained by good works and human effort (assisted by grace, of course). This is dangerous rot.

[1] Insensibility, Stoicism; cf. : Letter lxv, p. 162.

If you want me to tone down what I said, I can do it, if you send the MS. back. But I really do not want to! Of course, most of Balduke is beautiful reading, but *bonum* is *ex integra causa, malum ex omni defectu*. I fear the article is at best rather dull.

Ever yours affectly,

H. JOHN CHAPMAN.

Perhaps you had better anyhow send back the de Caussade article ; as it may need softening down. I want it to please the S.J.'s I don't like having enemies.

H.J.C.

XXIV: TO THE SAME.

Downside Abbey,

Oct. 9, 1930.   *Near Bath.*

My dear Thorold,

I have added a note of one page.[1] I had embodied more of the letter ;[2] but I did not like it on second thoughts. I do not want to look as if I denied that good works merit more actual grace *de condigno ;* as I hold this very strongly. I do not see that any apology is needed for falling foul of Balduke, as his view that ' desolation ' is our own fault is un-Christian.

I agree with you that there was a good deal of ' Stoicism ' in the desert, and that their mortifications were very like modern record breaking,—a kind of sport.

Ever yours affectly,

H. JOHN CHAPMAN.

---

[1] To the article mentioned in the previous letter.
[2] The letter to A. Thorold, dated 24th Sept., 1930.

Downside Abbey,
Oct. 15, 1930.   *Near Bath.*

My dear Thorold,

"I cannot always tell His Will (now) for the future ; but I can always tell it now (for now) " ; surely that is clear!

But you are quite right that a note is needed ;[1] as what I said can easily be misunderstood. I quite agree that some of de Caussade looks like *Illuminism*. I do not think it is really quite that.

1. In the case of a really saintly ' abandoned ' soul, its expectations in the long run will be fulfilled, and it will be seen that the results justify its confidence in God. But Caussade is emphatic that the soul itself will mostly be in darkness and perplexity, and it will seem like a kind of accident that things ever come right. The soul will not be conscious of being ' inspired ', but of Providence working, in spite of the soul's feebleness and ignorance. This is not ' illuminism ' but ' obscurism ' !

2. In the case of any one (any pious person) the proper thing is (1) to pray for guidance, (2) to act for the best, (3) to say that we have done God's Will, even if (*a*) we find that we had decided wrongly or (*b*) that (anyhow) the result is wrong.

For Caussade makes it so clear that God does not expect or want us to know and do what is most perfect in itself, but what, here and now, we suppose (after and with prayer and abandonment) to be best. Hence I do not think there is any ' illuminism '.

What I call Illuminism is this :—

(*A*) I pray, and then I make a decision which I call infallibly right in itself.

[1] To the de Caussade article.

(*B*) Or a Superior says:—"Whatever you do under obedience has God's blessing and will turn out a success ; *therefore* (!) whatever I order is infallibly right."

There is a lot of Illuminism about !

After writing so far, I have tried to explain the same in a note, which I enclose. Please read it and say whether it is right or wrong, or clear or obscure. I wish it was shorter.

I am not trying to give *my* view, but de Caussade's, which seems to me common sense.

One lives in perpetual doubt and ignorance what God's Will is going to be, but not what it is at this *individual moment :* that we always know, *because it is.*

Therefore the whole point of the " Sacrament of the present moment "[1] is that it is a (covering yet revealing) sacrament ; it is God's action, God's Will, or ' it is God '. All my duty is to keep in touch with Him as this moment passes into the next. My obvious duty may be *at this moment* to consider what comes next,—and not to know.

I am sorry this article has not pleased you much. I hope it will not prove obscure or misleading. If so, it had better not appear.

Ever yours affectly,

H. JOHN CHAPMAN.

XXVI: TO AN UNMARRIED LADY.

Downside Abbey,
Easter Tuesday, 1925. [*April* 14.]   *Near Bath.*

Dear Miss . . . .

I put your letter in my pocket, without looking from whom it came, and only found it this morning ; so please forgive my delay.

[1] de Caussade's term for his special doctrine of ' abandon ', see Introduction, p. 30.

I am not at all inclined to assume the rôle of a professional " director " to anyone. But I am quite willing to give occasional advice, for what it is worth ; and I can answer letters. Giving people advice sometimes helps them to know their own mind.

1. I do not think Fr. Baker is *invariably* reliable. But who is ? All books should be read with common sense. As to " living more with people ", it is not *in itself* good, if it means living less with God. Most people need quiet to be able to pray easily. But I should think that it would be good to avoid depression by reasonable distractions.

2. If your Mother needs you, of course that is a duty. And if it prevents quiet and prayer and Mass, obviously none of these are good for us, except when God wishes us to have them. If God wishes us to be " extroverted ", we must accept this with confidence.

3. No one goes in for contemplative prayer without violent trials. When these come, simply accept them as God's will, and as an absolutely necessary purification. When one is troubled by these thoughts, the only thing to do is to *despise* the state one is in,—to regard it as an illness,—as if it was someone else. Do not worry about your " mental balance ". Both Fr. Baker and Père de Caussade think that we may easily have to make an act of *abandon* that we are willing to go mad, if God wishes ! Only it comes to nothing, and it does not happen. It is a very painful state to be in ; but so much the better.

There is nothing to be done, but to accept all such sufferings passively, as if they were happening to someone else. Of course it is difficult,—in fact it is, in the main, impossible to do this ; for if we could *feel* (as well as believe) that all this was only a purification and did not matter, it would almost cease to be a pain, and would not purify.

But one must try to learn to live more and more by the *highest* point of the soul (or the " base " if you like, it means the same)—adhering to God without feeling, and trying to realise that the real " *me* " is not feeling and sentiment and worry and suffering, but a simple *intention* behind and above all the feelings—almost imperceptible, but the only real *ME*.

I think Père de Caussade's letters are altogether admirable. His treatise is more academic, and has some things which might be dangerous to follow. But his direction is quite safe. I know nothing so useful as those letters, for anyone who is in the " Night of the Spirit ", as you are.

I will try and come round. But, I repeat, I do not profess to be a " director " !

I am,

Yours sincerely,

H. JOHN CHAPMAN

The best way to bear trials is to say :—" I am ready to have as much more as God wishes. I want to be humbled. I do *not* want to be a great contemplative. I *want* just what God gives. I *want* to be dry and distracted. I want to feel in despair, even—if God wishes it.

XXVII: TO THE SAME.

Downside Abbey,
Near Bath.

April 27, 1925.

Dear Miss . . . .

What you describe seems to be not *abnormal* but *unusual*. It ought to be more usual, were there more detached people.

It is not a case of spiritual disease, but of spiritual growth; like (to take the first example that occurs to me) a child cutting its teeth, painful but necessary, and healthy and normal. Please understand that I am writing as a friend, not as a " director ". I do not pretend to special knowledge.

But I know that people who (like yourself) sometimes feel that they are off the main road, or isolated, or unlike other people, are often consoled by finding that others have had parallel experiences. Now I do not know that I can give you parallel instances : but I quote the nearest parallels which occur to me.

The Cloud of Unknowing, Ch. 36. especially " and mean by *sin* a lump, thou wottest never what, none other thing but *thyself* . . . it should be no need to bind a *madder thing* than thou shouldest be in this time ". (Fr. Collins's edition paraphrases, " should not lightly find a more foolish beast ".) Read also Ch. 40.

It seems to me that this perception of your own nothingness is not " horrible ", still less untrue, but a great grace. You know St. John of the Cross's favourite dictum, that the purer a ray of light, the less it is seen. So that, when you have this feeling of your own impurity, it is a proof that you are looking at the purity of God,—but without any consciousness of seeing Him, because the ray of light from Him is so pure that you only see it in its effects. One of those effects is the vision of your own nothingness; another is the perception of the (comparative) unreality of all finite things, when the infinite reality of God is unconsciously contemplated. (I should prefer to say " super-consciously ".)

When I said that the real ME is a simple intention, above all feeling, I meant " above all feelings of discontent, or despondency, or doubt ". If this idea of your own nothingness was a " feeling ", it would be imagination and delusion; I take it that it is really, as you say, "an experimental knowledge", that is to say, a super-sensuous perception and perfectly true.

But when you say, "a hideous mass of sinfulness", that can be taken in two ways: either (1) (rightly) to mean the 'lump' or 'mass' that we really are, or (2) as a description of *feelings left by this experience on the lower part of the soul* afterwards. If you have such feelings, causing depression or anxiety, disown them, pay no attention whatever.

And do not try to *use* the experience,—to meditate on it, or increase it, or diminish it. It is neither to be feared nor disliked on the one hand, because it is good and necessary when God gives it; nor is it to be wished for or encouraged, because we do not know *when* it is necessary.

The great thing is to *accept*, but nothing more. Never mix your *self* up with God's work. When one thinks over an experience afterwards one always distorts it somewhat.

So much for your adjective "abnormal". Next for your "looks uncommonly like *insanity*". (So does genius, so does enthusiasm or fervour.)

Here the quotation which occurs to me is from St. John of the Cross, who is discussing the beginnings of the "illuminative way"—(that is where you are !)

I can't find the one I thought I remembered, but this will do: *Dark Night*, Bk. II., Ch. viii, No. 2, "The soul . . . cannot pray or give much attention to Divine things. Neither can it *attend to temporal matters*, for it falls into frequent distractions", etc.

Don't mind feeling stupid, or as if your mind was going. (Why shouldn't it ?) It won't ! But it is inevitable that you should feel something of the sort. At least—I do not know, I am no authority—but I should think it is very ordinary in the "illuminative way". It is very unpleasant, and I expect many people feel it without supposing it to be in any way connected with "prayer". The explanation is obvious. The unperceived, infused contemplation occupies the mind, and it can't think of something else; but, as the operation in which it is engaged is either totally or partially imperceptible, the mind seems to be vacant and stupid.

Suppose you are immersed in a book, and someone speaks to you; you hear what they say without understanding it,—you have to repeat it again and wake yourself up before the words have any meaning. Much in the same way, if your mind is immersed in contemplation, you find you are stupid or crazy about something else; only the contemplation is always indefinite and often quite unconscious. Try to say the "Our Father", for example, and you can't imagine what the words mean.

Sometimes the 'contemplation' is a little more definite, and you get out into a desert, or into eternity, and the clock stops.

Are you to "shake it off" as far as possible?

When you have *some duty* to perform—I don't mean important, but anything you suppose is reasonable, and that God would therefore wish you to do—then you will naturally try to be *wholly* at what you are doing, and therefore will try to shake off what distracts you. Apart from that, simply accept it, and it will do you enormous good.

Finally: do not forget the distinction I tried to indicate above between

A. States of consciousness; that is, experience, experimental knowledge, state of soul—or whatever name suits it best, and

B. Your own reflections on these states, when you think of them afterwards :—or the *feelings* of anxiety or despondency, or of pleasure or calm which result from them, mostly in the lower part of the soul.

With regard to *A* : you should simply *accept* them, without thinking about them, reflecting on them, wondering about them ; not considering whether they are pleasant or not.

With regard to *B* : disown the reflections, etc., which you can't help making. Look upon worry as a temptation to imperfection. But in so far as anxiety, worry, reflection or pleasure are involuntary and unavoidable, they are almost the same as *A*. Simply put up with them. But do not reflect upon your reflections, or worry voluntarily about your involuntary worries.

But these involuntary reflections and worries are not *quite* the same as *A*. I mean, they are secondary, not primary ; not immediate states, but the result of those states. " *A* " is an involuntary state, because it comes from infused ' contemplation ' ; whereas " *B* " is an involuntary *action* (i.e. reflecting on " *A* ") of our own.

Consequently you *accept* " *A* " passively, but *put up with* " *B* ". i.e. (1) you let " *A* " come, and leave it alone, trying not to reflect upon it ; (2) you *disown* " *B* ", and leave it alone, for as long as it chooses to stay. Don't *fight* it, only disown it.

I think you will understand, but I will give the examples:—

" *A* ". I find I am not looking at God, but at a horrible nothingness, which is myself. Accept this as a fact that you do feel it, and that it is all right.

" *B* ". But you can't help reflecting on it : e.g. (1) it is unpleasant, (2) it may be bad for me, (3) it may make me ill, (4) perhaps I ought to fight it, (5) perhaps it means I am going mad, (6) shall I take a pill ? (7) am I so wicked that I am going to Hell, and that is why I can't think of God? (8) it must be bad, because I can't pray, (9) perhaps I am too religious, I am getting morbid, I must mix with others, and be worldly, (10) perhaps there is no such thing as religion.

Perhaps something like some of these thoughts *will* come, against your will. You *disown* them. You say (or mean, without words), " O God, You know these thoughts are against my will, I don't want them, they are not ME. The real ME is only the intention of suffering them as long as I can't help them."

If possible, laugh at them: don't fight them. Always say, again and again, that they do not matter in the least.

Of course "infused contemplation" is not *of itself* an interference with our ordinary consciousness; but, in the lower degrees of prayer it usually is (always, in fact, except when it is *very* feeble). Some would say that it is only in the "unitive way" that the impediment disappears. Poulain calls it the "ligature". Saudreau makes it the proof of the "mystical marriage" or "transforming union" that there is no impediment, so that it is possible for the soul to attend to God and to its ordinary business at the same time, without any lessening of the perfection of either.

I wonder ! I am inclined to think it is a question of degree. I should doubt whether anyone (except our Blessed Lady) could arrive at being so perfect that no amount of infused knowledge could distract them at all ! St. Teresa had ecstasies for years, after the time she thought they had ceased because the purification had gone far enough. But in lower stages the "inhibition" is always butting in when one doesn't want it ! Every moderately pious person feels *some* beginnings of the "ligature".

Lastly. You ask whether you love God less when you have less longings and anxieties. This is vague in itself. But in your case the answer is that more peace means greater love. As the vehicle goes faster it shakes less. The longings and anxieties are chiefly in the lower (sensitive, imaginative, emotional) part of the soul, or the lower use of the intellect; the highest part (or apex, or base, or centre) of the soul is the cause of peace.

St. Ignatius puts this in another way. He says that, in a bad man, the evil spirit tries to keep him in peace, the good angel tries to rouse him to anxiety. Contrariwise, in a good man, the bad angel tries to arouse anxiety, the good angel tries to keep him in peace.

May your Guardian Angel keep you in peace, though sometimes a peace you cannot understand!

I am ever yours sincerely,
(with apologies for lengthiness)

H. JOHN CHAPMAN

I daresay it is all off the point.

P.S. On reading over your letter and my reply, I am pleased to see that I have not really given you any advice. I have only said that (1) your *state* is all right, and (2) your *conduct* in it (accepting it) is all right. So that I am not interfering. God has done it all so far,—He gave the state, and through the state taught you how to take it.

But, thirdly, (3) there were your worries. God did not *do* those, but permitted them, for your profit. The pain of uncertainty and anxiety is a purification. St. Teresa's "Night of the Spirit" consisted mainly in the misery caused her by the friends and directors who told her the visions came from the devil, and the others who told her they were divine favours. It was like Barry Pain's story of the girl who was told by the great artist that her hair was divine, whereas the little boys in the street called out " Carrots " as she passed. She was so puzzled that she wanted to die,—so she dyed.

I can't help believing that St. Teresa got more good from her bad directors than from her visions ! (I am not including the mystical intuitions which were behind her visions ; for these caused the whole.)

Surely you have found yourself described and prescribed for in *The Dark Night*, Bk. II, and other places of St. John of the Cross. I suppose you understand his system : the Night of the Senses begins first, then the Night of the Spirit very soon after. They overlap, but the former gradually ceases to have any importance as the latter develops. *The Dark Night*, Bk. I, gives the *Passive Night of the Senses*, that is, how infused Contemplation acts in us to take away the use of our imagination, sentiment, and emotion ; Book II, how it purifies our intellect and will. The *Ascent of Mount Carmel* tells us what our conduct is to be during all this time : and St. John calls this the *Active Night*. The famous rules of mortification :—" In order to taste the Whole, seek to have no taste in any thing ", are the rules for the " active night of the senses ". Books II and III give rules for the " active night of the spirit ", i.e. to care only for the *indistinct*, not for visions and voices and pleasures.

I have just found the passage I wanted : *Mount Carmel ;* No ! I have lost it again. It is very elusive !

Here it is. *Mount Carmel*, Bk. III, Ch. i, No. 3. In D. Lewis's translation, (ed. by Fr. B. Zimmermann, 1906, p. 243) the remark is flat enough. But in the French rendering from the Spanish " Critical Edition " (by Chanoine Hoornaert of Bruges) it is worth transcribing.

" En effet cette union divine fait le vide dans la fantaisie et semble en balayer toute forme et connaissance pour l'élever au surnaturel, ce qui peut donner lieu à un singulier phénomène. Parfois, au moment ou Dieu accorde ces touches d'union à la mémoire, il se produit tout d'un coup une sorte de chavirement dans le cerveau où elle a son siege ; l'effet en est si sensible qu'on a l'illusion de la tête qui perd sa force, de la raison et du sens qui s'anéantissent. Cette impression est plus ou moins forte d'après l'intensité de l'action divine, et aussitôt par l'union même, la mémoire se vide et se purifie, comme je viens de le dire ; ses connaissances lui deviennent etrangères et parfois elle tombe dans un si grand oubli de soi, qu'elle doit faire effort pour se rappeler quelquechose.

" Cet oubli de la mémoire et suspension de l'imagination sont parfois si complets sous l'influence de l'union avec Dieu, qu'un temps notable se passe sans qu'on s'en aperçoive, et sans qu'on se rende compte de ce qui s'est passé dans l'intervalle. Comme l'imagination est parfois également suspendue elle n'est pas sensible à la peine qu'on veut lui faire, car il n'y a pas de sentiment sans images et sans pensée, et rien de tel n'est alors en activité. Or, Dieu n'accordera pas ces touches parfaites d'union, aussi longtemps que la mémoire, comme nous l'avons dit, n'a fait abandon complet de toutes ses connaissances perceptibles. Il est à noter que ses suspensions ne se produisent plus de cette manière chez les parfaits, l'union parfaite leur étant donnée ils n'ont plus à passer par l'initiation."

I expect this passage pretty well describes your frequent state. St. John of the Cross regards it as caused by " touches of union in the memory " or " perfect touches of union ", which take place in imperfect souls while being purified.

You seem to have this in a prolonged form. The mild forms, e.g. (1) feeling stupid, (2) distracted, (3) forgetful, are very common, and also a mild fear that the mind is going.

I suppose you understand that " le vide dans la fantaisie " and " la suspension de l'imagination " and " l'imagination . . . est suspendue " all mean the same thing. St. John of the Cross means that we can't use our reason in the ordinary way, because our reason works habitually by means of images (principally auditive, i.e. imagined words, also visual, i.e. mental pictures); consequently, when the imagination is empty and won't work, the reason is powerless, and can't think. [As a fact there is a higher use of the reason—without images—and this is precisely the 'infused contemplation': it is 'superconscious': i.e. we generally know that something is going on, but we cannot tell anyone else, or even tell ourselves, what it is, because we only describe by images. Hence, when we reflect upon it, and try to put it into words, we can only call it "nothing" or vacancy; only we *know* really that "nothing" means "the ALL", and that (as Aristotle says) there is nothing so knowable as the (to us) Unknowable. *Cloud*, p. 160.]

I am glad I found the passage. I looked for it in the English,—and of course it wasn't there. On the other hand there are many things in the English which St. John never wrote;—put in by Censors, to water down his doctrine.

I *meant* to write *two* pages ![1]

XXVIII: TO A LADY LIVING IN THE WORLD.

Downside Abbey,
Bath.

Sept. 27, 1920.

Dear Miss . . . .

God's Will for us is two-fold :—

1. His signified Will, including the Commandments, Counsels, and Inspirations. We correspond with this by the general active virtue of Obedience, which includes all the active Virtues.

2. The Will of His Good Pleasure, which we see in *all* the circumstances, both external and internal, of our

[1] The actual MS. fills twenty-five pages—Ed.

life. We correspond with this by the general virtue of Resignation or Indifference (St. Ignatius and St. F. de Sales prefer this name), or ' *Abandon* ', (for which there is no English word, it is Bossuet's as well as de Caussade's and Gay's term), or Conformity (Scaramelli).

Consequently, the whole of the relation of our Will towards God is expressed by these two Virtues, Obedience and Conformity.

Both for beginners and for imaginative people Obedience is the more important. For quieter and drier souls, after Obedience to the Commandments has become habitual, Conformity (or ' *Abandon* ') becomes the more prominent.

One reason is that Contemplatives become more sensible to the action of God's grace, which is always " pushing behind ". So that their obedience to God in little things feels more like non-resistance than positive activity. In reality the one act of giving oneself entirely to God's Will includes both Obedience and " *l'Abandon* " ; we are giving ourselves to God to do His Will and accept His Will in everything. The whole of this is called " *Abandon* ", because it is a gift of self to God, but more properly it is Obedience, since it is an act of obedience to God's wish that we should give ourselves to Him. It seems, therefore, that Obedience and Conformity are two divisions of a simple act which itself is either Obedience or Conformity, according to the point of view from which we look at it.

Although we may contrast Obedience as an active virtue with Conformity as a passive virtue, yet even so :—

(*a*) Obedience is passive in comparison with the activity of doing our own will, i.e. opposing and resisting God's presence (so to speak) when we have become sensitive to His grace ; and to *do* His Will feels like ceasing to oppose, refusing to resist.

(*b*) Conformity, on the other hand, though a passive virtue, is active, in so far as it is an act; i.e. to accept, to welcome, to abandon oneself to all the dispositions of God's Providence (all His arrangements, all He wishes us to suffer, all our own miseries, etc.), is an act, repeated, habitual, frequently unconscious, but still an act. (Just as the act of inattention to the world, which constitutes Recollection, is an act.)

" Abandon " is not pure passivity. It *feels like it*, but it isn't.

It is obviously to be expected that progress in union with God should result in less consciousness of effort to unite ourselves with His Will, and an increase of consciousness of His continual assistance. I don't mean " consciousness of " in the sense that we *know* He is " pushing behind "; rather we are often conscious of being pushed, without knowing that God is the pusher. But we no longer feel our duty to be activity (bustle, hard work, etc.) the day for that is past; but to remain united. At first our whole duty seemed to be to run hard to catch the train, but afterwards our chief duty seems to be to stop in the train. It carries us on in the dark, so that we can't see that we are getting any further, and our chief temptation is to get out at the next station, saying, " I should get on much faster if I walked."

Ever yours sincerely,

H. John Chapman, O.S.B.

XXIX: TO THE SAME.

Palazzo S. Calisto,
Roma, 14.

Dec. 23, 1920.
Dear Miss . . . .

It is quite right for us to throw our heart into our work and do it with all our might; but be quite detached from results. It does not matter whether we are praised and appreciated by human beings. All our work is for God, and through Him for our neighbours. The more disappointments and failures there are, the more we are thrown upon Him. Until we have had plenty of them, we never have a pure intention.

We have a *right* intention quite easily, but we have all sorts of other, minor intentions mixed up with it, until God has purified us. It is most important in all our pleasures and successes to have the habit of saying, " I am glad, I am immensely grateful ; but I don't *want* it, I only want *Thee*."

Never carry out any resolution made in prayer, without first testing it in a dry light outside prayer ; to see whether it is reasonable or really the best. You must have *plenty of time* for prayer. Recollection is usually impossible otherwise, and you will be driven to reading Novels! But when you have time to be alone with God and at peace, the temporal worries cease to be worries and become almost pleasures. But when you *can't* get time, then you have to try and be cheerful, and offer all you suffer to God *without feeling even that you mean it*. And then, later on, when you get some time again, you find that you have made progress in prayer without knowing how.

If one *felt* one was suffering patiently and for God, one wouldn't suffer so much. It is the feeling of impatience and division from God which *is* suffering, and it is most meritorious. So don't mind it. I think it is an excellent thing to laugh at one's self a little whenever one feels a martyr!

Ever yours sincerely in Dn̄o,

H. John Chapman, O.S.B.

97

Downside Abbey,
Stratton-on-the-Fosse,

Saturday, Feb. 23, 1929.   *Nr. Bath.*

Dear Miss . . . .

All you say in your letter is perfectly normal, and quite right and satisfactory. I can really only repeat what you say I said before (I have often said it, so I daresay I did) : that if you are carried in our Lord's arms, you will seldom see His face ! All the meditations with points, and the ordinary sermons, and the regular and admirable devotions, are meant for those who try to walk, holding our Lord's hand, and looking up into His Face. You evidently cannot do that.

You will gradually find that you don't want to, that you are infinitely better off as you are. You are in the dark, carried, and you don't need to choose and see your path.

But you must simply practise ' *abandon* ' (I wish there was an English word). I am always so grateful to you for introducing me to Père de Caussade. I think he is the best spiritual guide since St. Francis de Sales. His book on prayer is rare ; but Mr. Thorold has borrowed a copy from the Carthusians, and is going to translate and publish it.

I recommend you in prayer to think as little as possible, and say as little as possible. Now and then remain quite *idle*, as it were,—and get into the habit of doing this (a sort of suspension) if it comes easily, at any time in the day. The one devotion is simply God's Will. And when you want this and only this, then everything is included. You will find that you have *really* a greater devotion (say) to the Passion than you had before ; [Which is the greater love :—' I enjoy thinking about the Passion ', or, ' I can't bear to think about it ' ?]

Again remember that a distracted prayer is generally more humbling than a recollected prayer,—therefore it gives more glory to God and less to us, and we find afterwards that we have got more good.

I quite understand that you 'used to have a supernatural life', 'a spiritual life'. I hope that is gone for good! We have to become like little children. We have just the feelings which God gives us; and we thank Him for them, whether they are joys or temptations. We must not worry about our souls. We can't do much. We must remove obstacles (chiefly by continually humbling ourselves and being little) and God does the rest.

Therefore have *absolute confidence* in God, and none in yourself. Also *pray*, quite definitely and absolutely, for whatever you think God wishes you to pray for, whether for yourself or for others; and make up your mind that you will get it (not because you deserve it, but because God is good).

You are on the look out for 'consolation', merely because you still imagine that you are not serving God properly when you are in dryness. Make up your mind once for all that dryness is best, and you will find that you are frightened at having anything else! Embrace aridities and distractions and temptations, and you will find you love to be in darkness, and that there *is* a supersensible light that is simply extinguished by consolation!

You ask for explanation about the right use of *reason* and *feelings*.

1. *Feelings :* Protestants depend upon them. They are useful for beginners. They are not to be depended upon.

2. *Reason :* Necessary in theology, in teaching. Useful to show that the Faith is reasonable. Necessary for ordinary conduct. But in prayer only useful for beginners. We do not have to *reason* that God is to be loved, (except in early stages); or that the Passion of Christ, God and Man,

is the most wonderful event in history:—nor do we have to *reason* that we ought to correct our faults.

3. But we get the means to correct our faults, and love and glorify God by pure prayer—prayer of the will— pure intention without words. This prayer perseveres through distractions, and tends to become 'prayer without ceasing',—an intention of being united with God's Will at every moment.

As a fact we *are* always in touch with God; everything that happens is His arrangement, His Providence, and a means of grace, a push on to Heaven; only most people try to go their own way, and thus put obstacles to God's action. Once give yourself wholly to Him, and you realise that He is always working outside you by circumstances, and inside you by your thoughts and distractions,—unless you resist. This is the way of pure love. It is very dark and painful on the surface; but there is something behind which is really strength and peace (only those are not the right words,—there are no words—when you think of it there is nothing at all! But don't think,—and it carries you on!).

Ever yours in Dn̄o,

H. JOHN CHAPMAN.

XXXI: TO THE SAME.

Downside Abbey,
Stratton-on-the-Fosse,
Feb. 28, 1929. *Nr. Bath.*

Dear Miss . . . .

So many thanks for telling me of the translation of de Caussade's little book on prayer. I must try to get it. I wrote off at once to Algar Thorold to tell him; as he also thought there was no translation into English.

The two little books of Saudreau on Prayer, according to St. Francis de Sales and according to St. Jane Frances de Chantal, have just reached me to-day from Sheed and Ward. I recommended a friend of mine to translate them, as I thought they would be very useful. Try them, if you come across them.

I am sure the humiliations of the Catholic Evidence Guild must be very trying, and also very good for your soul! I suppose it is very necessary to go through a good deal, as the heckling on a pitch must be very difficult to bear patiently, and reply to gently and effectively.

Evidently your soul is getting on very well. We must not want to see our own progress, or ever to be self-satisfied (i.e. to be lukewarm). We suffer best when we resent and hate the suffering, and *feel we are bearing it badly*. (How admirably St. Thérèse of Lisieux teaches this : she puts the most iron heroism into sentimental language.)

I am,
Ever yours sincerely,
H. JOHN CHAPMAN.

XXXII: TO THE SAME.

Downside Abbey,
Stratton-on-the-Fosse,
Nr. Bath.

Dec. 30, 1930.

Dear Miss . . . .

Many thanks for your letter. I wish you all blessings for the New Year. I am so glad you are going on with all your Guild work and studies.

I quite agree with what you say about going on without any (apparent) help inside or outside,—and that it *is* the practice of ' *abandon* '—and that our Lady is taking care of us. We learn that our own efforts are of little avail, though we go on making them all the more,—and that God's support is not sensible.

But I find more and more that definite prayer for all we want is necessary. And our Blessed Lady *always* gives what we ask for reasonably. Everything is unexpected and disappointing : but, when we have realised this, the unexpected is expected, and disappointment is awaited, and almost welcomed as an old friend. God's will is all that matters. We have to be very small, like the Babe in the Crib. I am so very busy that I can't be very ' spiritual '.

Ever yours very sincerely,

H. JOHN CHAPMAN.

XXXIII: TO THE SAME.

Downside Abbey,
Stratton-on-the-Fosse,
Nr. Bath.

Jan. 8, 1931.

Dear Miss . . . .

I am so sorry to hear that your ill-health has begun over again, but I am glad you are taking care of yourself. No doubt daily Mass was too much of a strain. You evidently have to take things easy for a time. Don't worry your head with Higher Studies, if they tire you. Recreation of some kind will be better ; and, if you do it for God's sake, it will be quite as meritorious.

I send you an off-print of an article on Caussade, which has been reprinted, with slight alterations, as an Introduction to Algar Thorold's translation of his book on prayer. I send it merely as a recognition of the fact that you first introduced me to Caussade, and I cannot be too thankful to you for this. Have you got his book on Prayer ? Bremond has re-edited it in French, immediately after the English translation appeared; so I had not seen his Introduction, nor he mine.

Ever yours sincerely,

H. JOHN CHAPMAN.

XXXIV: TO A MARRIED LADY.

Downside Abbey,
Near Bath.

Jan. 20, 1931.

Dear Mrs. . . . .

I am glad you like my paper—though all the good in it is the quotations from *de Caussade*!

What you wrote to me, is what I feel. I suppose it is quite right to feel it. As you say, *de Caussade's* principles are obviously true. Whereas, on the other hand, it cannot be right to 'accept' one's imperfections and sins as coming from God! Hence the impulse to say:—"It is all very well for others, but I myself ought to meditate, and do violence to myself, and make elaborate good resolutions, or use 'particular examen'."

I think there is a two-fold answer:—

(1) If we are really uniting ourselves with God's Will, then we *accept passively* the duty of being active; whether active in external matters, or active about our own soul. We find God wishes us to be Martha, when we want to be Mary; and this happens every day in external matters. We throw ourselves into them because we do *not* choose them, but they are there to be carried out.

(2) But as to passive prayer, and 'accepting' our imperfection (sing.), and our imperfections (plur.) *after* they have occurred, I take it that we have to ask ourselves whether any other way is possible.

If we cannot 'meditate' as prayer—but only as preparation for a book or a sermon, or for a moment—it is no

103

use to ourselves to know *why*. [It is interesting theoretically, and it may be useful to others to find out *why*, but it is quite useless for *me*, except to free me from false ideas that I have got out of books.] We can't; there is the fact. So we do what we can; it is very little; it is humiliating; we should not like anyone to look into our minds while we are at prayer. But God knows we are acting as straight-forwardly as we can at the moment.

That the effect of this should be humility is obvious; and hence the result that we think we ought to be *doing* something, and that we must be in the wrong way, because we are so bad. But that is only a part of the paradox, that a saint usually thinks himself the worst of men, περίψημα πάντων, and that the way to sanctity is to think oneself worse and worse.

" I am glad you cannot see how badly I pray; but I really don't see what else I can do." This is what it amounts to. And, " Of course I do not correct my faults; I do not make elaborate plans and resolutions, and additions and subtractions; still I do not see what else I can do, except ask pardon and humble myself every time I fall; for I know all about it. I needn't meditate on my imperfections; and, though I doubtless have numbers of them that I don't see, yet God shows me quite, quite enough for the moment".

But this raises another question; *de Caussade* clearly would like to teach '*abandon*' to beginners! But then, would it be possible to have *begun* by being simple?

For we mostly find that we begin by methods and dodges, and scraps of piety, and meditations and considerations and examinations. There was little of all this before the 16th century, and none before the 13th. Is it all as necessary for everyone as it is good for some?

I can't answer this. And all that I have written before is only *quaerendo*. Theories are never quite adequate to life. Moral Theology seldom answers any difficult question, —nor does ascetical Theology. But in practice things work out more easily, as difficulties are so good for us; and therefore all difficulties are easy and consoling. And so on.

Forgive me for writing so much, as you know it all perfectly well, and can express it better than I can. You knew the answer to your doubts while you were writing them down.

And, conversely, I am quite content to feel doubts while I am writing the conclusive answer.

With many thanks, I am,

Yours very sincerely,

H. JOHN CHAPMAN.

Anyhow, it *cannot* be wrong to live in touch with God, by believing that all that happens outside us and inside us is His hand upon us.

XXXV: TO THE SAME.

Downside Abbey,
Near Bath.

June 9, 1931.

Dear Mrs. . . . .

I cannot possibly show you a way out. The most I can do is to show you where you are, *perhaps*.

So far as the information you give carries me, it seems that you have the simple experience that suffering is really suffering and that the chief feeling it causes is rebellion against it, and even against Providence for allowing it. Without all this, suffering would scarcely be suffering.

If we could always *feel* at peace in suffering, the suffering would be rather pleasant,—just as people 'enjoy bad health'. There is also another side,—that this revolt against suffering humiliates us, and shows us our own weakness. That is another great good, which our nature does not like.

It is all a nasty medicine, but works wonders. Only you will say :—'It would work wonders, if only I accepted it properly.' I should say :—'It would probably do you very little good, if you felt you were accepting it properly!' As I said, the suffering mainly consists in the natural surging up against it, and that is also the purification.

Just as we take medicine to cause what the Breviary lessons of St. Bede delightfully call '*indignatio stomachi*', —in a sense to make us ill—so God's medicine seems to stir up *bad* thoughts, feelings, desires, emotions, in us. They seem to go below the surface and to represent the real 'me', and the wish for 'abandonment' seems very hazy and unreal. I suppose the point is this : which do we *identify ourselves* with, the revolt or the '*abandon*'? If, with the centre of the soul, you hold on to the almost imperceptible acceptance of God's Will (manifested not only in the circumstances, but in your state of feeling), then that almost imperceptible acceptance is the real 'you'. It is a question of living in the '*fundus animae*', or apex, or centre (or whatever you like to call it), which seems a very frail life-boat in a stormy sea. But, provided we stop in the boat and not in the sea, it is all right.

You know all this as well as I do, and you could express it much better. Only do not worry at being worried ; but accept worry peacefully. Difficult, but not impossible.

Ever yours sincerely,

H. JOHN CHAPMAN.

Downside Abbey,
Near Bath.

Sept. 28, 1931.

Dear Mrs. . . . .

I don't think we should get much good from trials (or falls, or apparent falls), if we felt the better for them. Feeling is not very permanent.

It is better to doubt about oneself, and walk about in the dark, than to be pleased with oneself; for fear of having the least touch of the Pharisee.

Humility in oneself is not attractive, though it is attractive in others.

Phariseeism is most enjoyable to oneself, but not to others. If only one could forget oneself ! (that does not sound right). I always say that selfishness is the universal sin.

But do not be afraid of having ' another temperature '. We are in God's hands, so there is nothing to be afraid of.

However, I can't tell you anything you do not know.

I am,
Ever yours sincerely,
H. JOHN CHAPMAN.

XXXVII: TO A LADY LIVING IN THE WORLD.

Downside Abbey,
Bath.

June 23, 1931.

Dear Miss . . . .

I have not read Dr. Kirk on the Vision of God. St. Augustine held that Moses and St. Paul were raised to the Beatific Vision, and out of deference to St. Augustine, St. Thomas Aquinas admitted this : but St. Thomas held that both must have been for the moment " out of the body ".

But the early Fathers and Pseudo-Dionysius, and pretty well all the great Mystics and the scholastic theologians, agree in teaching that the highest ' mystical ' perception of God in this life (except for Moses and St. Paul !) is lower, *not only in degree but in kind*, than the Beatific Vision.

However a very stupid Carmelite writer 200 years ago, Philippus a SS. Trinitate, taught that the highest revelations of God in this life are *the same in kind* as the Beatific Vision of the next life, though obscured and diminished. He was followed by a Dominican, Vallagornera ; and Fr. Sharpe has taught the same in a book on Mysticism. But it is against all the best authorities.

As to visions, they are rarely to be trusted. Women have them for the most part, but not many men.

I am,

Yours truly,

H. JOHN CHAPMAN.

XXXVIII: TO THE SAME.

Downside Abbey,
Near Bath.

Sept. 4, 1932.

Dear Miss . . . .

I was away when your letter came ; and when I got back I was so busy with letters and visitors that I have only this moment read your letter. It looked as if it was not on ' business '.

It is common enough for those who have any touch of ' Mysticism ' (which I regard as having a natural base, though it is a grace if faithfully used) to be absolutely unable to find any meaning in vocal prayers.

If you simply read them without praying, you can understand them as well as any other book. But if you turn to God, all thinking and understanding stops.

I suppose this is because something else is going on.

The rule is simply:—*Pray as you can, and do not try to pray as you can't.*

Take yourself as you find yourself, and start from that.

Again: some day you may find the acts (or continued act) of love stops. It has gone—you can't find it. God is hidden.

Then you take that as His Will, and do the best you can in darkness and humility.

But do not worry yourself about vocal prayers. It is good to say some. But simply to stay with God is best.

As to stability. I quite agree with your answer from St. Benedict, whether it came from him straight, or not.

Stability to the Rule means (I suppose) stability in religious life according to St. Benedict's Rule. This includes stability of place, since the Rule insists that the monk is to remain in the monastery.

But I do not advise you to ask for ' revelations ', even of the most harmless nature!

I am,
Yours sincerely,
H. JOHN CHAPMAN.

XXXIX: TO A MARRIED LADY.

Downside Abbey,
Near Bath.

June 28, 1933.

Dear Mrs. . . . .

I do not like to give any advice to someone I do not know, and whom I have no duty to direct.

But I give you the general principle :—"Obedience is better than sacrifice". In order to be perfectly united to God's Will, we want to be rid of our own will.

Now in doing small mortifications to please God, you are giving up something you like, but You are making the choice yourself. But in obeying your Confessor, you are wholly giving up your will, and you are mortifying yourself more than by giving up some satisfaction by your own will. The little "sacrifice" you make willingly to God by some mortification you have chosen, is nothing like as pleasing to God as the 'obedience' to a man who represents God.

Therefore my advice is to obey! And obey without criticising your Confessor or doubting his wisdom. No Confessor is infallible; but what he tells you is God's Will *for you* here and now.

Believe me,
Yours sincerely in Dn̄o,
H. JOHN CHAPMAN,
Abbot.

Part II

LETTERS TO RELIGIOUS

Abbaye de St. Benoit,
Oct. 19, 1912.   *de Maredsous.*

My dear Father . . . .

I think after all Poulain's "Prayer of Simplicity" is all right, on the whole. But his *quotations* at the end of the chapter (they are omitted in Abbot Butler's reprint) have mostly to do with the Prayer of Quiet, and are wholly out of place.

I have been interviewing all the "contemplatives" I can get hold of. I have not found *one* who has had the Prayer of Quiet. This is annoying. But for the dark night of the senses I am getting plenty of material for study. I am so afraid of having directed people wrong, by general directions meant for everybody.

For instance, Father Baker makes an *absolute* distinction between "The Prayer of forced acts" and "The Prayer of aspirations". He is quite right. The former is non-mystic, and impossible to mystics (though they can get a close imitation of it !) ; and the latter is mystic, and impossible to non-mystics (though again they can imitate it almost exactly, but with *no fruit!*) If one tries the wrong method, one is simply like a hen sitting sedately and happily on a china egg. But I find it is very easy to make mistakes, and theorise without sticking to facts.

I don't believe there are more than ten or twelve monks out of the forty or fifty I have questioned who are in the Night of the Senses. But in enclosed convents I believe the percentage is much higher—from half to three-quarters. Only a few of them are very good. Some of the most saintly are not 'mystics' at all. It seems to me that people can get to very extraordinary sanctity, and wonderful love of God and familiarity with Him, by the loftier kinds of Meditation.

Yet what Bossuet calls "*la petite porte*" may lead them higher, with more suffering but much less danger. But it is all very puzzling. And I can't find anyone who knows *both ways* experimentally,—who has been in the one and has been transferred to the other. Most of the 'mystics' have *always* had the ligature, since they began to meditate. One or two have vague recollections of Meditative days. Hardly one of them knew he had the 'ligature' till I told him. The best formula is this :—

"Can you say a Paternoster slowly and with fervour, and at the same time understand what you are saying?" But sometimes the answers are ambiguous, and then there are other questions to be added.

Ever yours affec,

fr. JOHN CHAPMAN, O.S.B.

XLI: TO THE SAME.

Abbaye de St. Benoit,

Dec. 31, 1912. *de Maredsous.*

My dear Fr. . . . .

In consequence of the prayers said for me on the occasion of my feast, or from the fatigues of Christmas night, or from over-eating myself, I have had two days in bed. All over now. I took nothing but milk on the 28th in honour of the Holy Innocents!

I have at last worked out a theory of what Active Contemplation is, and why the authors squabble about it. Saudreau and Lamballe say it doesn't exist. Poulain includes some obviously mystical prayers under Simplicity. I have found an excellent little treatise by Thomas of Jesus. But my new discovery makes all clear.

1. There *is* a purely *non*-mystic "active" contemplation ; it is only a loftier sort of discursive Meditation.

2. There is a semi-mystical "active" contemplation. It is possible to contemplate *mysteries* (generally in a filmy manner, or in a large and intellectual manner) by turning the tap of mystical contemplation half-on. The habitual mystic will *never* do this in prayer, but only sitting or walking or in company, or (say) in the railway.

3. But *lots of mystics* don't know they are mystics, and *never* turn the tap full on. Hence they habitually exercise this contemplation of mysteries as their prayer.

4. It is the same as what Suarez considers to be *infused light* upon phantasms made by the *intellectus agens*.

Consequently it differs *toto caelo* from infused contemplation, in which the *species* are infused (in my view).

Hence the authors are all right, and all are wrong.

I need not say that St. John of the Cross is absolutely violent (in all his works) on the point that, in infused meditation, there must be *no* species made by the intellect (phantasms) at all. So the distinction between the three things is clear :—

(1) Meditation of a mystery, with occasional pauses — active contemplation.
(2) Contemplation of a mystery, without consideration —semi-mystical, (tap half-on).
(3) Contemplation of nothing at all (mystical).

No. 1 is Father Baker's "Prayer of forced acts", No. 3 is his "Prayer of Aspirations".

I don't think that there exists any real contemplation of mysteries in pure Mysticism; for visions, whether imaginary or intellectual, seem to be things which pass swiftly, as far as I understand,—so that they are not contemplations.

I don't look upon this theory as a theory,—it is mostly observed fact. I have interrogated several mystics, very searchingly.

I think a part of what Poulain includes under Simplicity, is certainly of this mixed character.

But he also includes the "*prière de simple remise*" and Bossuet's "Prayer of simplicity". Both are mere mystic contemplation. There is nothing in either to look at, no truth recognised or fact realised. *Wherever there is no* "*mystery*", *you have pure Mysticism*. There is a paradox for you!

In other words, whenever a person is using his intellect in the ordinary way, so that he "knows" something, he is not wholly (i.e. with the whole force of his intellect) in contemplation. But it is quite possible to use a part of the intellect for pure contemplation, and another part for active contemplation,—for saying the Divine Office, for any vocal or mental prayer, or for ordinary conversation, or writing.

All this depends on the level reached. In the lowest levels, it is hard, and needs practice. In the highest, it is habitual.

I used always to abuse St. John of the Cross. Now I find him the one author who knows his own mind. He is so clear and accurate.

I daresay this doesn't interest you!

Ever yours affec,

fr. JOHN CHAPMAN, O.S.B.

XLII: TO A CANONESS REGULAR OF THE LATERAN.

Abbaye de Saint Benoit,
Dec. 22, 1912.   *Maredsous.*

Dear Mother . . . .

I must enclose a line to you, to wish you and all the Community all Christmas blessings and graces. May we learn to become very little with our Lord, if He is to do great things in us, as we wish. If His love has drawn Him down from heaven so low, that He may make Himself like us, how much He must long to lift us up, and make us like Him. It is a cruel road that He has chosen, taking our miseries and our sufferings, in order to be able to give us His joy and His glory. He makes our road very easy in comparison, though we complain, and think He is very cruel to us. I always feel the Crib so sad, as well as so sweet. It is not like Easter, which is nothing but rejoicing.

I have come to the conclusion that one can remain united to God even when one goes to sleep in time of prayer. Don't laugh!

I say this, because I think I told you that, when one feels one is going to sleep, it is good to try and *think* some good thoughts, or even reason out something, in order to keep awake. If I said so, I was wrong. I see that it simply stops prayer dead ; so that thinking is more disastrous than sleep! I mean, quite seriously, that it is best to remain simply united to God's Will, (making any acts to fill up the time, that come of themselves, or none at all if none come) and not to mind if one's internal attitude is very much that of *trying* to go to sleep. But of course one can do one's best to keep off actual sleep by fidgeting, or changing one's position, and so forth.

It is possible that I did *not* give you the bad advice I have mentioned, but I believe I did.

I do not forget you all in my prayers.

I am always,

Yours sincerely in X͞ρο,

fr. JOHN CHAPMAN, O.S.B.

Isle of Caldey,
April 2, 1913.   *Near Tenby.*

Dear Mother . . . .

Many thanks for your kind letter. I am in an excellent position here for studying the development of prayer, as there are varieties of grade. I find that all confirms my own theories, and that some direction I have given is at once fruitful. This is most consoling, as it is so important to be able to give advice with confidence, and to be able to understand what people mean, even before they have explained. For the odd experiences of the beginner in contemplative prayer cannot be explained much better than the inexpressible experiences of the advanced.

I really had no theory worked out until last November ; and the reason that I am writing now is because I believe I can be much more useful to others now I have thought things out more definitely, with the help of two or three "contemplatives" who, of course, know much more experimentally than I do, though they are younger, and have not directed people, or very little.

The only good I did for you, so far as I know, was to answer your questions :—' Were you being idle in prayer ? ' and, ' Was it right to want God, and not thoughts about God ? '

I will give at the end of this letter (when I have found them) three passages of St. John of the Cross, which you will find useful for yourself and for others. A few sisters, who happened to speak to me about their prayer, would find the same passages useful, and the same advice.

---

[1] This letter is the original of the leaflet entitled *Contemplative Prayer*, which is reprinted as Appendix I of this volume, p. 287. It is referred to in several other letters also.

I only want to note one or two points. Ask me, if they are not clear.

1. All those who find it impossible to meditate—not from laziness or lukewarmness—and find they cannot fix their thoughts on a subject, or understand the meaning of the words, unless they cease to feel they are praying, are meant to cease *all thinking*, and only make acts of the will.

2. There is sometimes a period when meditation is sometimes possible, sometimes not. In this case use meditation whenever it is possible. This state will not last long.

3. Reading a little, or one minute's consideration of some great truth, or a few prayers, may be very useful to help recollection at the beginning of prayer. But they are not necessary.

4. *Let the acts come.* Don't force them. They ought *not* to be fervent, excited, anxious; but calm, simple, *unmeaning*, *unfelt*—for beginners. "Let us be thankful if we are like this for no more than twenty years !"[1]

5. The acts will be *always the same*. The first stage is usually :—" I am a miserable sinner, have mercy on me." But the principal stage consists of this :—" O God, I want Thee, and I do not want anything else." That is *the essence of pure contemplative prayer*, until the presence of God becomes vivid. (Then it may change, and praise or exultation may be the chief or the sole act. This is in the fully developed " prayer of quiet.".)

6. For those who have this *want of God*, interior mortification is as easy as it formerly was difficult. Any wilful immortification or imperfection stops prayer at once, unless it is repudiated.

7. The time of prayer is passed by beginners in the act of *wanting God*. It is an idiotic state, and feels like

[1] *Cf.* St. Teresa. Life. Ch. VIII, §I; and XXXIX, § 13.

complete waste of time, until, gradually, it becomes more vivid. The strangest part is when we begin to wonder whether we mean anything at all, and if we are addressing anybody, or merely using a formula without sense. The word "God" seems to mean nothing. If we feel this, we are starting on the right road, and we must beware of trying to think what God is, and what He has done for us, etc., because this takes us out of prayer at once, and "spoils God's work"; as St. John of the Cross says.

8. Progress may mean that *acts* grow less frequent, and we are conscious of one continued act, rather than its repetition.

9. Distractions are of two kinds :—

(*a*) The ordinary distractions, such as one has in meditation, which take one right away; and (*b*) the harmless wanderings of the *imagination* alone, while the intellect is (to all appearance) idle and empty, and the will remains fixed on God.

10. When these distractions remain *all* the time, the prayer is just as good, very often much better. The will remains united ; yet we feel utterly dissatisfied and humbled.

11. But we come away *wanting nothing but God*.

12. The whole value of prayer is seen in its results on the rest of our day. It ought to produce very definite effects :—

(*a*) A desire for the *Will of God*, exactly corresponding to the irrational and unmeaning craving for God, which went on in prayer.

(*b*) The cessation of multiple resolutions. We used to make and remake resolutions, never keeping them for long. Now we make only one—to do and suffer God's Will—and we keep all our old ones ; or rather, they seem to keep themselves, without any trouble on our part.

(*c*) Hence we have arrived at *simplicity*; all our spiritual life is unified into the one desire of union with God and His Will. It is for this that we are made, and we have found a loadstone which draws us.

As to progress in knowledge :—

(*a*) With some people there is *no* knowledge of God or of His nearness; only a blind certainty that He knows our want. (We cannot *think* of His being present.)

(*b*) Above this is a vague, indefinable knowledge that God is there. This should be preserved *all day long* by those who feel it. It grows more definite, yet remains indefinite.

(*c*) Again, there are *flashes of the infinite*, (I don't know what else to say), when, for an instant, a conception passes, like lightning, of reality, eternity, etc. These leave an impression that the world is dust and ashes. This effect must be carefully preserved out of prayer.

(*d*) In the developed prayer of quiet, the soul *does* know that God is there, without being able to say how. If it begins to know *what* God is, (again without being able to say); then praise and exultation tend to take the place of the want. The knowledge is much clearer after the prayer of union—but this is *very* rare indeed.

I think you may find some part of this useful to yourself and you might communicate it to several others. I have some in mind, but I don't like to mention names. But to those who can meditate, what I have said will be mere nonsense. But it is not nonsense to those who cannot think, and find that, by doing nothing and letting God work imperceptibly, they begin to live quite a different life.

Another point, which I omitted :—

Though, at first, *all* meditation seems impossible, still, as one is practised in contemplation, it becomes possible to meditate feebly and contemplate feebly at one and the same time. I mean that we *can* retain a filmy idea of some great truth—but then the tap is only half turned on of attention to God—unless the thoughts are merely in the imagination. This is good in hearing Mass, for instance, but not in the time of mental prayer.

Outside prayer, meditation should never be dropped, or the thought of all the truths of the Faith.

The simplest way of making an act of attention to God, is by an act of inattention to everything else. It is rather like the act of trying to go to sleep. Beginners want to be alone, or in the dark ; but practice makes this less necessary.

All this letter is *not* my theory on the subject, but a practical description. The theory does not matter much.

I did not at all intend to write at such length ; but having begun, I went on with all that came into my head. One can't say many of these things in public, as they are only of use to some : to others they may even be harmful. But in a contemplative Order few are capable of Meditation. Alas, some cannot meditate, and yet have so little generosity that they can't "contemplate". But it is contemplation which *gives* the power of being generous.

I have just thought of another point :—

Distractions. As these do not spoil our prayer, we ought to be perfectly satisfied to have them, as far as we can't help them. (I don't mean *be resigned* to them, but *will* them. A contemplative must never be *resigned* to God's Will, but *will* it.)

The result of this practice will probably be to decrease distractions, because it decreases worry. If we only want God's Will, there is no room for worry. We accept, willingly and joyfully, exactly the state of prayer that God gives; we *will* to have that, and no other.

At the same time we *wish* for Heaven—even for Heaven on earth—but to wish is not to will.

It is just the same out of prayer: we may *wish* for all sorts of things;—for a good dinner, cr more suffering, or the prayer of quiet—without imperfection. But we *will* to be as God's Will is for us—joyful, or suffering, or distracted—"only no sin", we repeat, "only no wilful imperfection".

I think this point, about distractions, is a great help to many people.

A real contemplative has been writing to me that he expected the Nuns of St. Bride's[1] to be converted; he was sure their prayer would force them to believe in the teaching of the Catholic Church without knowing why.

He says:—

"The basis of everything, the support and motive power, in fact everything that counts most, is found in prayer, and prayer understood in its most vague, formless, irrational, but most tremendously real form. It (prayer) seems, perhaps, to be nothing—waiting, mooning, dreaming—but yet, by its effect on our lives, we see it to be everything. It drives us on, and leads us to the state in which we have to accept the intellectual presentment of the Faith. . . . I think, somehow, it was this that brought me into the Church, etc. etc."

I think he is probably right. It is certain that this vague prayer throws a clear light on dogma; e.g. the

[1] The former Anglican community at Milford Haven, now at Talacre.

Incarnation, or the Holy Trinity, although we can't think of them in prayer. But, out of prayer they gain in reality, still more in unity. Don't you think so?

Forgive this considerable length. I often pray for you all, with affection and gratitude.

I am, yours sincerely in Xp̄o,

fr. JOHN CHAPMAN, O.S.B.

XLIV: TO THE SAME.

Isle of Caldey,
June 7, 1913.   *Near Tenby.*

Dear Mother . . . .

I always take this line; when people's imaginations are good and harmless, don't trouble them. Only teach them to be detached from these impressions. Probably they get much real good from them, a good which they would not get in any other way. They should humble themselves (so should everybody) and think that God does not judge them capable of walking by pure Faith, in the dry and dusty ways of simple devotion to His Will and His Glory; but gives them consolations, which are useful and good, even though they are by no means graces of the highest order. When I am told, for example, that Sister X has beautiful visions, but does not keep her rule, I am inclined to reply that, without the visions, she might keep it even less, and might lose all heart. [But, curiously, you will find another who has real mystical intuitions—the door seems to be ajar, she is always in the presence of God, without effort, without visions or impressions, or anything imaginative, she even suffers much, especially from the desire of God—*and yet does not keep the rule*, and is not edifying.]

Consequently, I am much pleased with people who have a rather imaginative prayer and much devotion, and yet are regular and charitable; I can think of one who is often almost heroic.

The great danger is that people love God for His gifts, and are always on the look out for them, and think all is lost when they have a little aridity; it is hard for them to learn to love aridity, to desire nothing so much as to be perennially dissatisfied with themselves, and full of an entirely vague and unsatisfactory longing for something unknown and unknowable. They have to learn this when they are plunged from time to time in the Obscure Night. But, generally, they are not long in it, and so are able to bear it. But, of course, they may have to go right through it, into contemplation, and the rules are clear enough in St. John of the Cross, (*Obscure Night*, Bk. I).

Some people have wonderful impressions of our Lord's presence, and it sounds exactly like the Prayer of Quiet: only it isn't ! There is the quiet, the cessation of " acts ", and the security that our Lord is there, and intense pleasure. It is good, but tiring, and should not be indulged in much. All these things are good, *as means*; provided they are only used as means, for serving God perfectly all the rest of the day. If people grow more humble and charitable, and punctual and prayerful; there is not much to fear. They are using the graces in the right way.

But there may be conceit, and wilfulness, and self-indulgence; then it is a different matter. Especially any pride is disastrous; and there are visionaries who always have admonitions about the government of the house, or warnings to give to their Superiors ! These are unmitigatedly bad.

As to the paper you sent, it seems all right. An imagination of our Lord's presence after Holy Communion (for instance) is a representation of something which is true, in a sensible way; and, if it is helpful, then let it go on. But never *strain* after it. This produces fatigue and dryness, and even disgust:—"I think it is the strained tension of prayer I am afraid of". Quite rightly. Meditation and imaginative prayer must be active, but not strained.

I am not infallible, unfortunately, and you must not take what I say for Gospel. But I think it is much what St. John of the Cross means; for instance in *The Ascent of Mount Carmel*, Bk. II, Ch. xvii. God deals with people *according to their nature*. If they are imaginative or senti-mental, He helps them in a suitable way, until they are detached and able to get higher.[1]

I think you meant to refer to the "Prayer of the enamoured Soul". It certainly expresses the essence of things. I ask your prayers, for there are many anxieties before me just now.

Believe me,
Ever yours sincerely in X͞p͞o,
fr. JOHN CHAPMAN, O.S.B.

XLV: TO THE SAME.

Isle of Caldey,
Near Tenby.

Aug. 20, 1913.

Dear Mother . . . .

The desire of doing and suffering the Will of God comes from Contemplative Prayer. It ought to grow

---

[1] A Religious who was for some years a penitent of Abbot Chapman writes of him :—" He had two principles which were set out with devastating clearness and—to use a vulgarism—were ' rammed home ' mercilessly. These were the two axioms :—' *Omne ens appetit suam perfectionem,*' and ' *Quidquid recipitur, recipitur secundum modum recipientis* '." The passage above shows how he interpreted and applied these axioms in practice.

until we feel that what we do is simply God's Will, not this or that particular action. The thing itself that we do is indifferent—what we notice about it is not its own individuality, but its generic character—it is God's Will. And if we are asked:—" What are you doing ? " we ought not to think so much :—" I am writing," as, " I am doing God's Will."

Yours very sincerely in Xp̄o,
fr. JOHN CHAPMAN, O.S.B.

XLVI: TO THE SAME.

Isle of Caldey,
Near Tenby.

Sept. 17, 1913.

Dear Mother . . . .

Some months ago I wrote you a letter about prayer. When it was finished, I read it through, and it struck me that it would save me a great deal of trouble if I had it copied, as I might want to say the same to other people. Brother N. made half a dozen copies with a typewriter and copying paper, and a good many people have found it useful. Brother X. has forced me to put it in *Pax*. I have altered a little. I send you a few of the off-prints, in case they may come in useful. I expect *very* few of your community can " meditate ".

I have read *Père Vallée* on St. John of the Cross with great delight. He is extraordinarily eloquent. I have written to Sister M.B. about the one passage which puzzles me, and seems all wrong. Everything else is most beautiful. I begin the Retreat at St. Bride's on Monday evening.

I am,
Yours sincerely,
fr. JOHN CHAPMAN, O.S.B.

St. Bride's Abbey,
Milford Haven.

Sept. 25, 1913.

Dear Mother . . . .

Only a line to thank you and Sister M.B. for your letters.
You quoted a very beautiful thought from *Père Vallée.* I
think the best explanation of the passage I found fault with,
is that it was taken down in shorthand and misunderstood.
Père Vallée would read it through, and read into it what
he really meant, without noticing that it is badly explained.

But what he *did* mean, precisely, I am not sure. Very
likely he meant that the contemplative dives below the
surface, and discovers the dispositions of our Lord's soul
by sympathy, in a way which the meditator (if there is
such a word) cannot. But he could hardly mean that
the contemplative does this in the time of contemplation.

Sister M.B. spoke of Bossuet. There are some good things
in his letters, both to Madame de Maisonfort, and the other
nun (I forget her name); and his simple method of prayer
(*oraison de simplicité*). It is reprinted at the end of some
French editions of Grou's " *Manuel des âmes intérieures.*"[1]

I am,
Yours sincerely,
fr. JOHN CHAPMAN, O.S.B.

XLVIII: TO THE SAME.

Isle of Caldey,
Near Tenby.

Saturday.

Dear Mother . . . .

I have not seen *The Dublin Review.* But I believe that
Mohammedan (Sufi), Brahmin and Buddhist mystics do

[1] A translation of Bossuet's *Method* may be found in the Appendix to the
English translation of Père Grou's work, *Manual for Interior Souls* (Burns,
Oates & Washbourne), p. 408.

arrive at very high states of union with God. This is surely possible for any *pure monotheist*, who retires from the world in order to live with God, in inculpable ignorance of the Christian revelation. Is he not in the position of Enoch, or Abraham, or Isaias?

These mystics, who believe in one God, have written their experiences in words that agree singularly with Rysbroeck, and St. John of the Cross, and the rest. The likeness is often most striking, in so far as I have seen quotations. Some day I must get hold of the books themselves.

Believe me, with best wishes for the feast,
Yours sincerely in Xp͞o,

fr. JOHN CHAPMAN, O.S.B.

XLIX: TO THE SAME.

Isle of Caldey,
Jan. 5, 1914. *Near Tenby.*

Dear Mother . . . .

I don't see why you should not answer any ordinary and reasonable enquiries, without difficulty. You are not answerable if a community is started, *nor is there any harm in Anglicans starting a community*. But of course you should plainly tell the enquiring lady that she is outside the Church, and therefore working in vain.

It might be well to explain to her also that Religious life cannot flourish where obedience is impossible. In Anglicanism everyone can choose even what they ' believe ' (if that *is* belief); and in a community obedience reduces itself to trust in a good Superior, and ' influence ' has to take the place of authority.

We want the authority of the Church given to our Superiors, and the approbation of the Church given to our manner of life. Otherwise we are only playing at being Religious; doing what we choose to do, because we like it.

As to your other question. I think it may sometimes be that *intensity* in prayer, which causes some slight fatigue, is a natural exertion on one's own part, which does not do any good to the prayer. It is better to be quite peaceful, without effort, except the effort to remain in peace. You see, what we do ourselves is tiring, and it is also absolutely an impediment to God's working in us. It *is good*, and does good; but it prevents a greater good. It is the partial substitution of emotional prayer for pure contemplative prayer.

When the will works, without the imagination and emotions, its action is almost imperceptible and quite quiet. There is usually no *pleasure*; only the satisfaction that all is right, and that one is occupied with what is the best of all occupations. I believe the effects are much greater, afterwards, than when there is some consolation, and some effort in the prayer.

But what you describe, suggests that the effort was rather in the trying to keep the atmosphere of prayer all day. That is a thing which *must not* be done with too much effort; for the attempt to be always conscious of God produces headaches, nerves, etc. I think the right way is (1) indirect, (2) negative.

(1) Indirect. Practise prayer, as much as possible, in the quiet way of contemplation: the effect follows *of itself*, out of prayer.

(2) Negative. Avoid distractions, as far as possible. Cultivate the habit of getting a few instants or a few minutes of *peace* as often as possible. It is like opening a window to let peace flow in: or, still more, like shutting a door to keep the noise out. But you can't *make* silence. You can *make* a noise. But you can only " make " silence

by stopping the noise, or stopping your ears. Hence the way to get that "recollection", which is simply interior peace, is not by any *positive* effort, but only by *negative* effort;—that is, the cessation of acting or thinking.

Consequently, it ought always to be a *relaxation* not an *effort*. Consequently, it ought never to cause fatigue, or overstrain, or headache.

I think all this is true, and I hope it is clear. Beginners have to meditate, work, tire themselves. But contemplation is rest, peace and refreshment; and its effect is extraordinarily strengthening. Just as the body is after sleep, so the will is after prayer.

Pray for me, as I have many worries.

Ever yours most sincerely in Xp̄o,

fr. JOHN CHAPMAN, O.S.B.

L: TO THE SAME.

April 7, 1914.   *Caldey*.

Dear Mother . . . .

I am sorry I misunderstood your former question. As you put it now, it is more difficult to answer.

The subsequent fatigue is due to no effort, but to the mere giving way to impressions that come. I should think, *probably*, that, if the impressions are very spiritual, it is all right; but that, if the exhaustion comes because there was some "sensible devotion" in them, they might as well be either resisted, or not too much encouraged. This is very vague direction! But I don't think it very much matters. I am quite sure that "sensible devotion" is *not* to be encouraged, and that pure spiritual devotion is to be accepted with joy. But it always seems to me that there is a good deal which is on the border line. In this case, I am inclined to think it does not much matter either way. One should not worry about it.

I imagine that, *if the fatigue is great*, and results in a *revulsion*, i.e. makes you less spiritual afterwards; then you can assume that there was *too much* sensible devotion.

If, on the other hand, the fatigue is not excessive, and spiritual fervour increases; the impressions are to be indulged in without fear.

This is the working rule which occurs to me.

Pray for us. If I may judge by myself, you will be very glad to have a peaceful time at X. I *hate* being a " Superior " !

Ever yours sincerely in X͞p͞o,

fr. JOHN CHAPMAN, O.S.B.

LI: TO ANOTHER CANONESS REGULAR OF THE LATERAN.

[No date, but after Sept., 1912.]

Dear Sister . . . .

A " state of prayer " lasts an hour, or five minutes, as the case may be, but it is seldom habitual, for people vary at different hours of the day. We cannot choose, but have to do our best, and take what God sends us. It is right, I think, to feel perfectly satisfied (after our prayer) that it *is* all right when it *feels* all wrong. We humble ourselves and say :—" O God, I cannot pray. I cannot even keep in Thy presence." Or, " I cannot pray as I did yesterday ; but I only want to do Thy Will, not to be satisfied with my prayer."

It is of the very essence of prayer that it does not depend upon us. It depends on circumstances—our stomach, our preoccupations, much more than on our will—for the character it takes ; and, naturally, on God's special grace. But possibly the *best* kind is when we seem unable to do anything, if then we throw ourselves on God, and stay contentedly before Him; worried, anxious, tired, listless, but—above all and under it all—humbled and abandoned to His will, contented with our own discontent.

If we can get ourselves accustomed to this attitude of soul, which is always possible, we have learned how to pray. We are never afraid of prayer, (do you know what that means?) and we can pray for any length of time—the longer the better—and at any time. We then worry no longer about our "state of prayer"; though, out of prayer, we long for more union with God. We can't help this, and it is right; and yet, in the prayer itself, we want exactly what we have and nothing else; just because we have God's will, and *that* is best of all.

I think you understand this already, as you said, most exactly and most clearly :—" I never feel that my prayer is a thing that I own as my possession; and, in fact, I would not even like it to be, if it could. I would rather take it like a beggar from our Lord, each separate time." That seems to me the real thing.

Ever yours sincerely in Xp̄o,
fr. JOHN CHAPMAN, O.S.B.

LII: TO ANOTHER CANONESS REGULAR OF ST. AUGUSTINE.

July 18, 1914.   *Caldey.*

Pax.

My dear Sister . . . .

We *must* have our times of desolation and trial. How can we show our love of God except by enduring? He showed His love for us by suffering.

Besides, it is such trials that make us humble—we begin to see there is no good in us, no devotion, no stability in good. That must make us see that God is everything.

The way to union with God is by humbling ourselves, by seeing that we have no goodness; and how can we realise this except by being dry and unable to pray or to be self-satisfied?

It is a great grace that God should humble us, and give us something to bear for Him. Of course you would like some other trial instead! One always prefers an imaginary trial to an actual one! Humble yourself; don't expect to be devout, or happy either; declare before God that you are incapable of a good thought; and you will find the only peace worth having.

Ever yours in Dn̄o,

fr. JOHN CHAPMAN, O.S.B.

LIII: TO THE SAME.

Palazzo di S. Calisto

Dec. 19, 1919. Roma, 14.

My dear Sister . . . .

I received your letter some days ago, and I really do not know what to say, except to wish you a very happy Christmas! I shall be here regularly, I suppose, from every November to July, going to Downside for the summer.

I was 3¾ years an army Chaplain, and have not heard much news. But at least, I have always enquired after the safety of your Convent. What a long trial you have had.

As for yourself, I am sorry that you have had to endure the same trial for so long; I had hoped that one or other would have been in another house. But the best thing to do is to make as light of it as possible. We should never carry any trouble with a heavy heart, but try to laugh at ourselves, and remind ourselves that others have worse sufferings. I know one *can't* always do this ; but one can do it from time to time, and even frequently.

As to prayer, I can only say that, if a simple resting in God's presence was once right for you, it presumably is so now. But I cannot know how far it went well with you after the Retreat, in 1913. Probably as you *read*, you cannot meditate, and therefore should " contemplate ". So on the whole I recommend you to try as before, on the supposition that it went well before.

The one real proof that you have the *right kind of prayer for you*, is not that it always goes easily and always succeeds, but that it really does you good and changes your life. The chief difficulty of contemplation is that a very little distraction by worldly things, and quite tiny unfaith-fulnesses make it stop suddenly, and it may mean some humiliation and some time before getting it back again.

Prayer, petition, recollection, an absolute giving of oneself to God, are necessary *conditions* ; but they are also the *results* of simple prayer. I don't think I even know the lives of the " *Mystiques de nos jours* " to which you refer. I like the old English mystics—especially *The Cloud*, and Richard Rolle of Hampole's *Fire of love*.

Ever yours in Dn̄o,

H. John Chapman, O.S.B.

LIV: TO A BENEDICTINE NUN.

[*No place or date, probably* 1915 *or* 1916.]

Dear Dame . . . .

The article in *Pax*,[1] of which a few copies were reprinted, was simply a letter to a Nun. (I have scarcely ever done such a thing as write to a Nun ! I always refuse.) I made

[1] This is the " Leaflet " called *Contemplative Prayer, a few Simple Rules*, it will be found in Appendix I of this volume.

a copy before sending it, in case I might find it useful for someone else, and I was urged to put it in *Pax*.

The Nun in question would easily understand what I meant by " unmeaning ", for she asked me, with some hesitation, whether it was wrong to say in prayer simply " *Nescivi* ",—and I said I thought it seemed an excellent tag.

I admit that, when the acts which are made in contemplative prayer express simply the attitude of the will; e.g. " I want Thee, O Lord ", or " I belong to Thee ", they *do* seem to mean something quite definite, in so far as they truly represent the attitude of the WILL. But beyond that, they are " unmeaning ", in so far as the INTELLECT has no definite idea of *what* the will wants, when it wants God; and no adequate conception of the idea of belonging to God—and so on.

And when the acts express, not the attitude of the will, but an intellectual idea,—e.g. " Thou art everything, I am nothing "; then they mean very little indeed that is definite.

My point is that the soul means *so much more than the words say*, that the words are rather suggestions than expressions,—they serve to keep the imagination quiet, by giving it a very little and very quiet work to do— whereas the higher part of the soul is really tense and energetic, perhaps fiery and passionate.

The words, imagined over and over again, may tend to be a sort of *drone*, which keeps the calm of the lower powers; while the intellect and will are occupied with something inexpressible, usually called darkness, sometimes called light,—but it really is the same thing.

I have with me one very dirty copy of the article which the Abbot of Downside[1] was so kind as to praise. So I send it, as I cannot get at cleaner ones in England.

H. JOHN CHAPMAN, O.S.B.

[1] In 1915 this was Abbot Butler.

P.S. When I said "idiotic", I meant that the world would call it idiotic! Also the soul itself often feels rather idiotic, and wonders whether it is not wasting time, knowing that, if it described its state to any sensible person, it would be told to go and do something useful, and not moon.

LV: TO THE SAME.

Pal. S. Calisto,
Trastevere,
Feb. 27, 1919.   *Roma,* 14.

Dear Dame . . . .

Your letter shows that you are doing well in soul, I am so glad.

The Anglican translation, "His banner over me is love", is given by Catholic commentators as the correct translation of the Hebrew. But the Hebrew of the Canticle of Canticles is very difficult and obscure, and St. Jerome seems to have helped himself by using the Greek. But the Greek does not mean "He set charity in order in me", and I cannot imagine how St. Jerome got hold of this sense. Another (English) mistranslation is the literal, "My Beloved to me and I to Him", which is not English, and means nothing. It is as if one translated the French, "Il est à moi", as "He is to me", instead of "mine". But on the whole, the Douay Old Testament is not at all bad. I always think St. Paul is the worst part, as it is almost incomprehensible unless one knows the Greek!

You ask if there are many Anglican conversions. I have no relations with the outside world,—scarcely! But I am told that conversions have never been so numerous as they have been since the war. Enormous numbers of people are favourable—in a general way—to Catholicism, and would like to know more, and are almost ready to be put under instruction, if only they could be got at. But a great deal is being done.

I hope *you* are doing a great deal. For one can probably —or rather certainly—do more to convert the world by keeping very close to God, and growing in union with Him, than by any outside work; though it seems difficult to believe it sometimes.

It is really best to preach a continual Mission to oneself than an occasional one to others! And it is not selfishness for our own soul; for if God wants souls, He first wants *mine* from me, and until I have given it to Him entirely without any reserve, I have plenty to do for Him, without saving others' souls. I am assuming that one wants perfection and union with God because *He* wants it, not because *we* want the rewards. And meanwhile, while we are trying to love Him more, He is doing more for our neighbours because we ask it, than we could do by our own activities. How one learns more and more that one can do nothing, and that God must do all!

Pray for me and I will pray for you.

I am ever yours, in Dn̄o,

H. JOHN CHAPMAN, O.S.B.

LVI: TO THE SAME.

Palazzo San Calisto,
Trastevere,
May 25, 1919. *Roma.*

Dear Dame . . . .

Before I had received your letter, I had naturally heard the sad news.

You ask why you are afraid of death. It is only human. St. Teresa describes her mental and even bodily sufferings, caused by her violent desire to die and to " be with Christ ".

And yet, she says, she still had the human fear of death. And our Lord chose to suffer this fear of death for our sakes. The separation of body and soul is a wrench. On the other hand, I know quite well what you mean about the feeling,—when you try to realise death—that there is nothing beyond.

The reason is plainly because *one cannot imagine it.* One tries to *imagine* a pure spiritual imagination of the soul without the body; and naturally one imagines a blank. And then one feels :—" There is no life after death "; and then one says to oneself :—" I am doubting the faith, I am sinning against faith."

All the time, one is only unreasonable,—trying to imagine what can be intellectually conceived, but not pictured.

It is different, I think, if you think of death naturally; not unnaturally.

(1) To die is a violence (as I said) from one point of view; but from another, it is *natural.* And to most people it seems natural to die, when they are dying. Consequently it is easy to imagine yourself on your sick bed, very weak, and faintly hearing prayers around you, and receiving the Sacraments, and gently losing consciousness, and sleeping in God's arms. (This is actually the way death comes to most people,—quite easily and pleasantly.) And looked at in this way, it does not *feel* like an extinction, the going out of a candle; it seems, on the contrary, impossible to feel that this is the end of one's personality. But what comes next? We leave that to God,—we do not try to *imagine* it.

(2) Only in prayer can you get near it—if the world ever falls away, and leaves you in infinity—which you can only describe as nothingness, though it is everything.

The moral of all this is,—do not try to *imagine* ' after

death ', for imagination is only of material and sensible things. Only try to realise what it is to be with God.

One's *terror* of death, after seeing a dead person, is merely because it is unaccustomed. If you were an Undertaker, you wouldn't feel it ! Nor even if you were a Nurse in a hospital. It is a thing to laugh yourself out of. But it does not matter much. Some people are afraid of mice or frogs. Some people are afraid of corpses. Some people are afraid of ghosts. Others can't stand the sight of blood. But you can get accustomed to seeing pools of it, and people blown to bits, and be cheerful and joking, and pass by taking no notice. It is all a matter of habit. The Chinese don't mind dying, provided they are sure of having a really nice coffin. I can't say the prospect would appeal to me.

These are gruesome subjects ! I think it is much better to be accustomed to them, and to take them as a matter of course. The worst of death is really the blanks it leaves in this world. But it often fills up blanks in the next world ; and we must rejoice when some one, dear to us, takes the place prepared " from the foundation of the world ", as our Lord tells us, for that soul ;—(at least He says " kingdom ", not " place " ; I am misquoting).

I am sorry to have been so long in answering. But it is an effort to write letters, when one is hard at work on other things.

Ever yours sincerely in Xp̄o,

fr. H. JOHN CHAPMAN, O.S.B.

LVII: TO THE SAME.

Downside Abbey,
Near Bath.

Oct. 13, 1925.

My dear Dame . . . .

It is all right ! You are in a perfectly normal state. Don't worry.

I have the advantage of remembering sufficiently your former letters. You were not without your trials ; but still you were ordinarily able to exercise the " prayer of recollection ", and you felt the spiritual effects of it in your daily life. That is the normal prayer of the entrance on the " illuminative way ". It has not the pleasantness of the " purgative way "—the striking meditations, the happy communions, the lights in prayer ; but it is comparatively dry and austere. Yet it has a higher happiness of its own in the almost imperceptible consciousness of union with God, which detaches us from the world and from our former pleasures, even from ' devotion '. It is good, thoroughly good, and causes us to make great strides in the service of God. We long to belong to Him wholly, to be entirely in His Will all the day long, and even to suffer for Him. A certain recollection and detachment are often easy, sometimes habitual.

That is, I think, the state you were often in. It is enormously higher than the " purgative way " of many devotions and good thoughts and pious exercises. It brings a wonderful *unity* into our spiritual life, and indeed into our whole life, which all *tends* to become a long act of uniting ourselves with God's Will.

But this is only the beginning of the *illuminative way*. We necessarily plunge into the " Night of the Spirit ". God takes us at our word. We offered ourselves to suffer His most Holy Will,—and He tries us. You will find it all described by St. John of the Cross, in the second Book of the *Obscure Night*. Some souls have internal sufferings only : others have these internal troubles largely caused by external troubles. In every case they are driven to the very edge of despair.

In the eighteenth century the commonest result was the feeling of being hated by God, and of being doomed to Hell.

In this century a very common form is even more horrible—temptations against Faith. You know how *Ste Jeanne Françoise de Chantal* and *Ste Thérèse* of *Lisieux* were sanctified by these—the former nearly all her life.

[What a cheerful and encouraging letter I am writing !] *You have got to go through some of this in whatever way God wills.*

Probably you will never again have that particular peace and prayer of recollection you had before. By this time it is as much past as the " Purgative way ", and its pleasurable sensations ; (you may never have had these). But you will get something so much better, so much higher (yet so much less tangible, describable, pleasurable), that you would never for a moment wish to go back.

The fact is that you are going on to God much quicker now. Just as it, no doubt, took you some time formerly to realise that the " prayer of recollection " was good, and not mere waste of time, or nothing at all,—so it takes some time to discover that we *are* really desiring only God's Will, and abandoning ourselves to Him when we cannot pray, when we are full of distractions, worldliness, temptations, revolts.

But I promise you that, after a time, you will come to feel that you are being taught, and taught efficaciously, by God Himself, *only to want His Will.* You thought you wanted it before, because you *felt* as if you wanted it. But when His Hand came down heavy upon you, and took away all the purely spiritual and excellent affections in which you trusted,—you found that you were trusting in God's gifts as you had them, and that you had not realised that *everything comes from God and is His good gift to the soul.* " All things work together for good for them that love God."

You began to learn this when God took away all the gifts which *you* thought were good for you, and bestowed on you all the things you were sure were bad for you. All you describe in your letter is God's gift to you. Thank Him for it. Faith tells you it is all good—only your response to it is imperfect.

[It is dreadfully hard. I am frightfully sorry for you while I write this. But God loves you much more! Trust in Him, that He knows what He is doing.]

We have to learn in practice what we always knew in theory: everything that happens is God's Will. God's Will always intends our good. God's Will is carving us into the likeness of His Son.

Every moment is the message of God's Will; every external event, everything outside us, and *even every involuntary thought and feeling within us* is God's own touch. We are living in touch with God. Everything we come in contact with, the whole of our daily circumstances, and all our interior responses, whether pleasures or pains, are God's working. We are living in God—in God's action, as a fish in the water. There is no question of trying to *feel* that God is here, or to complain of God being far, once He has taught us that we are bathed in Him, in His action, in His Will.

Now, what have you to *do*? I answer:—

(1) Be very careful about *external* duties: punctuality, obedience, regularity, above all charity to others and unselfishness.

(2) For the rest, DO NOTHING. Let God act. Tell Him continually (either by conscious act, or implicitly by leaving His action alone) that you have absolute confidence that He is doing right, that you *want* the state in which He puts you, and that you want no other; that you have no choice, that you simply accept and embrace without any pleasure whatever He sends you.

(3) Your *prayer* will consist in passing the time as best

you can—as far as possible by simply belonging to God, without acts—using acts to avoid distractions. At the end (and all through) you will be thanking God for giving you *this particular prayer* and no other; it will probably consist of (i) only distractions or worrying; or (ii) nothing at all; or (iii) utter misery, and feelings of despair; or (iv) that there is no God; or (v) that it is all dreadful, and waste of time and pain. And you will then (not at once) feel—in a higher part of the soul than you have realised before—how much better this is than what you used to have; and that you would rather suffer like this, as it is God's will, than have the most spiritual of pleasures.

When you begin to *live* in this higher part of the soul, you will have made progress, and will perhaps be worthy of having still more unexpected trials! Only *you will always have the necessary strength for them all*, so there is nothing to be frightened about.

Lastly—think as little as you can about all this. God is using the surgeon's knife,—you cannot help Him by watching it,—He could act better if you were distracted by something else! Try and get above yourself; laugh at your own troubles; say you know they will pass.

So they will: for it seems to be a fact that God *always gives breathing-spaces*.

Meanwhile, I tell you that it is all right. In the highest part of the soul you know this. But if God wants to try you by the feeling that all is wrong, then nothing that I can say will persuade you that it is right. But it *will* be all right, all the same. Say *Deo gratias* in your heart all the time.

I don't say, however, that you are not to pray for deliverance. Of course you must—but not absolutely— only saying:—" Father, let this chalice pass from me; nevertheless not as I will but as Thou wilt."

I don't suppose any spiritual reading will be of much use just now. But still I recommend very strongly *Père de Caussade's* spiritual letters (in the second volume of *Abandon*). There is an English translation now; but I have not seen it. You will see how much is headed " *Souffrances, afflictions, privations* " and " *agonie et mort mystique* ". You will find excellent instructions.

But you do not need them. For God is taking you in hand and teaching you. Be courageous. Let Him work. You can help by not interfering—that is, by not worrying or complaining, but trying to be peaceful and confident and content.

You will soon learn this, I hope, and then you will be unwilling to change your state for any other. But it will remain suffering, on and off—only you will be simplified and see God in it all—not the trial, not the suffering, but only God acting on your soul. I can't teach you this; but God will, by degrees.

Do not exhaust yourself by making *efforts*. You seem still to think that you can make yourself good! You can't. But God can, and will; though slowly, perhaps. We can prevent His action,—we can get in His way. But we can hardly help Him at all, once we are out of the " Purgative Way ". Try to be simply at His disposition, ready to be recollected or distracted as He wills; to feel good or to feel wicked (which is nearer to humility), to be wretched or consoled. I know the darkness is appalling sometimes ;—but it is the only way of learning that we depend entirely on God, that we have nothing from ourselves, that even our love and desire of Him tends to be selfish. The " royal way of the Holy Cross " is the only way. But you will find out that the darkness is God Himself; the suffering is His nearness.

I think that is enough. I seldom write letters, but when I do they tend to be long.

Don't talk as if few hungered for God as you do. God calls people in various ways, and some feel their love of Him in a different way. But I know people who have just the feeling of " hunger " you describe,—only more so. One is a Lady in the world ; another is a hard-working Priest. But whatever the exact way in which people tend to God, they get into the " Night of the Spirit " if they are to make real Progress. But do not think about it much. The less we look into ourselves the better.

I am ever yours in Dn͞o,

H. JOHN CHAPMAN.

(Note. This letter is a wonderful example of Abbot Chapman's sureness of touch and clearness of thought in these letters of direction. The MS. original covers no less than twenty-six pages of ordinary note-paper; but except for one place where he has inserted a couple of words to make the sense clearer, there is not a correction or an alteration in the whole.)

LVIII: TO THE SAME.

Downside Abbey,
June 12, 1926. *Near Bath.*

Dear Dame . . . .

This morning I happened to have a free Mass, so I said the Mass of our B. Lady for you. Otherwise I fear my prayers are not very valuable. But I promise them anyhow.

For I am very sorry for you. " Nerves " you cannot help ; and you are evidently physically bad with nerves. So far as this physical side is concerned, do not make too much effort ; violent efforts to control yourself only make your nerves more jumpy ! It is safe to say :—" I *am* nervy, and I must put up with it, for the present." So much for the physical side.

As for the spiritual side, it is largely the result of the other. But God uses these things for our spiritual good. Consequently you must pray God to take away your nervousness and the resultant temptations against vocation; and also, on the other hand, accept it all from God's hand, willingly,—taking it with both hands.

This is very difficult, because it involves being *two people!* But we *are* two. There is the natural self, which is rebelling all the time, and the higher self which says :— "I don't want this; I hate it, it is not me; but I accept it as a trial, a suffering."

The difficulty is that the other self replies :—" But I *am* rebelling, and I want to leave Religion. I want all sorts of things."

We have to take care to live on the higher plane. But *we can't feel we are living on the higher plane*, except from time to time. On the contrary, the trial consists in the fact that we feel, very vividly, that the lower self is the real self; whereas we only know most obscurely and indistinctly and *elusively* that the higher self is the real self. *Otherwise there would be no suffering* and therefore no purification.

Consequently your spiritual state is all right; though your physical state is not.

As to the two "Nights" in St. John of the Cross. They are not consecutive; so that we do not pass *right through* the 'Night of the Senses', before we enter the 'Night of the Spirit'. Only we *enter* the first before we *enter* the second. We enter the second long before the first is completed, and the two purifications go on side by side. St. John of the Cross distinctly teaches this, and so does experience; only he treats of the two separately for the sake of clearness and logic.

How soon the darkness of the spirit begins, and how dark it may get, will be different in different cases. But anyone who uses the 'Night of the Senses' as an entrance to pure contemplative prayer, will find himself in spiritual darkness much sooner than he likes. The more terrible and black the darkness, the greater the purification, and the closer the union with God.

Of course we have to co-operate. But passively in the main, by not giving up prayer, confidence, courage. Only a great part of the trial is regularly this : that we believe we *are* giving up confidence and courage, and are wasting our time in prayer.

I simply ask you to *believe* what I say : that God is purifying you, that you are perfectly safe in His hands, that it is the devil who wants you to worry about worrying. You can't *feel* this, or the trial would cease. But you can act upon it ; and that is what matters.

I gather that you have less sensible, or super-sensible feeling of desiring God's Will than you had when you wrote before. If this is so, it is all to the good ! Accept what God wills ; even *accept not being able to feel that you accept*. But trust (without knowing that you trust), and go on. It will all come back some day, but in a different and much higher way.

As to prayer ; don't wish for any prayer except what God makes possible to you.

God bless you,

Ever yours in Xp̄o,

H. John Chapman.

I write this advice ; but of course I know you cannot *feel* that you take it. Your trial consists in feeling that you *can't* take it.

LIX: TO THE SAME.

Downside Abbey,
Near Bath.

June 19, 1926.

Dear Dame . . . .

I am quite sure you have made the right resolution. It needs courage. But it has certainly been a disastrous mistake to shorten the time of prayer when it does not go well. And the use of books or meditation instead is mere waste of time.

I quite believe that more prayer will be good for your nerves, and strengthen you. But the temptation comes very easily, that one must meditate, and not waste time. If prayer becomes only acute suffering, so much the better, I suppose.

The only thing is to take life as it comes, with the greatest simplicity. Providence arranges everything, so all is right in the end. Meanwhile, if we worry, we must try also to take that fact with simplicity, however paradoxical it sounds.

Don't read *de Caussade* or any other book, if it does not suit you ; (it is his *letters* that I recommend, not the treatise on ' *abandon* '). It is always difficult to find ' spiritual ' reading.

As to Holy Scripture ; again, take whatever you like best. I find nothing to equal St. Matthew ! But one can get a great deal out of St. Paul (e.g. Ephesians and Colossians), by *thinking out* what he is trying to express, verse by verse.

Ever yours sincerely in X͞p͞o,

H. JOHN CHAPMAN.

LX: TO THE SAME.

Downside Abbey,
Near Bath.

Feb. 16, 1927.

Dear Dame . . . .

Best wishes and many happy returns. I am glad you like the ' Cloud of Unknowing ' ; it is extraordinarily like St. John of the Cross. It always seems to me absolutely good and satisfying, because (as you say) it is so simple. There is no question in it of " favours " and rapturous feelings. It leaves out the side which is God's side—what God may give to the soul—and simply takes the other, practical side—that the soul tries to give all it is and has. And that is all that we need worry about.

It seems to me that we have simply to accept, *without examining it*, what God gives us; to some it may be pleasurable, sometimes, but more often ' desolation ', which is worse when we worry about it.

As to the time after Holy Communion, I cannot help you ! because I find myself that it is the least pious moment of the day. I suppose there are two main reasons for this. First, and chiefly : because one is tired. But secondly ; because one expects something of oneself, and it doesn't come. We *cannot* call up feelings of love and adoration when we want to ; and they would be of little value if we could.

The only thing to do is to humble ourselves, and to say :—" You see, O Lord, how unfeeling and distracted and tired I am ; you see I hate it (only rather sleepily) ". Put up with it as a trial, and a great trial.

Do not worry about a thing like a new Breviary. If you thought it *reasonable* when you asked for it ; it is a mere scruple, worry and waste of time to regret, afterwards, that you missed the opportunity of a small mortification. The thought of regret is a good one, if it is merely a passing wish to have given something to God. But it is foolish to let it remain as a *real* regret ; as the thing does not matter, since there are abundant opportunities for similar mortifications.

Don't let us think about ourselves too much, or worry about what we might have done, or are going to do, or about what we feel, or do not feel. All this is want of straightforwardness and simplicity.

Not that we can *try* to be simple. God does that for us. But our part is (1) to think of others, (2) to be with God. And we should *hate* thinking about our own "spiritual state".

For our bodily health we must use ordinary prudence, ordinary food and exercise. But if we are always thinking about it, we become valetudinarians, and are never well! So with our souls—but even more so, for here God is our *Doctor*! He is not only the healthy air in which we live (which cures us more than any medicine); but He gives the medicine in the right doses, and we have only to accept it. Confidence in Him is what we want. Our dryness and distractions are *very* nasty medicines, though.

Many thanks for your good prayers.

Ever yours very sincerely in X͞p͞o,

H. JOHN CHAPMAN.

LXI: TO THE SAME.

Downside Abbey,
Near Bath.

Nov. 8, 1927.

Dear Dame . . . .

You write:—"I don't see quite how one can help taking self into account, when there are very definite things, the result of the uncomfortable, sticking *Ego*" etc. Of course one can't help it.

At first one passes some time in suffering from things which seem to come from other persons, or from circumstances outside oneself. Gradually one finds a great part (or all) one's troubles are in oneself! If someone pinches me, I suffer because my nerves are sensitive—obviously.

When we come to know that our whole environment and everything that happens is God's hand upon us, and that we are in touch with Him at every moment, because every detail of life is a means arranged by Him to lead us to Himself; *then* we find that our great trouble is *self*. Only the very top, or very centre, or very ground (as you please—these are metaphors), of our soul is quite united to God; and all the rest is horribly unquiet, and makes us miserable. This is an unavoidable process of '*purification*',—or Purgatory !

We used to think we were good,—now we know we are not. We suffer from this, and, as we realise our imperfections more and more, we seem to be going backwards. Only we have got to be *resigned* to seeing these imperfections. We must not make light of them, in the sense of not hating them; but it is quite good to laugh at them. The more we ridicule ourselves the better, as we see our constant failures.

It is not possible to make sensible "*acts of contrition*" for sins and imperfections which are not voluntary, or only partly voluntary. If we try, we only feel dry, and that we can't. So it is better to make "*acts of humility*": (1) either *laughing at* ourselves, for our failures, carelessness, want of love and so forth; or (2) say, " You see, O Lord, how silly I am,—this is all you can expect ! "; or (3) " I am delighted to see how imperfect I am,— reveal more to me of my wretchedness."

We say of course :—" You see what I am, without Your grace." Only don't think God is *not* giving you a great deal of grace. It is an enormous grace to be left to be conscious of our own want of recollection and want of energy. Earlier God had helped us, so that we thought we were continually united to His Will. We were grateful for so much grace, and expected it to continue, and to *increase in the same form*. But it doesn't.

It continues (only more strongly) by teaching us that we are not really yet *wholly* united to God's Will;—that is, not in the whole of our nature.

Hence this second state consists in a continual perception that we are wanting; that we are careless, half-hearted, etc.

Consequently the earlier stage was much more comfortable ; but, on looking back, we see it was a half-truth, or a tenth-truth !

The first stage :—" I feel I habitually am doing and suffering God's Will in everything."

The second stage :—" But I see this is only half-hearted and not thorough."

The third stage :—" *Habitually* I perceive that I am *never* really doing and suffering God's Will, except most miserably and imperfectly ; and I am, therefore, habitually miserable about it."

This means, obviously, a considerable *growth in grace*.

In the first stage we feel as if we were good, and we are not. In the third, we habitually long to be more completely united with God's Will, because we are beginning to realise, just a little, how much more is wanted. This is clearly a far closer union than the first.

Consequently we begin to realise that we can only get union with God by very unpleasant suffering, and not by very enjoyable feelings ! I gather from your letter that you are making real progress. All progress in virtue is progress in humility,—knowledge of our own wretchedness.

Only try to enjoy knowing it ! Thank God for showing it to you, and long to see it more and more.

[Only OF COURSE don't dwell upon it. All this introspection is unavoidable, but the shorter it is, the better.]

Fervour consists in dissatisfaction with ourselves—provided we also have confidence in God. But God has done so much for you, that you have every reason for confidence. He is leading you on to perfection " by ways that you knew not ". He never takes us by the way we should expect. So do not worry, but accept all your imperfections—when past or present—as inevitable, and use them as steps up. But future ones are neither to be wished for, nor to be worried about.

I don't suppose you can make many particular resolutions. General resolutions are ·best. Take your own imperfect state as God's Will, and hug the pain it gives you.

I pray for you. Pray for me.

Ever yours in D$\overline{no}$,

H. JOHN CHAPMAN.

LXII: TO THE SAME.

Downside Abbey,
St. Luke, 1928. *Near Bath.*

Dear Dame . . . .

1. Any wilful imperfection, which we are conscious we have not renounced, will divide us from God in prayer. This is a mere fact of experience, isn't it?

2. Equally, *a doubt, a scruple about such an imperfection will have just the same effect as a real imperfection.*

Consequently you must ' form your conscience '; that is to say, you must make up your mind whether a thing is *clearly* against God's Will for you, or not. If it is not *evidently* against His Will, then be entirely at peace.

You have got permission for a few books, because you thought them useful. Then keep them, and look on it as a temptation to be anxious about them.

But if, at any time, you see you do not want them any more, get rid of them. But do not think it matters either way. Similarly as to giving small presents. If your Superior permits, then it is all right, and *do not go back over it again.*

You have been in ' desolation ', and you have been hoping that you had found the cause in some want of detachment from this or that. Probably you have been mistaken. The cause is more general: you need to *learn detachment from yourself,* and God is teaching you this

154

in the usual way, by letting you feel powerless to get to Him on account of your want of generosity. This is humbling you, and doing you good. When you are quite convinced that you have nothing, not even a gift of prayer, and when you are quite resigned to feeling quite as unworthy of prayer as you are incapable of it, you will have gone a long way.

Meanwhile, thank God for all the trials you have to bear. You are in a perfectly good state, on the way to perfection; and you must simply accept the way along which God leads you. He will make it plain to you what He wants you to offer to Him. I do not think it probable that most of the small matters you mention are what He wants you to give up. I think it more likely that *He wants you to learn to accept the state of dissatisfaction with yourself in which He has put you.*

Don't ask or worry about any kind of prayer or recollection or union, but wish for exactly what God provides for you *at any given moment.* " Take no thought for the morrow." Trust in God. You are at each moment in touch with Him through all the arrangements of His Providence, and these include your own state and your own feelings at the moment that you are trying to unite yourself with His Will. If you do your best, at that moment, the result (however dry, weak, unsatisfactory) is just exactly what God wants you to have here and now. Worry is useless and harmful. Try to be absolutely at peace, because you are satisfied with God as He is to you at this moment.

I don't agree that monastic poverty is different from Franciscan poverty, except in unimportant matters.

(1) They beg—we give.

(2) Theoretically their convents belong to the Pope. In practice this makes little difference.

(3) In many countries they are not allowed to *touch*

money. So some one has to go to the Railway station with them, to buy their ticket—which is awkward.

Otherwise, they seem to act just as we do. They need many things for their use, and have them. Of course some Poor Clares, and more Carmelites occasionally do not get enough to eat. But some Benedictine nuns are even worse off, because they do not beg.

1. We are bound to possess *nothing*. We can have what is useful with permission. So much for the Vow.

2. The Virtue of Poverty means complete detachment : we are not to depend on things, but they on us. (1) This is a thing we can practise, as beginners ; (2) a little further on towards perfection it is more like a gift, not to be obtained by practice or activity on our part, but merely by loving God more. So you will get detachment from *things* and from *self*, by merely giving yourself to God, and *accepting yourself* as you find yourself to be. We all have one unpleasant person to live with, whom we can't get away from—ourself. Put up with yourself, and take your own hated imperfection and weakness as an unpleasantness you have to bear with. It is very hard, but it is really a very perfect act of love to God.

I daresay this won't help you. God is leading you all the time. The only fault will be if you are restless, and want to do something of your own. Let God do it.

Ever yours in Xp̄o,

H. JOHN CHAPMAN.

LXIII: TO THE SAME.

Downside Abbey,
Feb. 28, 1929. *Near Bath.*

Dear Dame . . . .

Please accept our sympathy in the loss of Sister . . . .
I have asked for prayers for her soul.

This is another trial for you, as an addition to what you had from God already.

Do not think that the right way to bear a trial—or many trials together—is to love God so much that you can bear the trial with joy ; *so that it ceases to be a trial.* On the contrary, it is obvious that the essence of a suffering of any kind is that we suffer from it ! We hate it. *We long to be rid of it,* or even we feel life impossible, or even the goodness of God incredible, so long as it lasts.

1. If we can say, *quite calmly* and *with the whole of our self,* that we are glad of the suffering, then (of course) it has ceased to be a suffering ; we have arrived at a sort of superhuman courage and firmness, which makes us despise it, and it is of no more importance. This is an excellent *human, physical* perfection : we should aim at it, no doubt. But it would be ridiculous to *expect to attain* it. In all serious cases it is impossible. It is desirable, just as good health is desirable,—but not necessarily attainable.

2. Besides this human (or superhuman) and physical contempt of suffering, which we ought to aim at but cannot expect to get, there is a higher and better method. It is, to recognise that we are meant to suffer, and that it is our nature to *resent* the suffering and to try to get rid of it, and that this worry and anxiety about it is the chief part of the suffering.

Our Lord has taught us this very plainly by His example. In the Agony, He did not say :—" I suffer, and I *rejoice ;* I only want to suffer more " (as Saints have sometimes been inspired by grace to say). But He prayed that the Chalice might be taken away,—to show that the feeling of hating suffering, and feeling it unbearable, is *a part of perfection* for us, as it is a part of our weakness of nature. We have a right and a duty, when we feel this, to tell God what we feel, and ask Him to remove the pain : but we must add, as our Lord added :—" Not my Will but Thine ".

Consequently it is not against 'perfection' that we should feel suffering to be intolerable, and tell God it is intolerable; only we must add *with the highest part of our soul* that we trust in God, and are willing to suffer as long as He chooses, and that we know He will give us the necessary grace.

Now this 'apex' of the will, or 'centre of the soul', or 'base of the soul' ('apex' or '*fine pointe*' in St. Francis de Sales,—base, '*fundus*' in Blosius,—'centre' in many writers,—but all mean the same thing) is not perceptible, or scarcely perceptible.

When mental suffering clouds our soul, it seems as though we were not making any effort to unite ourselves with God. That is the culmination of the trouble. We feel utterly floored, cowards, incapable of prayer; and we want to say:—"My God, My God, why hast Thou forsaken me?"

This again is obviously a perfection. Only if we did not feel it to be almost like despair (because the giving ourselves to God is not perceptible) it would not happen.

It is better for us, *and more perfect*, to suffer, feeling our weakness and helplessness, bearing up somehow, half-heartedly, feebly, than to suffer courageously and magnanimously! We have to *aim* at this last, but not to expect it.

We aim at it, and quite rightly:—

1. By trusting in God with the *whole* of our self, as far as we can; usually we can't! But so long as the 'apex' of the soul sticks to God, it really does not matter how little we *feel* that we trust.

2. By *despising* the suffering, whenever we can: trying to forget it, to throw ourselves into whatever God sets before us to do; by living for others, not for self; by remembering that so many have much worse to suffer, without so much help from God.

But we *need not expect* to be successful in these efforts ! We have only to repeat that we want God's Will.

You are not cowardly. No *feelings* of cowardice are cowardly. It is the giving in to them which is cowardly.

Don't worry about death. Usually when people come to die, they are either unconscious, or else quite peaceful, feeling it perfectly natural to die. But when we are *well*, it is naturally repugnant to us.

If we try to *imagine* it, then of course we can't ! We only imagine an abyss of nothingness which terrifies us. It is absurd to dwell on this, as it is a false imagination ; or rather, it is a failure of imagination. So, when the idea comes, laugh at it, and say to yourself :—" I am afraid, *not* of death, but of an absurd misrepresentation of what death is ! " But always turn back and say :—" I *do* want God, and only God ; and death is the way to God ".

Again, I hope you will take great care of your health. When you are physically stronger half the mental distress will go. Meanwhile God wants you to have it, and He is doing great things in your soul by this means. I daresay my advice will not do you much good. For if God wishes to act in your soul, nothing that I can say will prevent His doing it. But in that case all is right.

As to prayer. You have to use the prayer which God gives you. If, at the end of the time you have given to it, you only feel that nothing has happened, and that you are humbled ; be quite satisfied, and be *really* humble, and say to God that you desire nothing more.

It would be a dreadful thing to spend time in prayer because we enjoyed it. We have to do it for God's glory, not for our pleasure.

Ever yours in D$\overline{no}$,

H. JOHN CHAPMAN.

Downside Abbey,
Near Bath.

Sept. 11, 1929.

Dear Dame . . . .

I am sure you are all right in God's hands, though He is treating you very roughly. I can quite believe that you have felt often that you were distracting yourself unnecessarily, when you might have been praying. And it may be quite true.

On the other hand, to feel entirely unspiritual, to cease to wish for prayer and so forth, is a very good state to be in, and quite necessary for your spiritual progress.

The only thing that matters is the 'fine point' of the soul, and you have to learn to live by that, and not by any feelings, even of the most spiritual kind. Our Lord will strip you of all this spirituality, until you not only are sure you have no 'spiritual life', but also know that you ought not even to wish for it ! It must be enough for you to be exactly in the state in which God puts you,— that is, in the state in which you find yourself.

In prayer you can give yourself to God with all your incapability of praying, and offer Him all your dislike of spiritual things, and all your feeling of longing for what is purely natural ! Hug it, even. The more you are stripped of all satisfaction and self-satisfaction, the more pleasing you are to our Blessed Lord.

I think it is clear that all is going well with you.

As for your health, do not worry about it, but do not neglect it. It is your duty to take great care of it, *for the sake of your sisters*, not for your own sake. If you get ill, you will give a great deal of unnecessary trouble to others ; so you should prefer to take rather too much care of yourself than too little.

I do not expect to be able to console you. For, if God

wishes you to remain in your present, most valuable, state of desolation, you will *feel* the truth of what I tell you. But you are certainly learning it gradually.

I pray for you.

Ever yours sincerely in X$\overline{\text{po}}$,

H. JOHN CHAPMAN,
Abbot.

LXV: TO THE SAME.

Downside Abbey,
Near Bath.

Nov. 21, 1930.

My dear Dame . . . .

I am very sorry for you; and yet I am quite sure you are going on all right. Thank God for all your troubles, even for ' temptations ' against faith. These are the hardest of all, only they are *not* temptations. For they only mean a feeling as though you did not believe. When one finds this feeling painful and unbearable, this is a proof that one does believe, and very much.

St. Vincent de Paul said that St. Jane Frances de Chantal had a very wonderful degree of faith, though for years she felt as if she had none. It was St. Vincent who prayed that he might have another man's temptations, if that would deliver him, and then felt as if he had no faith— and wrote out the *Credo*, and put it on his breast, with the understanding that, every time he put his hand upon it, he would mean that he believed it all. A very good practice. (I don't know about " in his blood ", which seems a superfluous detail.)

I advise you always to despise and laugh at temptations about faith, as they are only feelings, and merit no attention whatever. In so far, however, as they are intensely painful (because they seem to dry up all devotion and to make prayer feel ridiculous), you can thank God

161

for them, and say you are ready to bear them for the rest of your life.

It is a great grace to feel you are 'a repulsive object', whenever you go to prayer. If you do not like seeing yourself as repulsive, that must be partly pride ! but chiefly mere nature. The great thing is not to look at yourself at all. The most universal of all sins is selfishness. Worry about our own soul is generally mixed up with selfishness. We want to be holy (we think) only for God's glory, but we want our own satisfaction as well. It is so difficult to realise that we can never be really holy as long as we are self-satisfied ; and that our great aim should be to enjoy being dis-satisfied with ourselves, until we can arrive at that complete detachment in which we do not care about ourselves at all, and only want to save our souls or be perfect, just as we should wish to save other people's souls for God's sake. (Of course I do not mean that we are to cease to love ourselves, just as we love our neighbour.)

I do not like *The Kingdom of God in the Soul*, by Father John of *Bois-le-duc* (or Balduke). He is full of beautiful things. But he thinks we ought to aim at unclouded union with God in this life, and he regards internal trials as our own fault. This is Stoicism, not Christianity.

Our Lord chose to feel internal sufferings for our sakes, and the culmination of them upon the Cross was the feeling of being forsaken by God. He is our model. If you wrote to me (as various Saints might have done) that you are so full of Love of God that you care for nothing but Him, so that you are 'confirmed in grace', that you have reached the 'spiritual marriage', with a continual sense of the Holy Trinity in your soul, etc., etc. ; I should most certainly write back that, if God seems to work such things in your soul, you should pay no attention to them, and consider your daily work and business. I should certainly (I hope) have written this to St. Teresa and I believe she would have been delighted, because she was really a Saint.

But internal sufferings are a much safer way, because they are the way our Lord Himself has shown us. God can lead us as He likes, and will. We ought not to choose, but to be carried in His arms. Of course it is not natural to like being carried. We want to walk and look about.

I am sure you know (as you say you know) that all perfection is in abandonment to God. It is not only external circumstances, but all the internal movements of our soul (except the deliberately wilful ones, when imperfections) are a part of His leading. Everything that happens to us, inside and outside, is God's touch.

I am,

Yours very sincerely in X$\overline{po}$,

H. JOHN CHAPMAN.

LXVI: TO THE SAME.

Downside Abbey,
Near Bath.

Dec. 7, 1930.

Dear Dame . . . .

Many thanks for your letter. I have nothing to add, except to say, God bless you; and I pray for you.

As to Fr. John Evangelist, I may be too hard upon him. Many excellent people admire his book. But I think the plain meaning of what he says is what I said. I have found other books of this Stoical school; they think we *ought* to aim at immovable perfection, and that it is our own fault if we do not reach it. This is very discouraging; and if there is some truth in it, at all events it is wrongly put! So *I* think; and I am not infallible.

Ever yours sincerely in X$\overline{po}$,

H. JOHN CHAPMAN.

163

Downside Abbey,
Sept. 4, 1931.   *Near Bath.*

Dear Dame . . . .

I shall not apologise for not answering your letter, as I daresay it was good for you. I was away when it came.

You seem not to have learned to think about other people, and not about yourself. Try to serve God for His own sake, as He wishes you to, and not for His gifts. What *does* it matter whether you enjoy your prayer, or are unhappy in it? What *does* it matter if you have all these feelings of having no Faith? (You know quite well that you *have* Faith; for if you had none, you would not mind having none: but your pain is caused by your " feeling as if " you had not any.)

You have not arrived at *simplicity;* you should take everything as it comes, and thank God for it. It is easy to be ' abandoned ' when one is quite comfortable. But it is difficult when God seems to leave us to ourselves. But I think God is much more with you than when you felt His presence; and He is working in you much more. All these trials are helping you.

You say they do not make you humble: but if you thought you were being made humble, you wouldn't be.

There is nothing to be frightened about, or to worry about.

You will find in St. Teresa of Lisieux's account of herself (so much better than other people's rather soapy lives of her), how much she suffered from the want of ' feeling ' faith, and from being apparently left by God.

Internal grace is generally imperceptible, so do not try to feel or see. It is far better to walk in darkness, and to trust in God.

Ever yours very sincerely in X$\overline{po}$,

H. John Chapman.

LXVIII: TO THE SAME.

Downside Abbey,
Near Bath.

Nov. 15, 1931.

Dear Dame . . . .

I send another copy of my article on *de Caussade*. It *is* the Introduction to the English translation of his book on Prayer ; only, in the published volume a note is omitted, and a bit is added at the end. I am glad you begin to find *de Caussade* useful.

It was not necessary to humble yourself by writing to me about what you call your sins. I am very glad you had so sensible a director as Abbot Smith.[1]

It was a clear temptation when you felt inclined to give up prayer because you had humiliating trials and feelings, and felt as if you had consented. I hope you *never* look back over them. There is no good reason to expect the trials to recur. Thank God that He brought you through them, and do not speak of them again.

As to Fr. John Evangelist, I quite agree that he has beautiful things and uplifting things, and I am glad you and anyone else should find him helpful. But his definite promises are (I am sure) a delusion, and therefore likely to bring despondency to those who believe them.

You ask whether it is right to use a recollected prayer when you are passing an hour before the Blessed Sacrament exposed. Of course it is quite right! Offer your recollection in God (or God in you) to our Lord as praise. What could be better ?

The idea that you ought to be distracting yourself from prayer by 'thinking' about the Blessed Sacrament is absurd. You praise It by kneeling in adoration, and uniting yourself with God; and by realising that all your

[1] Rt. Rev. Dom Oswald Smith, first Abbot of Ampleforth.

thinking would not realise anything at all of the reality of our Lord's gift.

You speak of Death. It is natural to wish to avoid death, and it is a duty; just as our appetite makes us remember to eat. But, when it comes to the point, people who are dying usually have no fear of death, because *then* it is natural. When we are well it seems, and is, unnatural! Therefore there is no object in worrying about it. We fear it now; but when it is near we shall probably welcome it.

Ever yours very sincerely in X$\overline{\text{po}}$,

H. JOHN CHAPMAN.

LXIX: TO THE SAME.

Downside Abbey,
Near Bath.

May 23, 1932.

Dear Dame . . . .

It is not a sin to give up 'the prayer of dark Faith'; sometimes it may be impossible, or too painful. But it is better and safer to stick to it as far as you can. But don't worry yourself by thinking out an ideal of what you ought to be or feel, and then get unhappy because you cannot realise it in fact! Start from what you are, and accept what God gives you; and do not imagine some futile perfection, which is not what God puts in your reach.

As to thinking you 'are unfit for a close union with God', of course you are; and that is why it is worthy of God to give such a union to those who are unworthy. But do not think you know what this union 'feels like', or what it implies! God gives it in His own way, not in our way.

All we know is, that His Will is the Rule. We must be guided by events and by His Providence, seconded by our own earnest prayers; and God will unite us to Himself in the way He thinks proper, according to our character, and the circumstances around us which He has arranged. I am glad you realise that St. Francis de Sales is a terribly hard master, though so gentle in manner!

I really do not think you need any help from me. You understand what God wants of you. Do not think too much about yourself, or that it matters much whether you are dry or consoled; whether you can or cannot pray, etc. For you know that it does not really matter. But it does matter, very much, that you should take what comes from God with thankfulness and simplicity.

Do not mind actual temptations. I do not think they will harm you ever. I am sure they will humble and purify you. When they are not there, forget them altogether.

Have plenty of courage, God is stronger than the devil. We are on the winning side.

Ever yours very sincerely in Xp̄o,

H. JOHN CHAPMAN.

LXX: TO THE SAME.

Downside Abbey,
Near Bath.

Sept. 2, 1932.

Dear Dame . . . .

I found your letter on my return from a fortnight's holiday. Since then I have been to Buckfast, and Bishops and Abbots have been here, and taking up my time. Besides, it takes a long time to read one of your letters. I have to read each sentence several times, before I can guess what the signs stand for! So much for my apologies for the delay.

I have no copies left of my article on *de Caussade*; but the article appears as a Preface (slightly altered) to Thorold's translation of *de Caussade* on Prayer. That is a useful book to study, as it gives so clearly the points where the Quietists went wrong. But it is not in the same line as the treatise on '*Abandon*' or the letters; these are much more indispensable. Still, it is not bad to have a copy of each.

As to my writing on Prayer—I have for many years intended to write a book on the Spiritual Life in general; but it is very difficult to find the time. I *may* do so, and I *mean* to do so. But when?

I think meditation, in the strict sense, sometimes helps towards 'nerves'; especially when people try hard to think and imagine, and can't! But I agree with you that pure prayer is—and ought to be—somewhat of a cure for nervousness. If it is properly exercised, it means rising above the worries of the reason, the imagination, the emotions, the nerves. It cannot always stop them from bothering; but it can look down upon them as an interesting phenomenon, as if it was all going on in some beetle, which we were examining with a magnifying glass. This makes them less important, and gives them a chance of boiling without scalding us, and even of quieting down much quicker. And the habit of prayer and *abandon* ought to keep the nerves quiet, and discourage the surging up of nerve storms.

In so far as these are a disease, they have to be borne by the sufferer, and borne with by others; but I am sure they are lessened by unselfishness, by not thinking about self, by not worrying about one's spiritual state, and by '*abandon*'. For 'nerves' generally mean that people are thinking about themselves: just as hysteria and neurosis, and all these nervous complaints, come from people thinking about nothing but their own bodily complaints.

We can usually feel *some* pain or discomfort, if we try to feel it. But usually we have no time!

I am sure you can realise that you know much more about prayer than you did when you had more 'consolation'. God has taught you through suffering and desolation; and you are beginning to feel that you are generally nearer to Him when you are distracted or dry, than when prayer comes easily.

We cannot help thinking our own opinion is right, otherwise it would not be our own opinion. It is not always possible, or always right, to try and change it so as to agree with a Superior. But it is always right to *submit* it and give it up, believing that the Superior's opinion is a Divinely ordained circumstance, which we must not only be resigned to, but accept with both hands, even while we are sure it is mistaken, and may have disastrous results! But if Superiors are not infallible, neither are we; and Superiors often have reasons, which they cannot publish, for what they do or order.

I am *very* grateful for your prayers, as I need them very much.

Ever yours sincerely in X͞p͞o,

H. John Chapman.

LXXI: TO THE SAME.

St. Catherine's Lodge Hotel,
Kingsway,

Friday, Feb. 17, 1933.   *Hove, Sussex.*

Dear Dame . . . .

I am here for a few days to recruit.

Your letter suggests that you are all right, in a very normal state of 'desolation'. And you seem to take the right means to regulate it. It is all a question really of accepting God's action upon us, and being satisfied with it. He knows best. We must not worry, but simply try to serve Him in what little ways He allows us to do so. It is a great privilege to serve without pleasure or reward. It seems dull and commonplace, and that is just the trial.

I do not think much or little intellect is of any importance in spiritual matters. But we have to use just the gifts which God gives us, in the way which He sets before us.

All this is very obvious ! But great truths are obvious, and people obscure them by little devotions, little anxieties, etc.

You ask whether I like Rysbroeck. I confess he is rather above me. Some parts are wonderful; others are so very 1, 2, 3, that they lose interest. I admire him more than I use him ! All these questions are a matter of personal attraction, I suppose. And at different periods of one's life one has found different authors attractive. St. Francis de Sales has lasted out all others with me, and has gone on all the time.

I have really nothing to tell you; and I do not think you need any advice.

Ever yours sincerely in X$\overline{po}$,

H. JOHN CHAPMAN.

LXXII: TO THE SAME.

Downside Abbey,
Near Bath.

May 27, 1933.

My dear Dame . . . .

You really do not need any advice; for God is leading you. It is good to stick to prayer without feeling. But do not distress yourself about it.

At other times, say to yourself that it is all right, and that you do not want consolation. And go on quite simply without worrying.

Ever yours sincerely in Xp̄o,

H. John Chapman.

LXXIII: TO A CANONESS REGULAR OF THE LATERAN.

*Commissione Pontificia
Per la Revisione Della Volgata,
Palazzo-S.-Calisto-Trastevere,*
March 24, 1922.   *Roma* (14)

Dear Dame . . . .

If I happen to pass through Belgium—which is not very likely—I will do my best to stop at Bruges. That is all I can possibly say !

I don't like *thrusting* myself on any one ;—but if Divine Providence so arranges that I am asked for advice, I try to give the best I can.

I think it quite probable that a very holy Jesuit (and some are very holy) would fail to understand many nuns in an enclosed Order. But I believe Reverend Mother would help you more than most experienced directors.

From what you write, I gather that Our Lord has given you a great deal of grace, and now is dealing with you in the usual way. You have felt, in the past, that you were making progress and improving, and that God had led you into a new way.

But after some time it *always* happens that one seems to return to the rut of common life. Provided you have the same desire to be all for God, what *does* it matter how you feel ? Except that this sort of feeling of dryness or dissipation is founding humility in you—We have to

171

accept from God with absolute submission (and with what joy we can) not merely our sufferings, but :—

Also *ourselves*, all our inborn and ingrained weakness and selfishness and incapacity.

And also the *poor amount* of sanctity we see in ourselves.

If we were always sailing along in a fair wind, we should have very little to suffer, and very little to make us humble. It is when we *can't* pray, and can't *feel* we want only God's will, and can't even feel humble (and so forth), that we are being purged and moulded and made into what God wants us to be. We are like little children being washed and having their hair brushed by a nurse; they don't like it at all, and think nurse is very unkind.

Do you ever read Père de Caussade's letters (l'Abandon à la Providence Divine) ? some of them might help you.

You say "unable to go on, and unable to go back". Yes, you can't go back,—but you *are* going on, if you learn to accept *exactly the* prayer that God gives you *here and now*. It is quite right to wish for higher union with God, and to envy those who have attained it ;—but *here and now* I must wish for *exactly* the state God wishes me to be in, whether it means distractions, or discouragements, or sleepiness, or merely emptiness. Nothing matters but God's Will; and we do not want simply God's Will, if we are *really* dissatisfied with what we get from Him.

It is the habit of referring everything to God's Will that we must acquire. And we should be always at peace, if we had really acquired it. As far as I gather from your letter, there is nothing going wrong. You feel sometimes, I expect, like a watch which has run down,—you want winding up ! You do try, I know, to care only for God's Will. But you do not always realise, perhaps, that He leaves you just as you are, for your good. And yet, of course, you do know it. In fact, you know already all

I can say to you, only it is sometimes useful to be assured of it by someone else!

When one is in a kind of " desolation " the only thing is to wish to be there and remain there. It is the only *means of union* with God. If you know " The Ascent of Mount Carmel " you will know the doctrine that the only means of Union is the stripping of self, and that illuminations and inspirations are cheering and helpful, but are not *union*; union is the imperceptible giving of self to God,—the only perceptible part of it is the leaving of everything else. When we have no comfort in God, *but want it* more than everything, then we are probably more united to him than at any other moment. Saint John of the Cross's doctrine is austere, but Saint *François de Sales* teaches exactly the same in a more cheerful manner, and so do all the saints.

So we must aim at being in the desert, *in terra deserta et inaquosa*—and not at any consciousness of God's grace and Presence. One is inclined to say " I am so weak, I can't go on like this! I must have some consolation, or I shall merely fall, and grow worldly ". But God knows best. Absolute and complete confidence, trust, abandon, is what we need.

I apologise for writing such obvious truths! Please pray for me and I will pray for you.

Yours sincerely in Dño,

H. JOHN CHAPMAN, O.S.B.

LXXIV: TO THE SAME.

Downside Abbey,
Stratton-on-the-Fosse,
Near Bath.

F. of Corpus Christi, 1922.

My dear Sister . . . .

I have no reason at all to think that you would get any good by seeing me, but I am quite willing to answer your letter, as it does not seem to raise any special difficulties, and I therefore hope that I shall say the obvious thing.

God is dealing with your soul very directly; your business is to let Him do just as He pleases, and to thank Him for all he does. As far as possible, you should not be simply *resigned* to any state in which you find yourself, but accept it with both hands and embrace it, whether it is pleasant or unpleasant.

The better state is probably the state of "absolute exterior and interior suffering" of which you speak; for God carves a statue "in the likeness of His Son" out of the cold and hard marble which we are by nature, and to do this, He has to hit us hard. But He gives a respite now and then, a breathing-space and a rest, to let us feel that all this hitting is only from Love. The one thing is to have entire confidence in what He does.

Only we must not try to act ourselves, as if we could intensify and improve God's action:—

(1) This is obvious in times of "consolation"—we must not be attached to the joy of God's Presence, or even seek it assiduously, or mind when He leaves us: or we run the danger of loving His gifts more than Himself. We ought *only to let them come*, not encourage, or pray for more light than He chooses to give, but feel ourselves wholly unworthy.

This is an austere doctrine; but it is easier than it sounds, precisely because anxiety to get and to keep the sense of God's Presence or tranquillity of mind is one of the chief causes of desolation.

(2) In times of desolation we must try to be equally detached from our own feelings. We must always have in our minds the intention of accepting the state we are in:—"O God, I am distracted, without devotion, full of temptation, extroverted, worldly,—but I don't like it

—I am ready, therefore, to remain so, as long as it is Thy Will." We must always go on praying not to sin, not to give way to wilful imperfections,—and if we do give way we can thank God for the humiliation that results. But all the time we must try and not take ourselves too seriously,—laugh at ourselves for the state we are in, and laugh at ourselves for minding it.

Because the great principle is that all these commotions, all these consolations, are effects in the *lower* part of the soul, and do not in themselves matter in the least; they purify and strengthen the lower part of the soul, if they are patiently and lovingly accepted.

What *does* matter is the upper part of the soul; but that is something which we can't *feel*, but only *know*. But we have to make sure that the highest part of our soul (or the deepest, if you prefer this metaphor,—St. Francis de Sales says:—"the highest point", Blosius says:—"the depth"—it is the same thing) is united to God, and *nothing else matters* at all in this world. The right intention is the only way I can describe it. *The essential interior act* of religion is the giving ourselves to God, turning to Him and remaining turned, uniting ourselves to His Will and renewing this union as often as we think of it, or simply remaining united. When this essential act is going on in the point of the soul, all the rest of the soul can be in a disturbance, unrest, rebellion, misery—it does not matter,—on the contrary, the "point of the soul" accepts it, embraces it, wills it.

Our advance in the practice of spirituality is the gradual increase of the habit of living in the spirit, not in the flesh,—that is, identifying our real self with the "point of the soul", not with all the emotions and imaginations which trouble us. The real "I" is the will which gives itself to God, (the emotions and imaginations are not *me*, they are in me, but are not under my control) feelings come and go; but my whole business is to concentrate my will on God. That is pure charity.

There are two kinds of love :—

(1) The love which wants to *get*,—it is good, but imperfect.
(2) The love that wants to *give* :—That is charity.

We must not think that distraction, dryness, desolation, is merely a state of trial which we pass through on our way to perfection—Perfection in this world is not a calm union with God, unless God so wishes. Our Lord suffered temptation and desolation to show us that they are not incompatible with perfection, but *are* perfection.

Progress will mean becoming more and more indifferent as to what state we are in. We ought to care less and less about our own souls, except about that higher part in which we ought to live united to God. We must not worry about perfection even; simply be what God enables us to be at this moment.

When we realise that God is not only in every external event, but in every internal event,—I mean in every involuntary feeling we have—we realise that, at every moment of our life, we are *in touch with God*, and His hand is on us; we have only to be carried in His arms. Our one care must be not to jump out of them, and try to walk alone.

I hope you see why I don't think you would get much good by talking about yourself. *Don't look into your soul*, but look at God. Don't ask yourself whether you are distracted, or at peace ;—but, if you can't help noticing that you are full of distractions or worldly thoughts, just say :—" What a pity I am like that to-day ! How silly I am ! " And add, as the case may be :—" God is not angry, but amused at me, as it is not my fault ", or " it is largely my fault "; and in either case renew and intensify your acceptation of what has happened, and then *think of something else*. Look upon it as a temptation to think about your state. It is always mixed up with self-love. Laugh at yourself, and then think of God,— or (out of prayer) of what you have to do.

There is a danger of " devout people " living for themselves instead of living for others. In prayer, of course, your own soul (the point of it) and God are enough; but outside prayer, charity to our neighbour is the whole of virtue, and includes everything. Give the supreme point of your soul to God, and all the lower part to your neighbour. Always try and forget your own sufferings or your own joys; *minimise* them. Try to think other people's joys are more important, and their sufferings much greater. We ought not to concentrate ourselves on our own spiritual life, but think about God and other people. Just as a Mother does not think about her love for her child, but about the child, so we must not think about our love for God, but about God. But we can't think too much (when we have time at least !) of His love for us.

I pray that you may get the grace of not minding whether you feel love of God or not, or whether you feel commotions or rebellions or not; but *that you may feel that to cling to God in absolute detachment is all you care for in this life.*

You will find roughly the same teaching, I believe, in St. Francis de Sales, in Ste. Jeanne Françoise de Chantal, in St. John of the Cross, and in the letters of Père de Caussade (L'Abandon à Dieu). The letters in the second volume will probably be useful to you, if you have not read them.

You don't need to be " put right" you *are* all right. If you doubt it, offer yourself (an instantaneous act) to God entirely,—and you *are* united to Him. There is nothing so simple as the spiritual life. It has no difficulties, no troubles,—these are all in the lower, the unspiritual part of us. You belong to God. Let that union be your real life, and look down on all the rest. Make light of it, whether it is good or bad,—whether it is floods of light, or darkness and devils,—it is all God's touch, whether caressing or hitting you hard; have confidence in it, and pay no attention to it; be sure it is all right, and try to forget it; it is God's work, not yours, so don't interfere with it, or look at it more than you can help. I repeat: *minimise* all that happens in your soul, although you must maximise God's love to you. " *Abandon* ", humility, charity, those are virtues; anxiety, self-dissection, wondering what God means, wanting to know whether we are making progress, these are very nearly vices.

God is everything, and He is all Love as well as all Power. We are nothing, and deserve nothing. And He loves us in our misery, and is bringing us to Himself in His own way—not in our way.

Let us try to be humble, to be nothing at all. Then we shall be simple, having only one act,—doing God's Will, and only one " passivity " embracing God's Will.

Believe me yours faithfully in Xpo,

H. JOHN CHAPMAN, O.S.B.

LXXV: TO AN URSULINE NUN.

Downside Abbey,
Jan. 14, 1925. *Near Bath.*

Dear Sister . . . .

Father . . . . has shown me the end of your letter. You say in it :—" I just sit there and wish to be united to Him, without effort on my part; but I am not sure if it is right."

Of course it is. Don't waste your time by taking a book. Don't worry to *think* or meditate. The object of meditation is to arrive at loving. Of course love does not consist in feeling, so it is not necessary (or even desirable) to have feelings of consolation in prayer, or even facility.

As for distractions; you must simply accept them as God's Will, unless they are wilful. No doubt they are due not only to the imperfection of our nature in itself, but to our own past carelessness; but as we cannot help having them here and now, we must resign ourselves to them, and even accept them with both hands, just like any other suffering. We must wish to have the prayer that God gives us and no other. A distracted prayer, a desolate prayer, a happy prayer,—we must take everything as it comes. For our union with God consists in *doing* and *accepting* His will, moment by moment all through the day. Nothing else matters.

So long as one *can* meditate in the time of prayer, one is obliged to exercise some activity in thinking. For this we use the imagination, so that we are conscious of doing something, and it is a satisfaction to feel that we are active in God's service.

But when we pass on to " Contemplative Prayer " (and we can't help this advance, since meditation becomes always too difficult and unfruitful, and sometimes utterly impossible) we use the *will* almost only; and, as this is the higher part of the soul, we have no *feeling* that we are acting. We seem to be idle, mooning, wasting time. But though we cannot *feel* that we are active, we perceive, when we reflect upon it, that we are really *intensely active*. To *sit and want God intensely*, is obviously an intense act of the will. In order to concentrate on this intense act, we want to stop all other action. Mere bodily action, such as walking about, may impede it a little; but *thinking* impedes it a great deal, or even stops it entirely. Why?

Of course, because *thinking* is directed by our will; and if we use our *will to think* of certain subjects rather than others, our will is occupied in keeping our mind to the subject; and therefore less occupied in loving God.

The harder we try to keep our mind on a subject, the more intensely our will has to keep us to it, so that it cannot turn simply to God.

Hence the *distaste for meditation* which we are conscious of in the time of prayer. We want to use our Will to "want God", and not to keep our thoughts in order. We want to be "wanting God", and detached from everything else. Hence we *want* to let our thoughts run about by themselves (I think you will recognise what this means) and not to control them; in order that our will may turn wholly to God.

The result is naturally that, while our will is making its intense (but almost imperceptible) act of love, our imagination is running about by itself, just as it does in a dream; so that we *seem* to be full of distractions, and not praying at all. But this is the contrary of the fact. The distractions, which are so vivid to us, are not *voluntary* actions, and have no importance; whereas the *voluntary* action we are performing is the *wanting* God, or giving ourselves to God.

Hence the chief trouble in prayer is to keep from worrying about the way in which the imagination flies about. The best and usual way to keep it quiet is to repeat certain words, texts, ejaculations; just as we try not to listen with our ears, or as we shut our eyes (or look at the Tabernacle or a crucifix) so as to avoid distractions,—so we have to try and stop our imagination by repeating words.

But the *real prayer* is the *act of the will* (wanting, loving, etc.) behind all this. You cannot *feel* this act of the will; but you can know it. What you *feel* is in the lower part of the soul (imagination, emotion) and does not matter; the activity of the higher part of the soul you do not *feel*, but you *know* it. You may *feel* distracted, despondent, miserable, or you may *feel* full of love or desire; but all this is unimportant. What matters is the act of the will (which you *know* but do not *feel*) which accepts all these feelings from God, and gives you to Him to be His, and to have and to be only what He wills. We have to learn to live by this higher part of our soul, and to pay no attention to anything else.

To show you what I mean, I will point out that this contemplative prayer *stops dead* when we (by a wilful imperfection) refuse what God asks of us. That is to say, when we are *not* giving our will to God.

Consequently, I have really only to say to you that your prayer is good. Go on with it. Any Benedictine will tell you so. It is the usual prayer of all but beginners, among Religious who are not very active.

Only, if a Director is not accustomed to this kind of prayer, he cannot understand it. You will find it in plenty of books :—e.g. Bossuet's *Manière courte et facile pour faire l'oraison de foi et de simple présence de Dieu*; St. Francis de Sales' letters, and those of St. J. F. de Chantal ; Père de Caussade, S. J. "*L'Abandon*"; and in almost all spiritual books not meant for beginners. But no one should try to start upon it, except because he *cannot* meditate, and is in the 'Night of the senses', or he will be really wasting his time !

Ever yours sincerely in Xp̄o,

H. John Chapman.

LXXVI: TO THE SAME.

Downside Abbey,
Near Bath.
Feb. 1, 1926.

Dear Mother . . . .

I can only give you the most obvious answers.

Clearly you do not fail in your vow unless you do so *quite* wilfully and knowingly. So do not worry about useless thoughts, with which you idly amuse yourself before you advert to the fact.

But as to the vow itself, I cannot give you any advice about the wording of it. If it makes you at all anxious or scrupulous, you ought *certainly* to modify it. But otherwise it would be best to leave it as it is. Only take it *roundly*, in its most general sense,—that you wish to do exactly God's Will and nothing else.

Next, you ask whether you fail in your vow when you struggle, without complete success. Well, it seems to me that what God wants us to do in this world is to struggle. As to success, that depends upon Him, chiefly. If we were always *successful* in overcoming our temptations, we should have no humility. To *try* is perfection, since it is what God wants us to do.

To show outwardly the signs of the struggle is not from an internal imperfection, if it is not wilful. As to the *pain* remaining, that is all right, and good for us. It would be very pleasant if (after a struggle) one could always submit, and either enjoy it or forget all about it. But it is just the continued pain afterwards which purifies us. It is not an imperfection to find it painful to submit to God's will. Our Lord showed us that, by His Agony in the garden.

If your Superior imputes wrong motives to you, or humiliates you unjustly, *there is no sin whatever* in justifying yourself. Sometimes it may be a duty to justify oneself. But where it really does not matter much either way, then you have, on the other hand, a perfect right to mortify yourself by saying nothing. If you feel that God *wishes* you to accept the humiliation, and to put up with your Superior's less good opinion of you, then do so quite simply, knowing quite well that it will be painful and worrying;—only, *if* you feel you are right to do this, do it cheerfully; offer it to God, *make light of it*, and try never to think of it again. And when it recurs to your mind of itself and pains you, use it as a mortification by laughing at yourself, saying:—" How silly I am to mind a little thing like this, and to care what people think of me!"

But I don't give any rule as to whether you should or should not justify yourself. That must depend on the circumstances. In most cases you would probably say casually that you did not mean any harm, had a perfectly good intention—(I mean laughingly and cheerfully). It would be a mistake to make slight matters tragic.

If it were a more serious matter and involved a sin (I mean, if you were accused of a *sinful* deed or intention), it would need a very special inspiration not to justify yourself. Saints have sometimes allowed themselves to be calumniated without defending themselves. But as a rule it is merely disedifying to let it be supposed that one has committed a sin! Any ordinary humiliations take quite simply and thankfully; but of course they will hurt.

If it is your duty to give counsel, give it whenever you think you ought. But do not worry if it is not taken, if you have done your best. Still less should you worry if it is not asked. [But if you think the Reverend Mother ought to ask more advice, you can (of course) suggest this to a higher Superior, or to the Bishop at any Visitation.]

I am quite sure your Superior and you are right, that a *perception* of the Presence of God cannot be acquired. I add that it would be rather presumptuous, as well as foolish, to try.

A mere habit of *remembering* that God sees us, of renewing acts of faith to that effect, *can* be acquired. Many books recommend it. But, in practice, it is dangerous to some people, like other anxious attempts to *force* our mind. People get nerves and " break their head " so easily.

The natural thing to do is obviously to acquire the habit of looking up to God, praying to Him, at *any* moment (not at every moment, but in intervals); but without any foolish attempts to *imagine* or *feel* His Presence. For this does not matter in the least. The feeling is an enormous help, if He gives it; and if He does not, we are better without it. I hope I have answered what you wanted.

I am, ever yours sincerely,

H. John Chapman.

LXXVII: TO A SERVITE NUN.

Downside Abbey,

June 10, 1929. *Near Bath*.

Dear Mother . . . .

The state your soul is in is God's Will for you, here and now. Do not worry about any half-intended weaknesses, for these are doubtless the very failings God means to cure and purge away by the trials He gives you in love. He uses the results of our weaknesses as the means of purifying and strengthening us. It seems a paradox, yet we find it true in fact.

It is a great grace to be ' left in blackness ', and ' to feel like a blind person '; precisely because it makes you want God. You will pray better like this. Only God does it, and you will feel you do nothing.

I am glad you feel you ' are standing still ' in your spiritual life. I should be still better pleased if you felt you were losing ground ! Whatever makes for humility is so much to the good.

184

I pray that your pains of body may stop, so that you may do your necessary work. I do not dare pray that your spiritual troubles may pass. Let God do His will in you, and He will always supply all the help you need. I think you are in a good state, and perfectly safe in God's hands.

I am sorry to write in such haste. I need prayers very much. I ask the prayers of all the Nuns on Tuesday, for a conversion. I ask most earnestly.

I am,
Yours very sincerely in Xp̄o,
H. JOHN CHAPMAN.

LXXVIII: TO THE SAME.

Downside Abbey,
Ash Wednesday, 1931.   *Near Bath.*

Dear Mother . . . .

It is much better to remain with God, apparently doing nothing in particular, than to make the grandest and most elaborate Meditations. Meditation is usually necessary in order to induce souls to love God, and to give themselves to Him. But at that point—when it *begins* to be reached—the power of meditation usually stops, and something better begins.

But this kind of formless prayer may be very painful, or full of distractions. But do not on any account give it up, or try to meditate; you will merely waste time.

I send you two articles of mine. I am also sending you two little books by Saudreau, as a present.[1]

[1] *Mystical Prayer* according to St. Francis de Sales; and *Mystical Prayer* according to St. Jane de Chantal. Both by Auguste Saudreau, translated by A. E. H. Swinstead. London, Sheed & Ward. 1929.

Père de Caussade's ' *Abandon* ' has been translated ; it is published by the Catholic Records Press, Exeter. *De Caussade* ' *On Prayer* ' is being translated by Algar Thorold, with my article (altered) as a Preface ; it will be published by Sheed and Ward, about Easter. You will find it very useful.

You will find *Ste. Jeanne F. de Chantal* more definite and useful than St. Francis himself.

Write and ask me anything you want to know. I am always glad to hear of and from you.

Your letter shows that your soul is prospering.

Ever yours very sincerely,

H. JOHN CHAPMAN.

LXXIX: TO THE SAME.

Downside Abbey,
Dec. 29, 1932. *Near Bath.*

Dear Mother . . . .

I am very grateful for your prayers. I wish you all the blessings of the New Year. I am glad to hear that your health is better.

I expect that it is all right, when you tell me that your ' prayer is methodless and often meaningless.' God gives you, by it, the good He wishes you to have. Anyhow you have the prayer which He gives, and you ought to be perfectly happy with that.

I am,

Ever yours very sincerely in Xp̄o,

H. JOHN CHAPMAN,
Abbot.

Downside Abbey,
Near Bath.

April 20, 1929.

Dear Mother Prioress. . . .

I have a great heap of letters to answer. People are very kind. It is really a great blow to become Abbot. There are so many useful things I wanted to do. I shall value your prayers, if you will bestow them on so unworthy (and therefore suitable) an object, that I may not do much harm.

I am, ever yours sincerely in X$\overline{\text{po}}$,

H. JOHN CHAPMAN.

LXXXI: TO A SECULAR PRIEST.

Downside Abbey,
Near Bath.

May 28, 1933.

Dear Reverend Father. . . .

I have read your letter with great interest. It seems to me that, in such a case, the vocation to the Secular Priesthood, which God has given you, is 'in possession', and that you should throw yourself into your Apostolic work with all your might, for God's glory. The desire for Religious Life, at the bottom of your heart, will be an incentive to fervour.

If, however, the desire should persist for a long time, and your Confessor, or other advisers should think it your *duty* to consider seriously the trying of your vocation in Religious Life, it would be best to choose an Order and a house, and pay a visit, a long one if possible, to discover whether a closer knowledge bears out your ideas, and whether Superiors would approve of your vocation. For all this, Prayer is the principal matter.

I am afraid my advice is rather obvious and trite ; but it is, perhaps, none the worse for that.

I assure you of my prayers, and am,

Yours faithfully,

H. John Chapman,
Abbot.

Part III

LETTERS TO A JESUIT

LETTERS TO A JESUIT

The first letter of this series is unfortunately, not forth-coming.

LXXXII: TO A JESUIT SCHOLASTIC.

Pax

Erdington Abbey,
Birmingham.

Oct. 10, 1911.
(*St. Francis Borgia.*)

My dear . . . .

Many thanks for your letter. I am much relieved to find that it[1] was not too much off the point, for after all I know little of you. But it is a great point to have a foundation laid. I know, at least, what I have to assume about your position with regard to the world.

As to the help you explain that you want, I can do nothing until more ground has been cleared, if then. So I proceed to clear some ground. I have two lectures to give. This is to be the first!

I start afresh from the point that you have *looked into Philosophy to find the answer to the riddle of the Universe.*

(*a*) *Some* modern non-Christian philosophers do try to give it. They have helped you here and there; but they don't satisfy you with a system and first principles,

[1] i.e. Dom Chapman's first letter to this correspondent.

191

(β) Scholastic philosophy does not try. It refuses to try. It asserts that it cannot. You were disappointed in it, because you looked into it for what *it professes not to give*.

(γ) But Theology *does* give the answer, and that is why Scholastic philosophy refuses to give it, but only prepares the way.

I proceed to explain these statements :—

THEOLOGY declares that man's experience is not homogeneous; it is twofold, *natural* and *supernatural*:

1. Man was made for a *supernatural* END.

2. He is endowed with *supernatural means* to it: GRACE and REVELATION. It is obviously not possible *in practice* to disentangle the Supernatural from the Natural. The two are warp and woof from which our whole experience is woven. But it *is* possible to do so *in theory*, and SCHOLASTIC PHILOSOPHY deals ONLY with the Natural, and therefore *c*ot with life in all its complexity as we know it, but with the world as it would be without revelation and without grace (of all kinds), which are disturbing factors.

[You may say, such an *abstract* science is an absurdity. Then so are pure Mathematics. In applied Mathematics all sorts of disturbing factors come in, some calculable, some averageable, some quite unknowable beforehand, for which a margin of power has to be left, etc.

Or take the parallel case of Ethics : it is obvious to distinguish the natural law, the positive divine law, and positive human law, *in theory*. In practice, however, it is frequently doubtful under which head a law is to be catalogued.

Or again : some cases cured at Lourdes may be wholly matter for the science of medicine, others partially, others *not at all.* The science of medicine must *omit these* from its data.]

The crucial instance of this abstract nature of pure philosophy is in *Natural Theology*, which is a *part* of philosophy; its subject matter is what man can know of God *without revelation and without grace* ; whereas it is (really) OF FAITH that it is within the power of every man to have divine faith (of some kind) and that no one is ever without ' sufficient grace '.

Consequently ' Natural Theology ' is a science entirely in the air. It never exists in practice; it only theorizes as to how much man's unaided reason can do in this direction. But it does not deny (indeed, as a handmaid to Theology it emphatically asserts) that just as, on the one hand, most people are far too muddle-headed to arrive at God clearly in this way—they may be polytheists or anything—so, on the other hand, they are never without some supernatural assistance, whether of teaching, or tradition, or internal light, or what not.

Consequently there is not and never has been in the world such a monster as a professor of purely natural religion. A human being falls lower or rises higher, but is never a simply *natural* man.

One who has a *lower* religion (e.g. fetichism, polytheism), could never make the abstract science of ' Natural religion ' ; but it is possible to those who have a higher religion, i.e. one which includes all that unaided reason can teach, *plus* a great deal more. Therefore Christian philosophers disentangle, in theory, from Christianity as a whole system all that part which, by unaided reason, a perfectly reasonable and unprejudiced philosopher might theoretically have discovered for himself—though no one has actually been clever enough, or unassisted-by-grace enough, to succeed in doing so. I hope this is all quite clear.

Now for examples :—

A. THE EXISTENCE OF GOD. Scholastics agree that the
'*quinque viae*' of St. Thomas are valid proofs (against
Kant). On the whole they are inclined to reject the
Anselmian argument. Many of them restrict the argument
from conscience, though they admit its partial validity—
and so forth.

All these agreements and disagreements concern *what
man can know by unaided reason*. Being Christians, all
these philosophers assert much more, but not in philosophy,
but in theology ! viz., that every man can have the *certitude
of faith* with regard to God's existence (whether you
call it faith, or quasi-faith) ; that no man can be saved
without it (in some form) ; that it is a gift of God, higher
than reason, etc.

Further, that God gives proofs of His action, by revelation, by miracles, by internal motions (light to intellect,
warmth to heart), that He reveals the supernatural in
visions, the future in prophecy, that He even shows
Himself (in some lesser way than the Beatific Vision,
sicuti est) to some souls in this pilgrimage, etc., etc.

But Natural theology leaves all these data out of account,
just as medical professors must omit the healing of De
Rudder's *tibia* from their data.

B. THE ARGUMENT FROM CONSCIENCE.

We spoke of this. I fancy that one can harmonize Billot
with Newman on these lines: Billot is speaking of conscience
as found in all men by philosophy—and he is possibly
quite right in restricting the argument by various limita-
tions—Newman, on the other hand, is speaking not of
the abstract philosophical argument, but of the practical
conviction caused by a conscience enlightened and
strengthened by interior grace. In his own case this

seems to have been very strong. I daresay the same was the case with Kant and with Webb.

There is no fault to be found with either position. Scholastic Philosophy takes up an impregnable position: " The argument from conscience for the existence of God must be considered at its lowest, as it can be seized by a person who has natural conscience without any special grace ". Newman would say:—" I am appealing to the enlightened consciences of devout Christians, as it is for them I am writing; and I am sure that for most of them the voice of conscience manifests itself as the voice of God."

To resume:

The Vatican Council has defined that there is an absolute distinction between the natural order and the supernatural order.

A. Scholastic philosophy deals with the *natural* only.

B. Theology (including Dogma, Moral theology, Ascetics, Mystical Theology) deals with BOTH, having previously used Philosophy to disentangle the *natural* for her.

C. Modern non-Christian Philosophy deals with both.

Consequently, you see, modern philosophical systems are parallel to *Theology*, not to *Scholastic Philosophy*. It is, therefore, most unfair to compare them with Scholastic Philosophy in the way you have done.

But compare the modern philosophy with Theology: Both profess to take for their data the whole of life, the whole of the universe and God, the whole of experience.

But the non-Christian, or the non-Catholic

(*a*) does not have *all the data* before him. Of a great deal he is simply ignorant; a good deal more he denies.

(β) He is unable to make the *distinction* between the natural and the supernatural. Therefore his conclusions are all vitiated to the Christian.

I explain :—

(α) Not all the data. He knows less about the religious consciousness, because he has not the inner experience at his disposal which the Church has accumulated in Moral, Ascetical and Mystical Theology. He has not the understanding of sin, repentance, fear and love of God. He rejects (probably) the miraculous. He does not know or admit faith and hope, the Incarnation, the value of prayer,—except in a half-hearted manner—and so forth. He does not see the miraculous in History—e.g. the dispersion and persecution of the Jews ; the unity and continuous identity of the Church, etc. ; and so forth, and so forth.

(β) He explains conversions, or gifts of the Holy Ghost, or Faith, all on natural grounds, as a part of human nature. He insists that answers to prayer, miracles, etc., are a part of the settled order of things. He omits, or denies, the facts that are most awkward, etc., etc. Now religious facts are *historically*, *socially*, *politically*, *psychologically* of enormous importance. Hence he *cannot possibly* reach right conclusions.

To resume :—

But I fully admit that, compared with modern philosophy, Scholasticism is wilfully at a disadvantage—so it is unkind to compare them.

(1) Scholasticism has put aside all questions of faith, grace, graces : saying they are not its business.
(2) Philosophy of the moderns denies these questions to be faith or grace, but includes a lot of the data. Hence

it can attempt a synthesis of the κόσμος, whereas Scholasticism cannot.

Again :—

(1) In Scholastic Philosophy you look in vain for ' the religious consciousness ', for intuitions of God, for a description of the ' prayer of union '.

(2) In the moderns these are included (in so far as they know or admit the evidence for them) as a part of the data on which they work.

Consequently :—

A. You looked in vain into scholastic manuals for what you wanted.

B. You found something of what you wanted in the moderns, but not all.

C. But Theology would have given you all.

I think this is important, if you will receive it ; for it is the real answer, I believe.

Example :—As a fact you *did* find yourself in St. Teresa, more than in Joachim ; and so forth.

I hope this long rigmarole explains why, in my former letter, I insisted that :—

(1) Scholastic philosophy is ancillary to Theology— being a propaedeutic and a method.

(2) That you must look forward to the study of Theology.

For Theology is not an abstract Algebra like Philosophy ; it is a concrete science embracing the whole of life, and it issues in action : i.e.

(a) Dogmatic Theology is pure science, but it is directive of (β, γ, δ) Moral, Ascetic, Mystic Theology, which are *arts* as well as sciences.

Therefore, if you had not found Scholastic philosophy to be a dry skeleton, you would have been grossly mistaken !

Modern philosophy has more body, is more full-flavoured. It has some excellent points. Scholastic philosophy has learnt much from it of late years : [e.g. too much used to be put down to miracle—some miracles (e.g. faith-cures) can be explained naturally. Phenomena of consciousness and sub-consciousness. Physiology, Anatomy, even Evolution, have helped greatly : e.g. in St. Teresa's time all trances, visions, locutions, were put down by Confessors either to God or the devil—St. Teresa herself had sense enough to see that nature does a great deal. Moderns all agree about this. So we often, to-day, put down to the stomach temptations which used to be ascribed to the devil. Irritability, desolation and aridity are often cured by a pill, or a little rest]. So hard is it to disentangle the natural from the supernatural.

So one may learn much from Kant or Hegel : equally, no doubt, from Joachim, or Jacks, or Webb, or Bergson. *But it is simply impossible that Spinoza, or Hegel, or the rest should account for the world as it is*, if they abstract from Revelation and do not admit grace to be grace.

But there are many things in modern psychological and intuitionist and monist philosophies which the Catholic critic *denies in philosophy but admits in theology* : e.g. arguments for the existence of God from universal consent, from cosmic emotion (!), from religious experience, and especially from *the inner need of man*.

These are not *valid proofs* in philosophy, but they may figure among the *motiva credibilitatis* in the treatise *De vera religione*. And the very scholastic who denounced the French apologetic " Method of immanence ", in so far as it claims to supplant all others, will the next minute quote with approval the first sentence of St. Augustine's

" Confessions ", that man's heart is unquiet until it rests in God, as an argument for the necessity of religion. [It is quite parallel to the way Kant destroys God, the world and the soul, in the *Kritik der reinen Vernunft*, in order to restore them by the practical reason.] There is much more I might say.

But take the main point :—

Scholastic philosophy *denies* that man knows God except by argument from creatures, *per viam negationis* and *per viam eminentiae.*

Theology *asserts* that man must and ought to know Him also by faith; that he can know much more by revelation; that he may and should arrive at communion, through the sacraments, through mortification, through prayer; that he can have, in this life, divine unions, and locutions, and spiritual marriage.

I might reproach you for looking for consolation in philosophy and not in Christianity. But I think there are too many obvious *excuses and explanations.*

A. A first draught of Philosophy is very exhilarating, not to say heady. One expects to find answers to everything. So did I when I read for ' Greats '.

B. You actually found some approximations to what you looked for in the recent philosophies—enough to encourage you to hope to find more. Besides, you compared them (unfairly, as I said) to Scholastic philosophy, and found the latter wanting (as it professes to be).

C. You were half timid, half modest, I believe, in wishing to find your experiences understood, commonplace, labelled, rather than at once believe that you had the state I have pointed out to you. I suppose you always suspected it; but *you* did not tell me: *I* had to tell you. I fancy that, at first, at all events, you *wished* to believe that many good half-Christians, or non-Christians, were in a similar phase. Later you realised that it was a 'state of prayer'; you rather gave me to understand that it was 'la quiètude' (which it certainly is not, in any sense of the word) and you wished to suppose it not so far from what the 'intuitionists' describe. But they attribute it, surely, to *all* religious persons!

I imagine the above to be your excuses. I daresay you could give a clearer account, if I have been right in my diagnosis. But a conjectural diagnosis is liable to considerable error! Don't be angry if I am usually off the point.

Another important point is, I think,

(1) That modern philosophers are inclined (after Hegel) to make Religion a part of philosophy, or subject to philosophy.

(2) Scholastic philosophy *does* make natural religion a part of philosophy,

(3) but it makes theology (= revealed religion) the whole of life; with philosophy as something inferior to even a part,—only ancillary.

That is another reason why you remain unsatisfied. To the ordinary Protestant, religion is a detail, though an important detail; a part of life, but an interesting and consoling part. To the least practising Catholic, it is quite well known (even when the knowledge is thrust aside) that religion is the whole of life, embraces everything,—that God's demands are paramount—that eternity is everything, this life nothing.

Don't you see how these pious philosophers—monists, idealists, sentimentalists, intuitionists—fail entirely to recognize what every Catholic recognizes? Perhaps you will say, at once, that I am mistaken. But yet I believe I am right.

Reasons for this—the first that occur to me :—

(1) If we hold that the next life is eternal and depends on this, then our whole view of life depends on this one point. Do these philosophers approach everything from this point? Surely NO.

(2) The end of man, why he is here. Do they answer that? Only a few of them. Fichte is the best; yet he is a " mystic ". As a philosopher he is nothing; a dreamer.

(3) The question of ethics. If they depend on *divine sanction*, the whole of life is altered. Not all admit even this. Kant does; but even he seems wanting here from the Christian standpoint.

(4) Do they recognize the essential weakness of man towards good, his absolute need of God, not as a vision but as a *helper*? Much more, do they understand what SIN is? It is one of the primary facts in the world; and any philosophy which proposes to account for the world must put sin, guilt, repentance, in a prominent place.

You see, my complaint is that the philosophers philosophize as if there was nothing in heaven and earth which is not dreamt of in their philosophy. Whereas humble Scholasticism says there are lots of things, and these the most important of all, which it must leave aside.

Consequently, only religion, only revelation, can explain things. Only God, who made the κόσμος, can say what He made it for, what end it is to serve.

Again; the reality of God, the nothingness of the world. This is asserted by Scholastic philosophy, and by religion as a logical deduction and as a revelation. Most people have to try very hard to realise it. It is a great grace to get even a little way.

But most modern systems seem to me to say just the opposite. You have materialists, or evolutionists, like

Herbert Spencer, at the one end ; the world is everything, God nothing. Or idealists, to whom our experience is everything,—whether the universe is an emanation, à la Bergson, or a self-existent entity, or a phase of God, or a mode of God,—all seem to think the rational κόσμος is *necessary*. They feel " cosmic emotion ". On a lower plane they are (like Mallock) impressed by the vastness of the universe, or (like Kant) with the starry skies.

The Catholic philosopher is primarily impressed by the fact that the universe, including finite minds, is so obviously CONTINGENT, so very imperfect ; even—so Chesterton says—" such a cosy little universe " ; that it manifests God so very poorly, that it is (as material, finite, contingent, mutable, temporal) the very *opposite* of the spiritual, infinite, necessary, immutable, eternal, which we call God.

So the philosophers (even idealists, who deny objectivity to matter) give a reality to the world which Theology does not. The reason obviously is that they do not understand that God's Reality is something quite different, and infinitely more real than what we call reality. Theology says that the material universe was created out of nothing, and that it only subsists by the sustaining power of God. It is the theatre erected for the combats of souls, and they too are from nothing. Only God has *aseitas*.

Philosophy would call your experience an interesting psychological state. Theology says it is a revelation of the true, and that all ought to believe by faith (and, if they can, realise in prayer) this reality of God and nothingness of all else. To the others it is an abnormal pathological case. To theology it is ' what ought to be ', though it seldom is.

I said to you that all ' idealism ' must logically end in *solipsism*. You tartly replied:—" I shouldn't mind much."

I think you are quite right; '*Una uni*', the Blessed Egidio used to repeat. *Una uni*, one soul to one God. Theology teaches us that the two great realities for us are God and our soul; the infinitely great and the infinitely little. *Here again* you are at one with Christian theology against the moderns, who all think *solipsism* ridiculous (as of course it is, philosophically) and assert that they are in no danger of it.

All the same, this is not your philosophy, it is your actual feeling, and practical conclusion. Theoretically you admit that other people *do* exist! The feeling that everything is a dream is not subjective idealism, it *is* solipsism.

Not that you feel *as if you* were dreaming. For, when we dream, we believe we are awake (except in rare cases, when we are only half asleep) and everything is quite solid. We know it was a dream because it vanishes, or because it doesn't correspond with our subsequent experience, or because it ends in the sensation of waking up, (sometimes, however, I wake up into a second dream !) I presume that you feel the world to be, not as substantial as a dream seems, but as unsubstantial as we recognize the dream to be when we have waked up. Hence experience is a weird flux under which the Ego remains stationary—because it is fixed on God. (Much as though we could anchor ourselves to the sun, and feel the world whirling round at 1000 miles an hour under our feet.) But I don't think that is even an impressionist picture of idealism as it is meant by idealists. However, that doesn't matter.

I wonder when this letter is going to end!

I hope you will gather that I have intended to justify your having found some (but not enough) consolation in philosophy.

But I told you I have a rounded theological theory of the world myself. I believe one ought to have one. The Creed only gives outlines. If you wish me to give some outlines of mine, I am quite willing to do so as Lecture No. 2,—i.e. " Letters to a Jesuit ", No. 3 ! But only if you think it likely to be of any use. I have no right to preach to you, and I have nothing original to say, (of course—else it would be heresy).

I don't see how to recommend you any work ; I don't know what you like. But surely there is no difficulty in finding something to work at. I really think you seem too vague about the meaning of life and the principles which guide us ; and yet I suppose them to be plain enough.

Of course all this long letter is not meant to help you for the future ; it is merely the only explanation I have to offer of the past, as a clearing of the ground. You are sure to have plenty to suffer ; but I don't see why it should be *internal* suffering. It ought to be easy enough to put *that* all right.

Don't be discontented at any little awkward effects— for a time—of so enormous a grace. Don't pity yourself, but pity those who fruitlessly envy you. To me it is a great source of joy merely to know that God does such things, and I speak to you as a poor old beggar in rags to a King on his throne.

I very much hope that, at least, this letter will answer one sentence of yours :—

" Philosophy can never *explain* my experience, but it can point out lines of possible explanation, and point upwards from below to what revelation sends down from above. If it does not leave room for it, or, negatively even, seems to discredit it, it [the philosophy] is discredited for me, and I go to one that promises better."

My answer is : *Scholastic Philosophy* is not discredited, because it refuses to explain. Modern philosophy tries to explain, but only partially. Only theology (including all parts) gives the answer.

A Christian cannot live by philosophy. Only the light of Christian revelation gives the end as well as the means of life. It is the same for you as for me and the man in the street. If one has more learning, another has more grace, it is all one.

If you can accept all this as *theoretically* probable, I will show you what I mean by Christian principles. But don't think you know beforehand. *Oremus ad invicem*.

Ever yours affectionately *in Christo*,

fr. JOHN CHAPMAN, O.S.B.

(Note. The original letter occupies forty-two pages of ordinary note paper, closely written.—Ed.)

LXXXIII: TO THE SAME.

Pax

Erdington Abbey,
Birmingham

Oct. 26, 1911.

My dear . . . .

It is not easy to say all I want to say. Anyhow, at best, it is only " my way of putting it ", and I am not even suggesting that you should take it cheap, secondhand, as it stands. You have to make it for yourself.

I will begin with my own starting point :—there is a lot of preliminary matter, before we get to the Christian religion.

A. At 12 (or 13) years old I felt that religion ought to be transcendent, infinite, necessary. I suppose the vague, unexpressed notion that was in my head was "The One" of Parmenides, and the idea that the ultimate explanation of everything must be "The One". Of course I knew nothing of philosophy, and very little of Christianity.

But this idea of the necessary and The One seemed to me a temptation to 'infidelity', for Christianity is a complexus of un-necessary, contingent, arbitrary facts and doctrines. The reply I gave to my own difficulty was that Revelation was not given for the sake of philosophers, but for the poor and unlearned.

I have never ceased to think this a complete argument —[only I should now add that the philosophers are not much ahead of the unlearned, after all].

B. "The Ethics of Elf-land," the second (?) chapter of Chesterton's *Orthodoxy*,[1] will excellently give my second point :—viz. the contingency, arbitrariness, surprisingness, of the universe we know; especially if that chapter is taken in contrast to the second part of Plato's *Parmenides*.

Now I have always felt these two truths with absolute clearness : viz. *A.* That God is τὸ ἕν the unchangeable, unqualified, infinite Being ;

B. That the world—κόσμος—is becoming, contingent, improbable.

C. When I started reading philosophy for "Greats" (more than twenty-seven years ago, alas!) I was agreeably surprised to find how many philosophers (from the Eleatics onward,—Plato and Aristotle to some extent,— the Neoplatonists vividly) had seen τὸ ἕν, the necessary, unconditioned. I had expected that everybody but myself would have been too stupid to see (this is still my usual attitude!). But the moderns seemed to have lost the idea. I don't see a trace of it in Spinoza ; he seems to try to get a 'One' which includes the κόσμος, consequently which has conditions, modes, etc. Therefore I am one

[1] Really Chapter IV.—Ed.

206

of those who do not see in Spinoza a man drunk with God, but an atheist. For his God is not mine. [But Stewart used to say that Martineau's criticisms were most unfair. Hegel defends Spinoza in more than one place. And perhaps Spinoza, when he 'contemplated', meant better than he said.]

I have always (consciously or unconsciously) tried philosophers by this test :—viz. whether they really knew what the ideal, necessary, one Being is, or not. Schelling (for example), with his stuffy little Absolute, is no nearer philosophy than the blankest materialist would be. Beyond his self-evolving universe, there would be an infinite, incomprehensible, immutable background. Hegel rightly said that Schelling's 'Absolute' came from no-where,— shot out of a catapult. I give Schelling as an example— it seems to me that many moderns are just as silly. I have not read Bergson yet—I understand that he actually allows free-will to God (and to animals). But I gather that he makes all things 'emanate' from God.

Still, the worst people are those who tell me I am a 'mode of the Absolute', or something equally childish.

D. Now, starting from these two fixed points :—

(1) God—The One, the All, the Immutable, uncon-ditioned necessary, etc.,

(2) The Cosmos, including matter and mind, and myself, —arbitrary and improbable and unaccountable ; there is but one solution possible, which I had from religion :—

God made the Cosmos.

Why? It was a *very* odd thing to do!

And what an extraordinary universe to invent! Just fancy inventing *matter !* and thinking of such a thing as time—or space! Very clever of Him, no doubt,—most ingenious, to imagine such extremely curious facts as co-existence and succession. But very arbitrary and absurd, —one might say, insane.

[I am trying to give you my feeling about " this cosy little universe "; but *do* read Chesterton's chapter on " Elf-land ".]

It seems quite evident,

(1) That no one can possibly say what it is for, except the Person who made it.

(2) That the Maker thereof is (in relation to it) an arbitrary Personality, an intellectual, free, will.

(3) That, presumably, it is not a machine wound up, which runs on of itself indefinitely, but one in which this ingenious inventor of it is much interested, and in which He works.

(4) He has made in it a number of self-conscious intelligences (I am one of them), who can act freely—not (apparently) adding by their actions to the amount of force existing in the world, but directing it arbitrarily at will.

(5) Presumably the Creator—as He is evidently, in relation to the whole, a magnified free will, inventive, arbitrary—also acts within the world in the same way ; not necessarily by adding new force by His action, but by directing forces, as human beings do.

[This is my way of looking at miracles—the Creator acting just as Creatures do. And, in this way, He manifests Himself ; just as I can prove my existence to you by speaking to you, or writing to you, or knocking you down (if I could).]

[Except by ' miracles ', external or internal, God has no means of making Himself known in His own world. The " impossibility " of miracles is another way of saying that everyone can act in the world except the Creator.]

If everything in the Cosmos was quite straightforward and obvious, if the planets all moved in perfect circles, and men did the same, it might be easier to suppose that God wound the world up, once and for all, and then left it to tick till it is worn out, or *ad infinitum*.

But the world is so surprising and so curious, that I could not easily disbelieve in the miraculous.

Now the miraculous is of two kinds:—*supernatural* and *preternatural*. [I propose to omit physical miracles, as they are not important for our purpose.]

Supernatural means (theologically) that which is *above all possible nature*, i.e. God, and only God,—(His essence, His action, or His purpose).

Preternatural means, above some particular nature : e.g. it is 'natural' for a man to talk, but 'preternatural' for an ass to talk.

Many things are preternatural or even natural *quoad essentiam*, but supernatural *quoad modum :* (i.e. because God does them, or because He intends them for a super-natural end, etc.).

So

A. The natural events of our life are *actual graces*, in so far as God's Providence intends us to use them towards our eternal salvation :—

$$\begin{cases} \text{natural } quoad \ rem \\ \text{supernatural } quoad \ modum. \end{cases}$$

B. Good thoughts, or feelings of fervour, may be in the same category as *A*. But they may also be *infused internal graces*,—action of God upon our minds and hearts:—

$$\begin{cases} \text{supernatural } quoad \ causam \\ \text{(preter)?natural } quoad \ rem \\ \text{supernatural } quoad \ modum. \end{cases}$$

[Without such internal *preventing* and *assisting* grace, it is OF FAITH that we cannot do any (difficult) good work ; nor, in the supernatural order (i.e. as of avail towards our salvation), any good work at all.]

These (*B*) are not physical miracles, but they are none the less miraculous. Our minds and hearts are *not* left to themselves, but God ' interferes '. [There are, of course, other higher graces and ' gifts '.]

C. Sanctifying (or Habitual) grace is *supernaturale quoad essentiam* or *simpliciter*—for it is union with God—a " created participation of His essence ", to use an incomprehensible description of a mystery (Billuart's, I think).

Now, when I did my philosophy at Oxford as a Protestant, I did not know what the ' supernatural ' was,—but I suppose I vaguely knew something of what I have just said.

But I knew (though I had *very* little religion) that religion had the first place. Though I really hoped (as you do) that Philosophy was arriving at something, though I was enthusiastic about it, though I loved (and love) Plato, and became (and am) an Aristotelian, and called myself (and was not) a Hegelian, I never doubted that Christianity must rule, and Philosophy be her handmaid. Yet I *did*, I confess, look to find an answer in philosophy to a great part of the world's riddle.

I think I was largely attracted to Hegel because he is Christian. Kant is the typical Protestant ; Hegel is nearly a Catholic. But his silly little SYSTEM repelled me.

It was just then that I began to have a little religion. I began to find the answer in Revelation, and ever since then I have lost my interest in philosophy, except as an intellectual exercise, or a means of refuting error.

I suppose I had been a Catholic about eight or ten years when I had satisfactorily worked out a theory of religion and the world for myself—a working theory, which had been, till then, implicit, but not thought out.

Much earlier, in beginning my Theology (I did no Philosophy, but read St. Thomas's *Summa* with commentaries, and occasionally got some help from Father Columba Marmion, the present Abbot of Maredsous), I had been helped enormously by the first part of St. Thomas. I had never before known what God is. I had realised His Transcendence as emptiness, not as fulness.

[N.B. Of course there are many odd and (*a priori*) most improbable things in the world besides space and time and matter,—such as colour and light, music, right and wrong (conscience), pain, wonder—and so forth— not to speak of the moon ; and there are many questions one might ask, which philosophy would find it hard to answer, such as why England is not an island (*sic*), why things don't fall upwards, why I cannot describe heat and cold, why things don't look larger in the distance.]

Now, I hope we are coming to the point, so I shall take a larger piece of paper :[1]

P.S. I think all this preliminary matter ought to be far clearer to you than to me. For you can better realise God's immensity, fulness, unity, transcendence, etc., and you can *feel* the unmeaning wildness, astonishingness, riot of phenomena,—a drunken dream, a fantasia, and so forth.

P.P.S. What comes next is only, I repeat, suggestion. It is incomplete as well as hurried. But note that it was written at least devoutly, and wants reading devoutly, and in a kindly and uncritical spirit. I am not infallible,

[1] The P.S. and P.P.S. which follow on the same smaller sheet at this point, were evidently added, after the whole letter had been written, when Dom John re-read it before sending it off. They are printed at this point, however, as they were evidently meant to be read before the "Theory" which follows on the quarto sheets, and occupies no less than thirty-six pages of these.—Ed.

and some of it may be unsound in wording. But I always *try* to be *orthodox*, first of all. For Truth is above Charity, and above everything paramount.

Part the First.[1]

THE END OF ALL THINGS

One must obviously begin at the end.

A. The *End of Man*, as man—which he *must* seek, because *omne ens appetit suam perfectionem*—is happiness, as Aristotle saw,—the exercise of his highest faculty,—contemplation,—on its highest object—God.

So far reason. But here we know God darkly. REVELATION ADDS: our END is not here, but in Heaven, the Beatific Vision—our Happiness, which we necessarily seek, is to be found not in any goods of this life, but only in *union with God.*

[The Beatific Vision is explained by St. Thomas: God unites Himself to our intellect as its *species.* Thus we are to know God *in the same way* that He knows Himself; our knowledge (and also our Love of God) will be Divine. Of course God *is* His own Knowledge, so that the Union is substantial not accidental, a true deification. If you ask in what it differs from Nirvana, I answer (with some hesitation) that it seems to me that the chief practical difference is that the Beatific Vision does not absorb the whole man into God, but leaves (nay intensifies) all his ordinary human faculties. It is an *addition* to his powers, not a substitution. The union is complete, but the human personality remains.]

B. The end of creatures, as creatures, is to give glory to their Creator. [They can be of no *utility* to Him, so it remains that they must be for His Honour.]

[1] The "larger paper", of quarto size, 8 in. by 6¼in., begins here.—Ed.

Gloria est clara notitia cum laude.

In intellectual beings, nature knows God's existence and can praise Him. Man as the microcosm (material, vegetable, animal and intellectual) praises God by seeing God's wonderful works, and praising Him for them (as in the *Benedicite omnia opera Domini Domino*).

By reason he knows this much; and that his great DUTY is this—to praise God, serve God, procure God's honour, work His will, promote His interests, etc.

(By grace) this becomes a passion; he sees that, to *know* God more and more, and to praise (i.e. love) Him more and more, is man's great work.

But here he can only know God *per speculum in aenigmate*.

Revelation tells us that, in Heaven, we shall know as we are known, and praise worthily. So our full duty will be fulfilled in Heaven, where we can know perfectly and so glorify perfectly, by means of the Beatific Vision and the Love that flows therefrom.

Therefore, *materialiter*, the end of man as a rational being, and the end of the creature as a creature, i.e. Happiness and Duty, are ONE; being attained by Union with God after this life.

C. The End of the Creator.

The end (I don't mean the point) of a poker is to make up the fire. The end of the maker of the poker was to gain a livelihood. i.e. *Finis operis* is not the same as *finis operantis*.

We have seen the end of the work (Man *A*, Creature *B*). Now what is the *finis operantis*, i.e. the purpose of the Creator?

Omnia propter seipsum operatus est Deus. He can have no end outside Himself.

Ipse prior dilexit nos. The end of the Creator is *love* (Himself, considered *formaliter* as Love).

CARITAS EST DIFFUSIVA SUI.

God has, from all eternity, all bliss in Himself. (As we distinguish attributes in God: one is His Happiness. We must express it to ourselves after a human fashion. Human happiness is to know and love God: God's happiness is to know and love His own infinite Fulness.)

[This is expressed in the TwoFold Procession of the Word and the Spirit.]

God saw that He could create beings capable of being raised to participate in this bliss, Therefore He made Angels and men, with intellects and wills capable of being raised (*potentia obedientialis*) to communion with Himself, sharing His Knowledge and Love of Himself, and thus participating in the Divine Life, the Divine bliss.

(God is *Actus purus ;* His communication of Himself, whether by grace or glory, is the communication of His *Activity*, not of a mere passive quality.)

Therefore again, God's end is attained (*C*) when we reach our end as

    A. Intellectual beings,
    B. creatures,

in the *Lumen gloriae* in Heaven. *Therefore* we are made for God—to be united to Him in Heaven. There to have the completion of

    1. our happiness (union),
    2. our duty (glory),
    3. God's purpose (love).

N.B. Of these three points, the third is the most important—God's loving purpose :—ἀγαπητοὶ νῦν τέκνα θεοῦ ἐσμεν, καὶ οὔπω ἐφανερώθη τί ἐσόμεθα. οἴδαμεν δὲ ὅτι ἐὰν φανερωθῇ, ὅμοιοι αὐτῷ ἐσόμεθα, ὅτι ὀψόμεθα αὐτόν καθώς ἐστι.[1]

---

[1] "Dearly Beloved, we are now the sons of God; and it hath not yet appeared what we shall be. We know that, when he shall appear, we shall be like to him ; because we shall see him as he is."—1 John iii. 2.

Herein is the threefold end of man : No philosophy could have worked this out, it needed God's revelation.

The end is *supernatural*—God Himself. And *it is a reward above all that any possible created being could merit* by its own powers. Hence the means to the end must all be *supernàtural*.

The complete union is reached by inchoate progressive union ; FAITH, an inchoate knowledge (supernatural) ; GRACE, an inchoate union, the seed of glory.

Part the Second

THE ORDER OF CREATION

Read St. Francis de Sales, *Traitté de l'amour de Dieu*, Book II, Chapter 4 : " De la Providence surnaturelle que Dieu exerce envers les créatures raysonnables." What I have to say is a kind of additional note to St. Francis.

A. The grades of Union.

Trinity, most perfect	(1) Three Persons in One nature : whose knowledge, love, happiness, is all in common ; in Whom all is one, except the opposition of relation.
Hypostatic Union, next in perfection	(2) Two Natures in one Person : so that God is Man, and Man is God, yet each nature is perfect, without mingling.
Glory, next below	(3) A human Nature and Person deified by participating in that eternal Act, which is the Divine substance— but retaining its human personality as well as its human nature.

| Sanctifying Grace, next in order. (This is not accurately defined.) | (4) An inchoate union of will (by charity) and intellect (by enlightenment=faith) to God, proceeding from an infused quality in the essence of the soul. Commonly described as *indwelling* (He in us, we in Him). |

B. *The order of intention* of the Creator.

The best is necessarily first in intention; the second best exists for it; so God's intention begins with Himself.

1. He first intends Himself as the end.
2. He next intends the Hypostatic union for (1), (so St. Francis teaches).
3. He next intends Glory, for the sake of (2)—(His Court, His Kingdom).
4. He next intends Grace, for the sake of (3) (all this wants thinking out).

This is THE SUPERNATURAL ORDER.

Below this comes Nature; therefore Nature exists FOR grace.

5. Next intellect (men and angels) for (4), (the subjects of grace).
6. Next sensitive life (animals, etc.) for (5), (they are for man, his food, his servants, and sensitive nature is a part of his).
7. Next vegetable world, for (6), (the food, scenery, etc, for (6)).
8. Next material world, (matter, space, time), the theatre in which (7) lives, and the material of which it is made.

This is THE NATURAL ORDER, in which all exists (in a ladder) for man, and man for the glory of God and his own happiness and perfection.

These Two Orders are not *contraries*, but *complements* ; each exists for the other and in the other.

(1) The natural *for* the supernatural : it was made for this and this alone, (just as matter exists for form) ; it is the support for it (just as bulk is the support for surface, or, if you prefer it, canvas for a painting).

(2) The supernatural order equally exists for the natural ; it is exactly adapted to it (as skin and flesh to skeleton). It does not hang in mid air, it is the perfection of nature.

[Just as Protestant philosophy makes soul and body two entities (a living body *plus* a spiritual soul !), so it makes the supernatural a sphere apart, and the natural a self-existent sphere.

Whereas Catholic theology makes the soul the ἐντελεχεία σώματος φυσικοῦ—the form of the body—; the body is not an entity, but an incomplete substance. Similarly it makes the supernatural order and the natural order all one entity, each incomplete without the other, interlaced, inseparable,

distinguished *realiter*, but

not distinguishable (separable) *in concreto*.]

I next take the four steps of the supernatural order in detail.

1. God the End. As the three Persons are one in Knowledge and Will and Essence, so our end is to be one in knowledge and essence and will with God.

(You know all that is commonly said about the *vestigia SS. Trinitatis* in man and nature. Hegel had some justification in taking the Holy Trinity as the root of his method and the skeleton of his system.)

2. The first-born, the Heir of Creation, πρωτότοκος πάσης κτίσεως. God *wills first* the most perfect created union, the Incarnation : (I am *not* a Scotist, by the way).

His Love consists in giving ;—giving Himself— giving life, giving happiness.

In the Incarnation is the most perfect gift of Himself possible (so far as we can see),—giving His own Personality to a created composite nature, (in which is summed up all the grades of the natural order) together with union with His Nature, and including both *glory* (Beatific Vision) and *grace* in the highest of all degrees.

All else is created for Him (Christ) : ὅτι ἐν αὐτῷ ἐκτίσθη τὰ πάντα, ἐν τοῖς οὐρανοῖς καὶ ἐπὶ τῆς γῆς . . .

τὰ πάντα	δι᾿ αὐτοῦ	καὶ	εἰς αὐτον ἔκτισται
ἐγὼ ἐιμι τὸ	Α	καὶ	τὸ Ω
	ἡ ἄρχη	και	τὸ τέλος
	ὁ πρῶτος	και	ὁ ἐσχατος καὶ ὁ ζῶν.

(*Apoc.* I. 18.)

Read Colossians I. (The second century Apologists, Paul of Samosata, the Arians, etc., understood it of the Λόγος. The Church has seen that St. Paul meant the Christ, the Λόγος—become—flesh.)

All was made *for Him in initio viarum.*

All ends in Him, (read 1 Cor. xv. 20-28, Apoc. V. 1-14, Hebrews i. 1-4).

He is the Head—in Him all things consist, συνέστηκε, in Him all are to be recapitulated ἀνακεφαλαιώσασθαι.

He is the Head of Angels and Men: *per Quem majestatem Tuam laudant Angeli, adorant Domina-*

tiones, tremunt Potestates, etc. Admirably worked out by St. Gertrude :—*All glory* goes up to God through Him. *All grace* comes down through Him.

3. The Angels and the Blessed in Heaven form His Court—they are His Kingdom. By His grace they have won the reward,—through Him they know, and praise, and enjoy—for only *in Him* are they there at all.

4. Grace. The primal union is union with God through Christ. All grace since the Incarnation is *gratia Christi ;* so was all grace after the Fall *gratia Christi* (*praevisis meritis*). The grace of Adam, the grace of the Angels, was all *intuitu Christi* (though not *per merita Christi*), for it looked forward to Him as its End to be reached.

Part the Third

THE WAY

God has not chosen to diffuse His bounty upon machines.

Three ends :—

1. Of Creator. He gives His joy as a reward, He gives Himself to those who accept Him freely.

2. Of Creatures. He asks for glory to be given Him by His creatures as a free gift.

3. Of Man. He wants man (and angels) to earn his own happiness, not to grow into it.

Therefore He made Man (and Angels) with FREE WILL, the highest point in the natural order, the most perfect resemblance to God.

[It is in fact a kind of *created Aseitas*, it seems to me. We should not have thought that God *could* create free wills, if He had not done so ! In fact strict Thomists still argue as if He couldn't ! *Praemotio physica* is only a way of denying that God *could* create us as Gods, having free determination, *aseitas*, in our own actions, within limits.]

[Naturally *intelligence*, and *free will* which follows it, being highest in the natural order, are the nearest to the supernatural order.]

The end of angels and men being glory, they could not be created *in it*, if they were to *win it*. When we *see God* face to Face, we shall *not be free* not to love Him. That which has no imperfection forces our love.

1. Therefore we could not be created *in glory*.
2. Nor could we be created *in pura natura*, for then we could have no means of reaching glory.
3. Consequently man was created *in gratia*, nature raised by grace to the obediential power of rising to glory.

      Hence MERIT : *in via.*

            FAITH : not sight.

Actual grace, praevenient and subsequent, as the viaticum for our journey.

The Way is a *Probation :* a journey *in patriam.*

The probation is one of *choice :*

      good   or *evil*

      to God or *away from God.*

Hence God puts us down in *any circumstances :* with all sorts and kinds of graces and helps, of temptations and obstacles.

Hence this *very odd world :* a novitiate for heaven ; (as odd as Manresa was in my time !).

[Here you can interpolate the whole doctrine of *grace*,

of *merit*, etc. It is very good to read at some time the Council of Trent, Session VI, *De Justificatione*. It is quite sound doctrine and very beautiful, more *orthodox even than* Bergson and Co.!]

The test is *our works*. Every man is judged according to his works. Were they done *for God*,

> *for good, in confuso,*
> or not?

The test can be applied to St. Thomas Aquinas or to Aristotle, in the same way; or to a medicine man in Central Africa, or to the Methodist Minister, or the footman.

Grace is given or offered to all, but in odd ways. We cannot judge. Fortunately it is not our business just now. Our business is on the contrary, *not* to judge, and we shall not be judged.

Some have more knowledge of revelation (all have a small minimum), just as some have more brains, or more riches.

It is an enormous advantage to be a Christian, a Catholic; to know, to see. To have explicit faith. To have a Church next door. To have a good Mother. To have a cross Master. To have only one leg. To have the prayer of union. All are graces.

> " Heaven, which man's generations draws
>   Nor deviates into replicas,
>   Must of as deep diversity
>   In judgement as creation be.
>   There is no expeditious road
>   To pack and label men for God.
>   To save them by the barrel-load.
>   Some may, perchance, with strange surprise,
>   Have blundered into Paradise.
>   In vasty dusk of life abroad,

They fondly thought to err from God,
Nor knew the circle that they trod ;
And wandering all the night about,
Found them, at morn, where they set out.
Death dawned ; Heaven lay in prospect wide :—
Lo ! They were standing by His side ! "

Francis Thompson.[1]

I couldn't put it so clearly !

Part the Fourth

THE USE OF EVIL

Hence the ORIGIN OF EVIL is explained.

WHAT GOD WANTS in this world is *what is* BEST.
Not physical beauty, of person or landscape,
Not beauty of poetry or music,
Not happiness of men (that is for afterwards),
Not beauty of intellect,
but *beauty of action, ethical beauty*.

Everyone knows that MORAL BEAUTY is the best thing
in this world. All the rest is FOR THAT. (So Fichte
was right—so far.)

What God wants, therefore, is good action, arduous
action, energy, perseverance, heroism.

This is the meaning of Life.	The victories of Martyrs over suffering,
	The triumphs of Confessors in temptation,
	The daily conquest of self,
	The turning to Him, the aversion from sin ; resistance, patience, war, work, suffering for justice, death for God's sake.

The world, as we know it, was made for this, as a

---

[1] Epilogue to *A Judgement in Heaven*, v : Works, I. p. 190.

theatre for combat : hence its oddness, its unexpectedness. The trial of this life lies in the unforeseen,

the improbable,

the inconceivable (too often !).

The very *arbitrariness* of the universe, as well as the slow grinding of its *unyielding law*, makes our probation.

God did not *make* evil. But He would not even have *permitted* it, says St. Augustine, were He not so great that He can bring good out of it.

The good we know—moral good, the highest thing in creation—could not exist without the possibility of *sin*, and the consequent necessity of *punishment*.

For, if *no one ever fell* in temptation, it would (on the average) not be real temptation ; nor could there be real fighting and real triumph.

Thus I am not a Scotist—so as to hold that God intended the Incarnation as the crown of His creation even had Adam not sinned. I agree with St. Thomas that this has not been revealed, so we cannot affirm or deny.

But I hold that we *do* know that *God intended what has happened*. He MEANT to permit sin. He meant His Son to be made perfect through suffering ; for He meant this for all. He wanted a real trial, real pain, real victory for the Saints.

Theology distinguishes in theory :—

A. INTEGRA NATURA, nature as it ought to be in man ;

Order
1. The Intellect, enlightened to know what is right.
2. The Will, obeying the intellect.
3. The Emotions, with lower passions, imagination, etc., perfectly subject to the will.
4. The Body, perfectly subject, beneath.

B. PURA NATURA, nature as left to itself,—sure to go wrong sometimes, right sometimes. Weak and wobbly; the intellect often ignorant, uncertain, or clouded by the passions. The will obeying the lower emotions, not the enlightened intellect. (Disorder)

C. STATUS ORIGINALIS IUSTITIAE, in which the *integra natura* was established and kept up by *very strong grace*, which enlightened the intellect and strengthened the will.

Adam began with *C.* By sin he lost the strong grace, and fell back to *B.*

But our state is a little better than *B*, for

(1) *actual grace* is assisting us to return as near as we can to *A.*

(2) *habitual grace*, given to a perfect turning to God, or by baptism, gives essentially the same union with God that Adam had, though without restoring integrity.

But the weakness, wobbliness of our intellect and will, as we have it from our parents, is the means of our trial; (i.e. the *vulnera*, or concupiscence, *ἐπιθυμία*, which is natural to *pura natura*).

The strength of our lower nature pulls us down—we want to live for this world instead of for God and the next world.

ταλαίπωρος ἐγὼ ἄνθρωπος. τίς με ῥύσεται ἐκ τοῦ σώματος τοῦ θανάτου τούτου;[1]

Part the Fifth

FAITH AND HOPE

A. FAITH is the door through which we enter the supernatural order. It opens into heaven. It tells us:—

[1] Rom. vii. 24. "Unhappy man that I am, who shall deliver me from the body of this death?"

οὐκ ἔχομεν ὧδε μένουσαν πόλιν, ἀλλὰ τὴν μέλλουσαν
ἐπιζητοῦμεν.[1]

B. Hence HOPE—the practical virtue,

consisting of $\begin{cases} \text{courage,} \\ \text{confidence in God.} \end{cases}$

We know God wants us to show our love *by fighting*
—*not by conquering*. He does not ask us to *get virtues*
(habits), but to do *virtuous acts*.

Every good action gets us

(1) Merit (1) of more habitual grace here,
        (2) of more actual grace to help,
        (3) of glory in heaven.   Besides
(2) satisfaction,
(3) impetration, both of these we can offer for others,
    living or dead.

Therefore each good action gives us

        (1) Closer union with God = more charity,
        (2) More hope to do better still,
above all   (3) The certainty of glorifying God more
        perfectly in eternity.

[I ought to have added earlier :—

(1) our love and praise of God in heaven will not be
free *quoad exercitium* in heaven :
(2) but the *act* in the *lumen gloriae* of the beatific vision
is *timeless, one,* (not successive).

(3) The *choice* to do it or not, IS MADE HERE BELOW.
Therefore it IS A FREE ACT, as having been chosen
freely and deliberately. Thus we freely give to God in
eternity exactly in proportion as we have gained grace
here ; i.e. all our good actions have an eternal value.]

[1] Hebrews xiii. 14. " We have not here a lasting city, but we seek one that
is to come."

[The amount of glory received and given=the amount of sanctifying grace at the moment of death.

Sanctifying grace can be *all* lost by one mortal sin.

Sanctifying grace cannot be partially lost. ALL is restored, by contrition or the Sacrament of Penance,—so it *never decreases*.[1]

We go on piling it up every moment that we live in a state of grace, except when we are committing venial sin. I follow St. Thomas in part, Suarez wholly, and not St. Bonaventure; i.e. the received view. I think no other is tenable to-day.]

FAITH tells us *the true values :* i.e. the answer to " *Quid hoc ad aeternitatem ?* "

HOPE tells us not to mind falls; God forgives them and forgets. But the merit of getting up again and again He never forgets.

[On Faith, which transfigures the world, read Ephesians I, II, carefully, meditating all the new, unclassical vocabulary, and the piling up of hyperbole—imagining yourself to be an Ephesian idolater, fornicator, idler, lover of wealth and this world, just converted, baptized and filled with the Holy Ghost. (This, by the way, is the way to study the Bible, and then apply it to ourselves.)]

Part the Sixth

CHARITY

(God's, not ours, which is not worth considering.)

A. The essential act—God is love—is explained in

1. the *notional* act=the *Spiratio* of the Holy Ghost from the Father and the Son as one Principle, = love proceeding from knowledge.

[1] See St. Francis de Sales. *Amour de Dieu,* IV, 4.

2. The act of love expressed in the Processions :—

(a) " The Father loveth the Son " (John iii. 35)
Omnia tradita sunt mihi a Patre meo. Luke x. 22.

In begetting Him, the Father ceaselessly bestows upon Him His whole Nature—and Father and Son are One. This is the model of love—the gift of all the Lover has and is, and union therefrom. (See St. Francis de Sales, *Amour de Dieu*, III, 12, and St. John of the Cross' Hymns, " The Most Holy Trinity " and " The Communication of the three Persons ".)

(b) And so again the Father and Son give their whole essence to the Holy Ghost, in whom the Unity of the Three Persons is consummated.

Each Person as a Nature is identified with the Others.

Each Person as a Person is distinguished solely by the relation (Fatherhood, Sonship, *Spiratio duplex*), the closest of relations—not a separation but a bond—knowledge—love.

B. God's love of creatures :—

Order of Nature
$$\begin{cases} \text{He gives them His image and likeness in the various degrees,} \\ \text{from matter (being)} \quad 1 \\ \qquad\qquad\quad \text{(life)} \quad 2 \\ \text{up to man (consciousness)} \quad 3 \\ \qquad \text{(likeness of His } \textit{Supreme intelligence)} \\ \qquad\qquad\qquad\qquad = \text{Reason} \\ \qquad \text{(likeness of His } \textit{Aseitas)} = \text{Will} \end{cases} 4$$

Order of Super-nature		
He gives Himself by grace	1
He gives Himself by glory	2
He gives Himself by Hypostatic union	3

227

Now Love consists in

(1) ceaseless gift of the whole self,
(2) identity of likeness in all but Person,
(3) absolute union—thereupon.

So

In Nature God gives	1. Being 2. Likeness 3. Conservation	from Himself. of Himself. in Himself,

" divinae consortes naturae " 2 Peter i. 4.

In Grace He gives	1. created participation of Himself. 2. His essential likeness by re-creation. 3. Union by (Faith, Hope and) Charity.

In Glory He gives	1. His whole essence, so far as we can take it in. 2. His perfect Image, ὅμοιοι αὐτῷ ἐσόμεθα. 3. Inseparable union, *Intra in gaudium Domini tui.*

In the hypo- static union He gives to Jesus	1. The Divine Person of the Son, identical with the Divine Nature. 2. His uncreated Image, χαρακτὴρ τῆς ὑποστάσεως αὐτοῦ. 3. His own inseparable Unity as God.

[In the Holy Trinity we find this threefold character of Love hypostatized,

Father	=	giving,
Son	=	likeness,
Holy Ghost	=	union.]

When we think of these things we ought to be rapt in ecstasy !

228

[But there is yet more :—

The whole order of Creation is a *manifestation of God's love* as a great play, with the universe for its scenery.

But besides Love in *Creation*,
        and Love in the *Incarnation*,
      there is Love in *Redemption*,

and it is *an essential part of the whole plan.* καὶ ἡμεῖς τεθεάμεθα καὶ μαρτυροῦμεν ὅτι ὁ πατὴρ ἀπέσταλκε τον υἱὸν σωτῆρα τοῦ κόσμου.[1]

"When we were yet sinners, Christ died for us."

But *I omit all this*, as too obvious.

You know the Catholic doctrine of the Atonement. You will see how it fits in. But I add certain *consectaria*.]

Difficulty :—

The ordinary person—and you yourself when not in a state of prayer—finds God far off—unimaginable, cold —a bare desert of perfection.

He prefers—with Omar Khayyám—a glass of wine, which is here and now, and warming : and love means something nearer, and lower, and hotter to him.

And God has answered.

He has translated Himself into human language—He has come—*in propria venit.*

> Ἦλθες, ὦ φίλε κοῦρε, τρίτῃ σὺν νυκτὶ καὶ ἠοῖ
> Ἦλθες οἱ δὲ ποθοῦντες ἐν ἤματι γηράσκουσιν![2]

(Don't be shocked—for the Saints use human language. Why shouldn't I use Theocritus ?)

We can join human love with Divine Love.

We can join feeling and passion to the " *amor aestimative summus* " which is necessary to salvation.

---

[1] "And we have seen and do testify, that the Father hath sent His Son to be the Saviour of the world."—1 John iv. 14.

[2] "Thou'rt come, dear heart, after three days and nights, Albeit one can turn a lover grey !"—Theocritus xii.

We can realise the infinite Love through a Human Heart. And, in this way, God answers our objections :—

1. We see God's generosity : making us to share His joy. Bestowing His Nature in grace and glory, and His Personality in the Incarnation.

But *it costs Him nothing*—He gives it out of His infinite riches—He rejoices to give.

Whereas, among men, the widow's mite is what we esteem, and what He asks—the love that gives and strips itself, and suffers in giving, and dies for the Beloved—that is the human ideal. Can He ask that of us, and remain afar in cold serenity ? Can he demand the lives of the Martyrs, the long torments of the Confessors, the hard work and fighting, which is His delight in this world, and for the sake of which He made the universe, and *simply look on*, as the spectators looked on and turned their thumbs, in the Coliseum, as the Christians fought with the beasts ?

And we do not understand a love which is intellectual, even infinite. We are accustomed to a love of feeling, a love which pines and weeps, which glories and triumphs.

2. God's reply is plain.

His Love costs Him everything, ἐκένωσεν ἑαυτόν, He gave up *all* His Glory, all His infinite Happiness, to bestow it on us.

[In the Holy Trinity the Three Persons give without losing, and refund without being impoverished in the perfect union of their *circumincessio*—περιχώρησις. But in the Redemption God leaves all—without leaving it —*Verbum supernum prodiens, NEC Patris linquens dexteram*—that He may win it all for us.

He gives more than the widow's mite, He strips Himself and goes up to the Cross with Poverty as His Bride, as St. Francis and Dante have sung. He becomes the chief of Martyrs, the example of the Saints—*dux ipse*

230

fuisti—He has fought in the arena, and has won the crown not only for Himself but for us. Whatever He asks us to suffer, He has suffered for us and in us. And His Love *feels*, weeps and sorrows, pleads and dies, and rejoices and triumphs.

3. And so, *in the Crucifix*, we see the Nature of God better than anywhere else.

(α) His Purity. This is what sin does to God. Wounds Him, slays Him. This is how God feels sin done against Him. " He cannot feel " ; but in God's infinite Perfection is the exemplar of all that we know as perfect, only in a higher way. So, in His impassibility, is all that is perfect in *wounded love*. In His fulness, Love is not an abstraction, but Love in the concrete ; Love hypostatic, Love including all acts and passions of Love.

(β) His tenderness. If He is to unite us with Him, He will first unite Himself with us. If we are to have His Nature in glory, He will have ours first, that the union may be complete *com*munion. He keeps nothing of Himself back from us ; He takes everything of us up into Himself—*ut homines deos faceret, factus homo*, (St. Thomas).

(γ) His Equity. What He demands of us, *that* He does first, as an example. What He demands of us, *that* He gives, by dwelling in us and doing it in us. What He demands of us, He does, and crowns it as if it were ours, but we in Him ; for in Him alone we are rewarded.

For we are not only His Court, His Kingdom ; but His Mystical Body, Himself. We are not only God's creatures, made for Him to exercise His generosity upon, but His Sons, *in Christo Domino nostro*.

[Sonship : *Filiatio est origo alicuius viventis a principio vivente coniuncto secundum rationem similitudinis.* (I quote from memory.)]

1. By *nature*, we are ' analogically ' *sons of God*. We are *viventes* from a *Principium Vivens* (God). We have a certain distant likeness in all our being ' especially in our soul '.

2. But we are *adopted*. [A man cannot give the *origo* to another man's son,—nor personal likeness of feature or character. But he can give external likeness, in social position, rights, riches, inheritance, by a legal fiction. But God is already our original whence we proceed; and He can give to us His Nature, His likeness. So the adoption is not fictitious but real; " *filii Dei nominamur et sumus* ".]

3. By being made one with the Incarnate Son. We are made His mystical Body, and so we have His Spirit—His grace.

4. So we become Children of God:

(1) By grace, really but not sensibly.
(2) By glory, fully and inseparably and in enjoyment; and by being first united to His Humanity, and so Children of Mary.]

I think this is enough ! But, of course, there is any amount to work out.

Holy Mass—for example—e.g. work out " *Unde et memores . . . tam beatae passionis . . . resurrectionis . . . ascensionis* "—and you understand better than out of certain helpless controversies, [*sic*].

The Sacraments : [for an example of *devotional dogmatic Theology*, take the lessons, by St. Thomas, for the Second Nocturn of *Corpus Christi*, and St. Thomas's Hymns. In another style, Dom Fromage's introduction to the feast in Dom Gueranger's *Liturgical Year* is very good. So is the Fourth Book of the *Imitation*.]

Obviously *Ascetica* have to be worked out in the same way. I always tell people that our spiritual life must be managed, like the War Office, *on business principles*. We must not waste time in deciding on the pattern of a brass button. We must organise battalions, store supplies, arrange transport,—and understand both strategy and tactics.

I will suggest *one* useful division.

Our *Duty* is union with God's *Will*, by our free will, on earth ; in order to win union with God's *Nature* for our nature, in heaven.

God's Will towards us is :—

(1) *Voluntas beneplaciti*—(permission).
(2) *Voluntas signi*—(precepts and counsels).

Hence two general virtues—including all others :—

(1) Conformity (Rodriguez's name) or Indifference (St. F. de Sales' and St. Ignatius's name) or *Abandon* (Mgr. Gay's name).
(2) Obedience (*a*) to commandments of God and of the Church,
            (*b*) to counsels, according to our state,
            (*c*) to inspirations, according to super-natural prudence.

Also (above) our duty is summed up in giving ourselves to God, as He gives Himself to us.

Every one *ought* to be able to *direct* himself in ordinary things. A good director has *to teach us to walk alone*. So study *Ascetica*.

Warning :—But there are bad books (e.g. silly, French piety) and *nasty* books (e.g. De Lugo, *de Eucharistia*).[1]

[1] For the explanation of these words, *vide* infra. Letter xci, p. 266.

One must read with caution.; very critically, very humbly (i.e. always inclined to disagree—for fear of not following the Saints and Doctors).

For *devotional dogmatic*, I fancy I have learnt most from

(1) St. Francis de Sales' *Treatise of the Love of God*. (It ought to be read right through, as it is a system; and it is the greatest work of genius in Theology since St. Thomas, and one of the most learned.)

(2) St. Gertrude. (Blosius is nice.)

Of course, too, *very* much from Abbot Columba Marmion.

I recommend you to try Mgr. Gay, " *Les vertus chrétiennes.*" For Ascetics, I like old Rodriguez—he is very sound. In another style, Grou, " *Manuel des Âmes intérieures.*" St. Teresa (e.g. Chapters 4 and 5 of " *The Foundations*)."

I also recommend the Gospels, for *Ascetica*. I haven't found anything else so good!!

For Dogma too, St. Paul (especially Ephesians, Colossians, Philippians),

St. John (Gospel, Epistles, Apocalypse),

Hebrews,

1 Peter (best of all).

I always preach this sort of dogma (End of Man, Order of Creation, etc.) in giving Retreats. I go on to the virtues, especially *Hope*, (Courage and Confidence) as that is what everybody needs most in this life.[1]

Why have I written you this maddeningly long letter? Because I assume that you get no Theology. The ordinary Jesuit Scholastic is expected to get all he needs out of his meditation book—he is to study and digest it—

[1] The " Theory ", written on the larger, *quarto*, sheets of paper, ends here. What follows is written on the ordinary sized note-paper, like the first portion of the letter.—ED.

and then there are Retreats. But if you don't meditate, you get *nothing* ! for Rosary and Litanies don't give you much.

A Priest not only has ' done ' his Theology (often he has ' done with ' it !) but he has *Mass and Office*, giving him the long meditation of the ecclesiastical year from Advent to Pentecost, and all the examples of the Saints, and lessons from Scripture and the Fathers. All this works as meditation and spiritual reading.

I suppose you are aware that even the greatest contemplatives *must meditate*. Some people meditate during their time of prayer; and (though it seems rather waste of time) the Saints recommend the practice to those who can. But for those who can't or won't, there are other times. We preach (and we prepare our sermons) and this is *most* useful. We have spiritual reading. We can write books, or study. Especially, however, *think things out*, with the help of sound, orthodox theology. But don't go to anything but the best, the soundest; the Doctors, the Councils, the consent of the School.

Only don't read any books you don't *like*; it is always bad for the soul to read uninteresting spirituality.

As to your own experiences, they fit in very well with my scheme.

As I conceive the mystic state, it does not transcend the sphere of faith: for

1. Visions and locutions, if ' corporal ' or ' imaginary ', are simply one part of the ' miraculous ', when they are not delusions.

2. ' Intellectual ' visions and locutions are never new revelations.

3. The perception of God, which in its degrees is the essential matter, can never destroy faith by sight; for

God's existence and nature are not matters of faith (primarily) but of knowledge.

It seems to me that the perception you have is *not* of some new *kind* of union, which others have not got, but precisely a perception of the *union by grace*, which all *justificati* possess. Of course the perception leads to a greater degree of union ; but there is nothing new in kind.

So with " the unreality of the world in comparison with the Reality of God " ; you only *experience* what others know, by reason, must be. God helps you to realize, without trouble, what others have to try—somewhat vainly—to realize intellectually. You have got a short cut to Truth.

This ought to be a great help in Theology as well as devotion.

Theology, as we know it, has been formed by the great Mystics,—especially by St. Augustine and St. Thomas. Plenty of other great theologians—especially St. Gregory and St. Bernard, even down to Suarez—would not have had such insight without mystic super-knowledge.

But there is another side. If I should study all the publications of the Rationalist press, with a view to refuting them, and with a proper amount of prayer and humility, I should probably get nothing but good. But if I read them carelessly, for amusement : or if I read them seriously, with the intention of getting help from them towards a theory of life, I suppose I should soon cease to be a Christian. It is only when one has a safe, clear position of one's own, that one can afford to study the positions of others.

That is why, if you *do* want to read modern anti-Christian

Philosophy, you are bound *first* to know where you stand, by what standard you can judge them.

It is very dangerous to hold the Catholic Faith as a matter of " the religious Consciousness ". It is a matter of Truth or Falsehood. That is why I, for my part, should be horribly afraid of reading non-Christian philosophy, or science, or Biblical criticism, or anything of the kind— if I had not a definite and *reasoned* position to rest upon.

You may feel yourself more safe, and I do not doubt that this is the case, and that God has given you great graces, to which I do not pretend. But I must humbly suggest, whether it would not be best to be on the safest side; to wait for a philosophy until you have rationalized your religion ? (Not, anyhow, to try and explain your religion by an outsider's philosophy; which is to make philosophy the all-in-all, and religion its handmaid.) Catholicism claims that religion is all, and that theology embraces the whole of life.

As to your letter, of course I admit that scholastic manuals of philosophy are not always up to date; that the writers may be pig-headed. Nay, I *assert* that they constantly misunderstand the anti-christian philosophers whom they condemn.

I add to this, that the theologians are frequently pig-headed as well. If St. Augustine and St. Thomas contain heresies, why shouldn't the good manual writers make slips or nod ?

I don't want to answer or to criticise your last letter, because it is not only very clever, but very nearly exactly true. It only wants—I think—a little toning or a little addition or explanation here and there. And this will come of itself, and we shall find ourselves in complete agreement, if you begin from the theological end. It is merely accident—because you were doing philosophy—that you have begun from the other end. It is quite right to begin at that end—but not at that end *only*.

Of course about detailed philosophical points we needn't agree in the least. [As for idealism, I never saw the *real* arguments for realism till long after I became a Catholic—when I was teaching it ! I only saw the *reductio ad absurdum*. The idealists generally don't see it—I am sure you don't—and they never meet it ; and then they complain that the realists avoid *their* point. That is generally what happens in philosophical battles. Neither sees the other's point, neither refutes the other in consequence, and each marches off thinking the other is a fool!]

Some day, I do not doubt, you will have a more active life, and 'find yourself' in helping others. Meanwhile, every step you take to closer union with God will mean more trial, probably a vast and dreary amount of desolation. But you are near fire, and must needs be burnt to be purified. And I presume that nothing is more enjoyable than the pain of such a holocaust, with the prospect of emerging self-less at the end. Anyhow, for you now, the pain of God's absence is always better a thousand-fold than the pleasure of the possession of everything else that is.

God asks such different things of us. Some He wishes to have their content in the world, and work, and wives and children, etc. Others He calls to suffer much ; others to renounce much. Some to renounce all—gradually. It is very hard to know sometimes how far prudence or cowardice is telling us not to renounce this or that yet ; or how far self-love and presumption are urging us to imprudent sacrifices. But, at least, we know the principle —at all costs to do and suffer everything that God asks, as He has given us an example. I can't give you any

238

definite help. I can't tell you "the relation of the world, and beauty and art to mortification and asceticism" *for you, now*; nor can I tell you what to study, what books to read. Obviously I don't know enough about you, and anyhow you would have to find out for yourself. And I never 'direct' anybody !

I have never written so long a letter before.[1] I hope I never shall again.

Ever yours affectionately in Christo,

fr. JOHN CHAPMAN, O.S.B.

LXXXIV.

Erdington Abbey,
Birmingham.

Nov. 27, 1911.

Pax

My dear . . . .

When I detailed my own feelings as to the oddness of the world and its obvious 'contingency', I never meant to suggest that this view is exclusively right, or that it is inconsistent with the sense of God's presence in all His creation. I thought it was understood that I recognized that you had the latter view as a special gift, and that I have not. I merely described my own point of view.

Beyond this, I fear we do not quite agree ; as you simply reaffirm all that I have denied. So I will just restate my denials—and that is all I can do !

1. Christianity affirms that man has a *supernatural destiny*, to be realized in a *future life* ; that he might make happy guesses about this, but that it is not capable of being deduced by reason from anything we know by

<hr>

[1] The original MS. fills sixty-eight pages ; thirty-six of which are occupied with the " Theory " on *quarto* sized paper.—Ed.

nature;—it is not a *necessary* complement of this life, but a '*convenientia*'—although God made man solely for this end.

Hence, (α) this end could only be known by revelation, not by philosophy.

(β) No other explanation of the existence of man can be the right one.

(γ) Revelation must be, therefore, accepted as the only answer to the riddle of life, and as a truth, or truths, which are to be received before, and apart from philosophy.

This is, I imagine, the Christian position. [Please notice that I am not speaking of *religion*.]

2. Starting from revelation once given, Christians work out the relations of revealed truths with one another and with truths otherwise known. This philosophizing is *not* called philosophy, but dogmatic *theology*. In this rational system is given the outline of the answer to the riddle of the universe—including the *end* and the supernatural means, together with the explanation of the rational world, in so far as its origin and purpose are concerned.

3. This leaves for philosophy a perfectly free field—except here and there, where the *magisterium* of the Church happens to condemn this or that speculation as inconsistent with revelation. But the field of philosophy is carefully restricted to the '*how*' of the universe; the '*why*' is answered by theology alone.

So far, I suppose, you will agree, if you follow my meaning.

A. It follows that all non-Christian (and many semi-Christian) philosophies are, necessarily, wrong, whenever they propose *an explanation of the universe* which is a *Rival* to that which Christianity gives.

B. They are also, fairly often, wrong (although they do not profess to explain the universe) because they ignore, even without absolutely contradicting, the data of revelation.

C. Consequently they may be right when they are approaching the different parts of the subject from a wrong point of view; in this case they may be almost as misleading as when they are wrong.

I infer that non-Christian, semi-Christian, and non-Catholic philosophies *are all somewhat dangerous reading*, except to one who has already a *reasoned faith*; i.e. a reasoned outline of what Theology lays down. I think you must admit this.

This is really all I have been driving at, on my side.

Part II

But you, on your side, reiterate that you will not be told " to wait for a philosophy until you have rationalized your religion." You say, rightly, that " a rationalized religion is surely a religion, the supernatural data of which have been interpreted and co-ordinated in the terms of some philosophy".

Exactly; that is a rough definition of *Dogmatic Theology*. Now *you have not got to compose a new dogmatic theology for yourself*. That would be ridiculous, wouldn't it? But, I admit,—nay assert—that you must assimilate dogmatic theology like food, until it becomes a part of your substance, the framework of your thought; consequently you must make it yourself by thinking it out. I tried to give you an example, by showing how I myself present it to myself.

You went on:—" The problem exactly is to find that philosophy which, since it best, i.e. least inadequately, expresses a rationalized experience, is best suited for the reception and exposition of revealed truth." Now this might mean many things. The most natural meaning of the words would be that you and I and John Jones have got certain data from revelation, and have got to rationalize them. Good gracious ! The Church has taken nineteen centuries over it, and has not got very far yet ! It has cast off innumerable wrong explanations, as it fixed upon the right ones. You and I have simply got to take it,— or be Protestants.

As you don't mean this, I think you don't really mean the data of revelation, but the data of consciousness in the light of revelation ; for further on you say :—" Religion is practical : philosophy theoretical " ; and by ' Religion ' you evidently do not mean ' revealed truths ', but the relation of man to God in general. This interpretation of your words is all right, I think.

The result is :—

A. Start with a reasoned account of what God has revealed (i.e. Catholic Theology) as the basis, admitting that herein is the only key to the meaning of life.

B. Then, and then only, go on to explain by Philosophy whatever Theology has left unexplained. Thus philosophy becomes the ' handmaid ' of theology and not her mistress.

C. Among these things to be explained will be the phenomena of the religious consciousness. But before explaining any point by philosophy (especially when using a non-Christian philosopher as guide), take good care to see just how far theology has already (possibly) explained, or partly explained, or suggested an explanation.

D. Consequently : be *sure* of your theology, before you think yourself capable of choosing a philosophy. And remember that the non-Catholics are often dangerous, even when they are right.

If this *A, B, C, D,* in any way meets your case and your acceptance, I think we can be said to have come to terms.

Perhaps you will accept it, and add that you know your theology so perfectly that all danger is absent. But that is precisely the point which you have induced me to doubt about ! Don't be offended. I judged by your own statements. I believe you will find some day that there is much more in Theology than you think. That the saints who wrote it, and thought it, and rejoiced in it, were not such stupid old fogeys after all, and that they did not leave so many things unaccounted for as you may suppose.

I also think it highly probable that you are looking at some questions from the wrong end.

But notice that I have never accused you of holding wrong opinions about anything. Only I think you may be in considerable danger of wrong opinions, or at any rate of wrong points of view, if you read Catholic philosophy with irritation, and non-Christian philosophy with sympathy.

Just as I should wish to put off blowing up an inferior until I was no longer irritated with him, so I should avoid, etc. . . . [sic]

I repeat—I don't see how anyone can profitably, or even quite safely, study non-Christian philosophy, unless he has first made sure that he is *intellectually satisfied* by Catholic theology *as far as it goes*. I am by no means sure you can say this ; or that you quite know how far it goes.

I am glad Poulain goes well.[1] It is somewhat dry and methodical ; that is the chief fault. I don't agree, either, with *every* point. Is he right that there is ' ligature ' in

[1] The work referred to is *The Graces of Interior Prayer*, an English version of *Les Graces d'Oraison*, by the Rev. Aug. Poulain, S.J., which had been published by Messrs. Kegan Paul & Co., a few months earlier.

the prayer of quiet? It is a semi-voluntary ligature, surely. And I imagine that the 'ligature', even in raptures, is a purely natural effect of a supernatural grace. This he thinks improbable.

Evelyn Underhill's is the most readable—and I think the most enlightening—book on Mysticism, I have read. Of course it has some omissions from the Catholic point of view. But I think the authoress wanted to be read by non-Christians and semi-Christians. For example, she avoids saying that the 'transforming union' in the greatest saints is but a part of their exile, and that they all—Buddhists and Mahometans inclusively—look forward to heaven as the consummation.

Ever yours affectionately in Christo,

fr. JOHN CHAPMAN, O.S.B.

LXXXV.

Erdington Abbey,
Birmingham.

Dec. 3, 1911.

Pax

My dear . . . .

If you take everything I say in such a good spirit, there can be nothing more for me to desire. And don't forget that I don't profess to be infallible. Nor do I give you advice. Nevertheless, I am rather glad you are not going to read too much non-Catholic literature at present.

I have just run through a second time (as I have a second edition for review) an edifying little book: *Une Âme Bénédictine, Dom Pie de Hemptinne*, 1880–1907.

Though he was a monk of my own monastery of Maredsous, yet, as he came to the school, became a monk, and died at twenty-six and a half, all since I have been here, I have seen him, and no more.

He seems to have arrived at considerable holiness. His private notes are most edifying. There is no sign of his having any *extraordinary* graces; except a few hints, such as the statement that our Lord had just united his heart to that of His Mother:—by which he seems to have meant some definite experience.

But that is not what I wanted to say: but what Dom Pie's brother says of the Theological lectures at Louvain by Dom Columba Marmion.

" A la fois chargé du cours de dogme, et de la formation spirituelle de jeunes gens [about twenty ' theologians ' from Maredsous, at the Abbey of Mont César, Louvain,] le père Prieur leur rompait abondamment le pain de la vérité. Il savait par expérience que le demi-jour d'une atmosphère grise et terne déprime les âmes et les engourdit; il voulait la lumière, une lumière abondante, radieuse comme celle de l'aurore. Qualité rare: le professeur de dogme avait le don de faire savourer les vérités rèvélées et d'en dégager les conclusions mystiques. Au sortir de ces leçons, on allait, malgré soi, s'agenouiller au pied du Tabernacle ou se recueillir dans le silence de la cellule. La théologie était une préparation à la contemplation; on ne croyait pas vraiment savoir les choses, avant de les avoir digerées dans la prière. ' Nous avons terminé le traité de la Sainte Trinité ', ecrit le frère Pie, ' mais je ne le sais pas encore *par le cœur.*'" (p. 49).

Now Dom Columba is Abbot of Maredsous and he can't teach Theology; and probably nobody any longer teaches it like that. But that is what I hope theology will be to you. Centuries ago, Contenson wrote his *Theologia mentis et cordis*: an admirable model of method.

I *do* wish you could stay at Maredsous, and talk to the Abbot. He is more scholastic even than I am ; but there is no one who has such influence on souls.

[I remember, years ago, asking about his pupils at Louvain. He said, Dom C. had the prayer of quiet ; Dom I. was very holy—the best, it seems, by common opinion—but he did not mention Dom Pie. He made Louvain quite a school for saints.] He is an Irishman, you know ; no one gives such Retreats.

I still go on intending to read Jacks and Joachim, and anything else beginning with a J.

I hope you get on all right with your philosophers. If we could talk, I doubt not we should get on better ! At least *I* should learn much.

> Ever yours affectionately in Christo,
>
> fr. JOHN CHAPMAN, O.S.B.

Père Poulain tries to make out a *corporal* effect of the prayer of quiet. Someone told him it inclined the eyes to shut of themselves.[1] So do certain sermons.

LXXXVI.

The Abbey,

Good Friday, 1913.   *Isle of Caldey,*

[*March* 22.]   *Nr. Tenby.*

Pax

My dear . . . .

I have been meaning for months to write to you from Maredsous. Now I wish you a happy Easter. I came here on Tuesday afternoon, after a dreadful journey, to help Fr. Bede. We shall be here for a year, I presume. The ' monks ' are most candid, simple and hard-working. They seem to be really men of prayer, and—thank God —not in the least ritualistic.

[1] *cf.* St. Teresa, *Way of Perfection*, xxviii, § 6

Instead of the usual Benedictine (scamped) half hour of prayer, they have an hour every evening, besides the time for Communion (if no low Mass) in the morning (three-quarters of an hour). Some take another hour before bed. The ' solitaries ', who never talk except on Great Feasts, have more than four hours prayer a day, besides all the Office and Conventual Mass and Low Mass. I have not spoken to them about spiritual things as yet ; but Fr. Bede says that three out of the four are contemplatives. I hope they will help me. This is a truly contemplative island. I had a nice two hours to-day, in a cleft of a rock, where I could fancy I was the last man. I wish I could join the ' solitaries ', instead of being Superior and having to write books. But I don't wish to have what I wish, of course.

I hope you are having much suffering, and you have my best wishes and prayers for more of it. I wish you could come here, when you want a real spiritual holiday. But I daresay the philosophers are better for your soul.

About the middle of November last I took to studying the *commencements* of mystical prayer—and I have worked out a provisional theory, which has helped me very much. I talked a good deal to some Fathers at Maredsous, and they helped me. One (younger than you are) has a very marked prayer of quiet ; he immerses himself in God when he prays, and can remain recollected at all times. Two others have less, and seem to make a bridge between my way of doing nothing and feeling nothing (except distractions) and the real prayer of quiet.

I should like to write you my theory of this some day, when I have time. I am coming to the conclusion that the thin end of the wedge of mysticism is to be traced in most serious people who have an attraction to prayer. Only they want their attention drawn to it. Few Benedictines can meditate : and, in most cases, it seems to be imperceptible contemplation which prevents them.

You remember that I sent you a huge series of papers of theology—a theodicy—a theory of the world on the Christian hypothesis. *Now*, oddly, I can't say that *any* of that is my real spiritual life.[1] I did not know this till lately. It is my Faith—it leads me to God—it is most useful out of prayer. But in prayer always—and out of prayer also—the mainspring of everything is wholly *irrational*[2] meaningless, inexpressible. " I want God "— and the word " God " has absolutely no meaning. I find so many in this positively absurd and obviously mystical condition ; I suppose one ' contemplates' without knowing it. I wonder whether you have ever been through it. Of course it simplifies people's spiritual life into nothing but the desire of God's will. The whole object of life becomes to want nothing that is not God. *Only there is no reason for it*. The word ' God ' means *nothing*—which is, of course, theologically quite correct, since God is nothing that we can think or conceive. St. John of the Cross describes the state at length in three places. Hardly anyone seems to understand it. I could have been in it— with immense profit—twenty-two years ago, or more. But no one told me it was possible.[3]

So I mean to study up the subject, and eventually write something, after getting experience from others, and showing what I have jotted down to people.

You asked for a picture of St. Teresa [of Lisieux] ; I

[1] An interesting parallel to this—*parva componere magnis*—may be found in the reply which St. Thomas Aquinas is recorded as making to Brother Reginald, when the latter urged him to resume work upon the *Summa Theologica* after the great rapture which came upon him in the convent of St. Nicholas at Naples :— " I cannot, for all that I have written seems to me *now* to be but straw ! " (*v.* Acta Sanctorum I Martii, pp. 712, 713). But the Saint did not mean to imply that his theology was untrue or useless.

[2] " Irrational " in the sense of being *above* reason, not *contrary* to it.

[3] See on this point Note on p. 59, *supra*.

have one on the table, so I enclose it. She is very popular, because she is so pretty ! But you should read *Soeur Elizabeth de la Ste Trinité*, who is much more recent, and much more wonderful. The French edition is published at Dijon (no author). The English edition is called *Laus Gloriae* (Washbourne). If you have not read it, read it.

As an interlude during this letter, I have been instructing a good young monk how never to think about anything when he is praying. He is delighted at the idea. I explained to him how we ought to delight in being distracted, when it is God's will for us; this also pleased him. He is ex-master of novices ! Obviously not a contemplative yet, but in the Night of the Senses, like most monks. Pray for us here.

Ever yours affectionately,

fr. John Chapman, O.S.B.

LXXXVII.

The Abbey,
Isle of Caldey,
April 6, 1913.   *Nr. Tenby.*
Pax

My dear . . . .

I have just written a long letter to a nun, and it struck me that it might save me trouble for subsequent occasions if I had it typed, so I send you a copy.

I quite understand your difficulty in recalling past states of prayer. But you can certainly see the lower states more clearly from a higher point, and understand what is undeveloped. Please criticize what I have said. It is made up from the experiences of a great many people, and a good many have found the things I tell them to be useful. But if you think anything is wrong, say so frankly.

Read it before you go on with the letter.[1]

It is curious that it seems (perhaps only seems) to be possible to make progress in love without any progress in knowledge. St. John of the Cross insists so often that the purer are the rays of knowledge, the more imperceptible they are to the ordinary understanding. Hence to people (like myself) who have not learnt to use the ' pure reason ', there may be a great increase of imperceptible knowledge, producing perceptible effects on the will. For my theory is this :—

According to theologians, Adam in the state of original justice had not the wobbly state of *pura natura* which we have now, but *natura integra*, wherein all the faculties are ordered in one proper hierarchy ; the intellect supreme, the will following the intellect alone, and all the passions, emotions, and even the imagination perfectly subject to the will. This state was preserved in him by *actual grace* of great power. But they add that Adam had an *immediate knowledge of God*, not through creatures, but direct.

Now it is obvious that this knowledge of God gave the real light to his intellect, and its power to reign supreme. The will, having this direct knowledge of the supreme Object of desire, had the strength to govern the imagination and emotions.

Now perfection in this life for us consists in the *return to the state of original justice* by the grace of Christ.

Hence theologians and ascetic writers ought to point out (and they rarely, if ever, do so) that, in order to arrive at Adam's state, we *must* get back the direct knowledge of God which he possessed. It *must* be a part of God's dispensation towards us that we should have the power of regaining this gift, without which we cannot attain to the ordered peace of *integra natura*.

[1] The typed pages enclosed are a copy of the letter " To a Canoness Regular of the Lateran ", dated April 2, 1913, No. XLIII of this volume, p. 118.

Now *mystical intuition* is precisely the direct knowledge of God required. In practice it does lead, gradually, to *integra natura*. Its first manifestation is in an extraordinary strength which we find in our wills, after an idiotic kind of prayer of groping after God. It forces us to give up all wilful imperfection; it gradually enlightens us as to what perfection is.

Again, the saints regularly imply that this mystical knowledge is to be desired, to be prayed for, aimed at by mortification and detachment. They represent it as the normal means of attaining a perfection above the ordinary—of arriving at a real return to original justice.

Again, it is connected with physical phenomena, such as levitation, power of fasting or doing without sleep, facility of communication with God by ' locutions ', etc., prophetical knowledge, etc. These abnormal phenomena are not *essential* to it, but they seem to be an *integral* part of the highest forms, and not simply *accidental*.

But the grace of Christ carries us further than the grace of the first Adam; and the Saints seem to have had very much stronger forms than would be necessary for the first man.

Next : I take it that this power of mystical vision is not *supernatural quoad essentiam*, but only *quoad modum*. It is *preternatural* to fallen man; it was *connatural* to Adam.

The theologians say that Adam knew God by *infused species*, representing God. Hence there are three grades :—

1. To know God from creatures (natural to man in any state).

2. To know Him *directly*, by representative infused species.

3. To know Him *intuitively* by the *lumen gloriae*, " as He is ".

The second way is called "intuitive" and "immediate" in comparison with the first. But the third alone is strictly intuitive and immediate.

By *species* created things are known directly, for the species is the means of knowledge, not the object of knowledge. But as no *species* can represent God's infinity, a knowledge of God by *species*, though infinitely above a knowledge from creatures, is infinitely below the Beatific Vision.

I suppose all mystical knowledge to be by *species*: it is angelical knowledge (or diabolic, if you will). Pure spirits, the souls in purgatory, and nearly all the saints in Heaven, are obliged to do without the bodily senses and the imagination. Hence their *matter* of thought is immaterial, by immaterial species, unlike ours, which is abstracted from matter.

Adam had, then, the power of using his reason *pure*, without the imagination. We have lost this power. When we get it back we see God, Angels, etc., without effort!

But surely we still all have the faculty *in potentia*: it is obscured by the habit of using the imagination, '*convertendo se ad phantasmata*'. But children often have it (I had sometimes)—witness Wordsworth's Ode. And poets have it (Wordsworth, Tennyson, etc.). This does not appear to be supernatural, or even preternatural. But it is a gift peculiar to dreamers, to those who reflect, and abstract themselves.

It would seem that, by habitually taking our attention away from material things and from *species abstractae a materia*, it is possible to become sensitive to *pure species*, pure spirit, *formae per se*. This latent power is obscured by the habit of looking only at matter and abstractions ("*convertendo se ad phantasmata*"), but it is only dormant.

But by this means people do not seem properly to arrive at "a state of prayer". They may get a vague 'intuitive' sense of God's existence, with comparatively little love or desire of serving Him. They also seem to get a new relation to the natural world. They have feelings of the infinite,—perhaps even visions of angels, or demons ! But this is rather mere 'experience' than religion.

There is another way, which is the way of religion,—it is trodden by those who are seeking God, and seek Him *before* they have found Him by this mystical knowledge.

Buddhist, or Brahmin hermits, or Sufis, or Zoroastrians, have their own method ; by solitary life, abstractions, etc. But they aim at love and union, if they are really religious, not at mere knowledge for curiosity. What they want is not knowledge connatural to man, but a *special in*fusion into the, as yet, undeveloped faculty. In other words, they want a *grace*, which is preternatural (at least) *quoad essentiam*, and supernatural *quoad modum*.

Consequently they have two needs : *the one* is to develop the latent faculty by loneliness and abstraction, *the other* is to impetrate and merit the infusion of higher knowledge and love and union, by prayer and purity of heart.

Christians lay most stress on the second point,—prayer, good works, mortification of the passions. But the first, (long hours of prayer, asceticism), are not without their importance.

Hence Christians begin with *meditation*, which makes the soul realise the truths of natural religion and revelation, —teaches it to know that God is infinitely pure, infinite love, and infinitely desirable as our Great Reward,—to despise the world and its pleasures, to look within for the kingdom of God.

Thus 'introversion' begins ; and with it the strange cessation of meditation, accompanied by a dry but fervent longing for God. (See St. John of the Cross :—

Ascent of Mount Carmel, Bk II. Ch. xiii–xiv.

Obscure Night, Bk. I. Ch. ix–xiv, and

Living Flame, Stanza III, §§ 31–69, on the first blind guide, the spiritual director.)

St. John of the Cross teaches that the *cause of the impossibility of meditation* is the *commencement of contemplation*, but an *imperceptible contemplation*. Hence the soul imagines that it is idle, because the occupation of the intellect is unfelt. This explains the whole mystery.

The intellect has become capable of perceiving *pure immaterial species;* it has before it God as pure Spirit, by means of infused species. So long as it looks at God, it cannot use its ordinary power of working by phantasms (abstractions). But *what it sees cannot be translated into terms of phantasms;* therefore it thinks it sees nothing at all. [I will speak of "pure intellect" for the use of the intellect on pure species, and of "abstract intellect" for the intellect that works in the ordinary way.]

So :—

The *intellect* is occupied without knowing it, and cannot work in the ordinary way.

The *will*, however, always follows the intellect, and it *loves* and *desires* what the pure intellect is contemplating.

The *imagination* has no idea what is going on. The will is occupied, and leaves it to itself; so the imagination runs off as it pleases.

Hence an extraordinary state of things :—

1. "*Nihil amatum nisi praecognitum.*" Yet the will seems to be loving without knowing. It does not know why it loves, or even what it loves, because the knowledge, which the intellect has, is 'pure', and cannot be expressed in words or in any terms of the imagination.

2. There is a divided consciousness; for the will feels that it is fixed on God, yet the imagination runs off, and does what it likes.

3. The will wants to remain quite quiet, or in darkness and alone, in order to still the imagination. But the imagination wants to stir up the intellect and will, and goes on saying:—" This is only idleness, you are wasting your time."

Everyone who can ' contemplate ' knows this perfectly absurd, and seemingly idiotic state of things:—

(a) All ordinary knowledge has become useless; philosophy and theology disappear; it is impossible to *think* at all; no cleverness is of avail. " You may as well throw down your brains outside the door, when you go to pray," said Brother X to me. But this is not because the intellect is empty, but because it is full already, and there is no room for more.

(β) But the Will can work, provided it works towards God. It can make acts; humility, desire, love, etc. But, as God is hidden, its one repeated act tends to be:—" I want, I want "; without knowing what or why.

(γ) The imagination does little or no harm by its agitation. If the will tries to keep it in order, then the will itself has to detach itself momentarily and partially from God. So the imagination may run riot, but is best quieted by a short previous recollection, and by shutting the eyes, or being in the dark.

As the intellect gets accustomed to its new work, it can detach itself partially, so as to work the imagination and by the imagination: consequently can have the two taps (of contemplation and meditation) each half on. This is bad in prayer, but may be useful in saying beads or Office, etc.

Eventually it becomes possible to keep a little contemplation during work which is not too absorbing to the intellect.

Progress seems to be by

(a) the intellect getting more and more accustomed to its new work,

(β) by greater infusion of pure light.

The *conviction* of God becomes a *presence* of God, then a very definite (but entirely inexpressible and incommunicable) knowledge of God.

Then the *want* turns into praise : this is the developed " prayer of quiet".

Whether the same theory applies to " Union ", I do not know. I think not. For when " substantial touches " begin, they are said to be " in the essence of the soul ", not in the faculties, and therefore are not " species " in the intellect. But higher and higher species (especially the attributes of God) seem to explain ecstasies. And the ' transformation ' consists in part (at least) in the developed power of using the intellect in both ways simultaneously.

But " Union " seems to be something more (since God becomes subject as well as object).

The " Ligature " is easily explained in the lower stages. The impossibility of thinking ; the fog that comes over the imagination, divorced from the will and intellect ;— the physical results of the fixity of the intellect. Poulain thinks that the ligature cannot be the result of astonishment, because there is no astonishment,—all is calm and sleepy. But I hold that there *is* an unfelt astonishment and absorption of intellect and will.

This is still more true of the higher phases, and it seems to me that, in rapture and ecstasy, the bodily effects are one result of the astonishment of the intellect, which the imagination does not realise.

This seems to be confirmed by the opinions of so many saints, (e.g. St. Philip) that ecstasies are undesirable; and, of St. John of the Cross, that the bodily effects are due to the body's want of practice; it has not been spiritualized yet, to become an organ for the pure intellect. In the highest state, much higher communications produce no rapture, yet even in that state raptures do not cease, but merely become infrequent; since God can always give indefinitely higher species, to which the soul is as yet unaccustomed.

Ecstasies are not signs of great spirituality. A very slight communication produces one in a child. A feeble-minded person, like my dear St. Joseph of Cupertino, goes off more easily. I can tell you of a person raised eighteen inches from the ground in the transition from multiplied acts to a continual act of ' want of God '. This was some time ago; he does not know it; and he has not yet the developed prayer of quiet—only the arid prayer. So I think bodily effects may appear at any time. I can't explain them. But doubtless St. John of the Cross is right, in connection with the spiritualizing of the body to become a suitable organ. It is perhaps *more* than a return to Adamic conditions.

This is more than enough, for the moment. A good deal of this theory is quite doubtful to me; some of it is still vague. But some seems pretty certain, on the ground that it explains the facts.

I cannot accept the theory of the *Cloud of Unknowing*, that we cannot apprehend God with our intellect, but can apprehend Him with our will. For our Will doesn't apprehend.

257

I have nothing to criticize in your letter. I entirely believe all you say.

Ever yours affectionately,

fr. JOHN CHAPMAN, O.S.B.

LXXXVIII.

St. Bride's Abbey,

Sept. 26, 1913.   *Milford Haven.*

Pax

My dear . . . .

I have been forgetting to send you the enclosed off-print from *Pax*.[1] It is nearly the same as what I sent, type-written, before.

The Nuns here are *very* good. All are contemplatives, of course. How extraordinarily rare it is to find an enclosed Nun who can meditate ! And can one find (except by accident) a Little Sister of the poor who can ' contemplate ' ?

I take it that there are two necessary conditions :—

(1) Physical : separation from the world, in order to get that peace in which alone (for most people) the mystical sense is perceptible at all.

(2) Moral : to give the whole self to God, without reserve.

Many people do the second, as far as they can,—with less success, but perhaps more merit, than if they were mystics ; but the first condition is wanting.

There are exceptions : for to some (as to you, or to X.Y.Z.) the veil is thin. That is a metaphor : I wish I knew what the reality is which it represents !

[1] The leaflet, " *Contemplative Prayer*, A few simple Rules ". See Appendix I of this volume.

Is the " thinness of the veil " merely that there is an ' overflow' upon the imagination and emotions, so that the curiously (of itself) imperceptible action of the pure intellect is known and recognized ? Or is the use of the intellect itself upon God more complete ? I am inclined to believe in a third explanation : that the ' pure' use of the intellect (=mysticism) becomes perceptible and distinct to the consciousness, either when the senses and imagination are stilled, or (better) when they are purified and spiritualized. I believe there is real truth in Görres's rather grotesque doctrine of the spiritualizing of all the powers of the Saints by the mystical infusions. Some people are grosser and more material to begin with,— by birth and circumstances. Others are naturally good subjects. Anyone *may* become so, by quiet, mortification (interior, chiefly), detachment, etc.

But it is very difficult and vague. My *Pax* paper is merely what I have got out of many people, *plus* St. John of the Cross. Lots of Nuns, in various places, are enthusiastic about it ; so it *is* practical for an enormous number of souls. I only hope it is theoretically right also.

Pray for me.

Ever yours affectionately,

fr. JOHN CHAPMAN, O.S.B.

LXXXIX.

The Abbey,
Isle of Caldey,
Oct. 16, 1913.
Nr. Tenby.

Pax

My dear . . . .

It is difficult to find time for a long letter. I am glad you approve of my paper. I think it must be fairly right, because it seems exactly to suit such a very large number of people. Nearly all enclosed Nuns want this particular treatment.

What I meant about Görres is his long series of chapters on the miraculous effects upon the body, caused by the higher degrees of mysticism. They are rather grotesque as they stand. But there is truth in them.

I am glad you prefer my " third " explanation. [But there must be something in the idea of ' overflow upon the imagination and emotions ', unless I quite misunderstand St. Teresa, e.g. Fourth *Mansion*, Chapter i. Perhaps, however, this may also be by a spiritualizing of the lower part of the soul.]

When you speak of " the basic part in our personality ", the fund or apex of the soul; I don't know what you mean. Blosius talks about this ' *fundus* '; St. Francis de Sales about the ' apex '. But what *is* it, psychologically considered ? These seem to be metaphors.

Surely it is not the *substance* (i.e. personality) itself; but a faculty, the highest. Is it not simply the intellect working in the ' angelic ' way, and not by ' *convertendo se ad phantasmata* ' ?

St. John of the Cross speaks of God's " touches " as being in the substance of the soul, but does he not mean something different ? Or does Blosius (*Spiritual Instruction*) really mean the ' substance ' of the soul, when he says " blessed is he who finds this *fundus* in himself ". The thing always puzzles me very much.

I don't see how a ' substance ' can receive ' impressions ', except by an impressionable ' faculty '; nor receive intellectual impressions, but by an intellectual faculty.

As to preparation; I think for *ordinary contemplative prayer* preparation is possible, necessary, and really useful, if not infallible. But I imagine that the ' inrush ' of mystical experience is generally sudden, and without any visible *immediate* preparation. But, even for this, solitude and abandonment to God are a good remote preparation.

Most people who use contemplative prayer are unconscious of anything extraordinary, except (1) the curious inability to meditate, (2) the ease of remaining with God, (3) and sometimes an 'experience' that God is there. But there is nothing that surprises or troubles the soul, it all seems quite commonplace and ordinary.

From this I distinguish explicitly mystical states, which are uncommon, while the other is very common.

But the ordinary contemplative prayer seems to get *less* ordinary as it develops. It gradually makes all acts cease, and makes the soul in prayer receptive and passive, and absorbs the whole life, outside prayer. But even then nothing *happens*,—there is nothing to take hold of and say :—" This is a mystical experience ; this is a revelation of divine things." It is all so calm in progress that there is no landmark. At least this is how I seem to observe it in some souls.

I don't think I have answered some criticisms you made in April.

1. You said that *Praise* would be only complementary to the *Want of God* in prayer. I think this is true ; but souls differ, and it is quite right for a person like Brother X to praise God all the time, if he wants to. He says that, when he simply 'wanted' God, he made no progress. Brother Y, on the contrary, 'wants' God, and draws Him in all the time ; and then says he thinks he *must* die soon, because he wants Him so much. Both are very good. *Omnis spiritus laudet Dominum.*

2. You objected to my recipe of 'making an act of inattention' for the beginning of prayer. It is meant for those who have no perception of God's Presence, or very little. For those who have enough of it, you are

naturally right in saying that they must consciously attend to it. [But, after all, it is the same thing; since Ribot declares that attention to one thing is nothing else (physiologically and psychologically) than a detachment of the nerves and muscles from other things: e.g. to *listen* is to cease to look, feel wilfully, etc.; to *look* is to cease to listen. Try feeling a pulse, and you will notice that you feel and count, without *looking* or *listening*, though you still *see* and *hear*. Ribot says this is by *detaching*, the senses of sight and hearing, not by any *positive* concentration on feeling. I expect it is true.]

3. I said 'levitation' and other physical phenomena are an 'integral' part of Mysticism as a whole; meaning that they are *not* 'essential', yet are contained within it as parts of a whole. I meant that mystical impressions not only inform the soul with new knowledge and love, but have some effect upon the body, and that the *full* effect of the completest and highest forms will have preternatural effects upon the body. I think you agree that this is probable.

4. It seems to me a possible explanation that the mystic perceives God by *direct* knowledge (like the Angels, ' by infused species'; let us use the scholastic terms—they do not involve a theory, I think—they are quite plain sailing), hence he sees God *in his soul;* since God dwells there by grace.

Then (1) *The prayer of quiet*—in various degrees—is the mere perception of God. (2) *The prayer of union* is the perception of God, not merely dwelling in the soul, but one with it by grace. *It is not a new kind of union*, but a PERCEPTION *of the ordinary union which exists by grace*, and of course a new degree of that union. That is why it is ordinarily accompanied by a perception of God's presence in everything else: (i.e. it is a clearer knowledge of God—and a perception of *how* He is in things and in one's own soul). Hence follows a new point of view. The union being perceived, everything is viewed from God's point of view, and the whole of the soul's outlook is transformed, transfigured, almost reversed. (3) Then ecstasy occurs when God gives a higher degree still of knowledge, and *for this purpose* (in order that the soul may see Him undistractedly and therefore more clearly) closes up the senses and imagination. (4) As these become purified, the same, and even higher communications become possible, although the senses, imagination, emotions, remain free. Eventually, talking, working, sleeping are possible, while God is seen more clearly than in earlier ecstasies. (5) But, even in the highest stages, it seems that God can give communications so much higher than those to which the man is accustomed, that the silence of the lower part of the soul by ecstasy is needed. For ecstasies are rare, indeed, after ' the mystical marriage ', but they do not cease.

I said :—" God closes up the senses ". Whether the force of the communication does this (I think so), or whether it is a separate preternatural act of God to make the communication possible, I do not know.

It seems to me important to distinguish *mystical union* from *essential sanctity*. The latter is simply the amount of sanctifying grace in the soul, and this is simply the sum of all the good actions of the past life, *plus* the grace received in the Sacraments—(i.e. = merits, = right to glory, —the glory to be given by us to God through all eternity), —and this essential sanctity may be added to, or lost, but can never be diminished.

Whereas mystical union is an *actual grace*, hence a means of grace. It is not sanctity, but a new means of being sanctified, and consequently it does give (or rather

263

get) a new degree of that essential union with God by sanctifying grace, which *is* essential sanctity, just in so far as it is meritorious. We shall be " judged according to our works "—that is the essential point. And mystical union is (in so far as it is a vital act of response on the soul's part) a meritorious act, as well as an actual grace, and hence draws in more grace.

In fact, during prayer, there must be an immense increase of sanctifying grace,—drawn in all the time,—but that is the *effect* of the prayer, strictly speaking, not the prayer itself.

I say all this, because there are holy writers who talk about mystical union with God, as if it were something higher than sanctifying grace—which is surely wrong. For habitual grace is real, though unperceived union with God, sonship, charity.

The *Cloud of Unknowing*, published by Watkins, must be the edition by Evelyn Underhill, I suppose. I bought several copies of it. No book that I know is so like St. John of the Cross. Yet that Saint cannot have read it. It is very practical and simple for beginners.

Forgive haste and bad writing. Pray for me.

Ever yours affectionately,

fr. JOHN CHAPMAN, O.S.B.

XC.

The Abbey,
Isle of Caldey,
Nr. Tenby.

[Postmark]
[*March* 23, 1914.]

Pax

My dear . . . .

I have meant to write to you ever since Christmas. Only, as I could not write at once, there was no reason for writing on any particular day.

You wrote me an account of a very peculiar, and apparently very painful experience of the emptiness of everything. I have nothing to say about it, except that it was obviously good, as it made you pray with more intensity. But I do not recognise it as having been described by anyone.

It seems to be a perception of what the world is *apart* from God. Only it must be *incorrect*, as the world, however distinct from God, cannot be without Him. Still it must be a corrective, if it is true (as it is said to be) that the perception of God in all things tends to Pantheism. (I do not know that it *is* true.)

Have you read Rabindranath Tagore's *Gitanjali?* I think it most beautiful. I daresay he is not a *very* deep mystic, but his religion is real, as far as it goes, and the expression is sometimes wonderfully vivid.

I have found a nice book by an early Carmelite, Joseph of Jesus Mary. It is the best synthesis I have seen. It is an Italian translation from the Spanish. I found it among the books here. I wonder if I shall manage to get a copy. He has two parts : I. *Salita dell' anima a Dio*,—all about Contemplative prayer. II. *Entrata nel Paradiso*, about the mystical states.[1]

He rightly sees that all Contemplative prayer is *after* the " Night of the Senses ", and is the ordinary prayer of pious people. He also says " our venerable Father, John of the Cross ", is the great teacher of ordinary prayer,

[1] Don Francesco de Quiroga, in religion Fra Joseph de Jesus-Maria (1562-1629), was the first official " Historian-General " of the Spanish Congregation of Reformed Carmelites, and won a great reputation by his writings both historical and mystical, especially by his Defence of the teaching of St. Teresa and St. John of the Cross. The volume here mentioned is an Italian translation of his most important spiritual work, in two parts, I. *Subida del Alma a Dios que aspira a la divina union*, II. *Entrada del alma a Parayso espiritual*. After the author's death his mystical writings were attacked by the Capuchin, Felix Alamin, but after examination by the Inquisition both in Spain and at Rome, these were approved, while Alamin's own work attacking them was condemned.

as St. Teresa is of the higher ways. I was delighted with this, as it is my view; whereas most people think St. John of the Cross is too lofty for anyone to read. He seems to me to be two-thirds for beginners and one-third for saints. Nothing much for people between the two.

I hope you are getting on well with Theology, and like it. Pray for me.

Ever yours affectionately in Christo,

fr. JOHN CHAPMAN, O.S.B.

XCI.

Downside Abbey,
Jan. 23, 1915. *Near Bath.*

My dear . . . .

If I do not answer a letter at once, it gets put off indefinitely. I was really delighted to hear from you, though I do not seem to show it. I am waiting here till Thursday, to try and finish an article which I foolishly (after refusing) consented to do on ' Catholic Mysticism ' for Hastings' *Dictionary of Ethics.*

The reason I disliked de Lugo, *De Eucharistia,* many years ago, was because he seems :—

(1) to take a materialised view of the Blessed Sacrament, trying to show (almost) that transubstantiation is possible or conceivable. Whereas I prefer St. Thomas's view that, while no one can show that it is impossible, no one can show that it is possible. He has ideas about what matter is, and matter in two places at once, which I not only disagree with, but also thought entirely out of place in a discussion about the ' immaterial ' presence

of Christ, after the manner of substance under the accidents. What annoys me is, when perfectly simple Christian truths are turned into scholastic absurdities and ingenuities. A good theologian, however ingenious and subtle, ought always to keep hold of the simple truth which his elaborations are merely guarding, not explaining.

(2) I don't like his doctrine of the Eucharistic Sacrifice. But I was not certain that Franzelin, who professes to follow him, has not exaggerated him. I doubted, I remember, whether De Lugo is so near heresy as (to my mind) Franzelin is. (N.B. I like Franzelin immensely elsewhere.)

I think you are right that *Gitanjali* is more charming than deep. I should like to find the letters of M. de Bernieres.

Do read the first and (especially) the eighth homily of St. Macarius of Egypt. You will find him in the *Patrologia Graeca*. Palladius says that ἀδιαλείπως ἐξίστασθαι ἐλέγετο.[1] The eighth homily is a personal document worthy of St. Teresa. The apophthegmata and second letter (and all the homilies) have beautiful things.

Ever yours affectionately,

fr. JOHN CHAPMAN, O.S.B.

XCII.

Downside Abbey,
Near Bath.

Oct. 1, 1920.

Dear Father . . . .

Have you read *The Philosophy of Mysticism*, by Edward Ingram Watkin? The book is good, on the

[1] " He is said to have lived in unbroken contemplation."

whole, I think. But I find it dull reading. It is very long-winded.

I *do* wish there was a certain, recognised Catholic teaching on the subject. All recent books disagree with each other, and I disagree with all of them ! It is extremely tiresome, and even practically worrying, as one is obliged to give practical advice sometimes. Also, I get more and more to the view that St. Teresa and St. John of the Cross are *absolute opposites*. Are they therefore irreconcilable ? Of course I always follow the latter, and discard St. Teresa as dangerous. I want to find a Hegelian synthesis of opposites.

When Algar Thorold was staying here, the other day, he lent me two volumes of Clement Webb's on the Personality of God. They are *extra-ordinarily good for a non*-Catholic philosopher. I wish I could go and see him and talk, before I return to Rome. I shall leave Downside in a fortnight or so, on my way to Rome.

I am surprised to find how many good monks, who use a kind of prayer of aspirations, are frightfully prejudiced against " Mysticism ", and dislike the idea of darkness, ignorance, fog, etc. ; and either call St. John of the Cross exaggerated, or won't read him. Personally I think they are quite wrong, and I agree with St. John of the Cross's denunciations of ignorant directors. But there must be *something* right in the attitude of such excellent people. And I suppose St. Teresa would have said the same thing, wouldn't she ? One can't imagine her approving of anything she couldn't see or feel very vividly. She would have made fun of St. John of the Cross's books, as she did of his letter ! It is all very puzzling.

Ever yours in Domino,

H. JOHN CHAPMAN, O.S.B.

Downside Abbey,
Near Bath.

Oct. 6, 1920.

Dear Father . . . .

Bad people love bad Mysticism, because they think it is occultism or magic. Good people dislike it for almost the same reason ! They say :—" The Incarnation shows that we must go to God through material things (Sacraments), and the senses and the imagination. We *must* use our reason in prayer (even if we can't !), that is what God gave it us for." It is not easy to give them a plain answer ; for they are often very good and very clever.

As for Watkin. I think he has explained St. John of the Cross in a modern way very well ; and has made a very good attempt at *uniting* the ' mystical way ' with ordinary Christian life. But it is a first attempt, he has no precursors, really ; and hence not always quite convincing. A great deal seems to me *probable*, not self-evident.

But the problem of *reconciling* (not merely uniting) Mysticism with Christianity is more difficult. The Abbot[1] says St. John of the Cross is like a sponge full of Christianity. You can squeeze it all out, and the full mystical theory remains.

Consequently, for fifteen years or so, I hated St. John of the Cross, and called him a Buddhist. I loved St. Teresa, and read her over and over again. She is first a Christian ; only secondarily a mystic !

Then I found I had wasted fifteen years, so far as prayer was concerned ! Naturally I had a gradual revulsion against St. Teresa !

[1] (?) Abbot Marmion of Maredsous.

269

Of course St. John of the Cross read and approved St. Teresa's works. He recommends them in *Spiritual Canticle XIII*. But there is a great contrast.

St. Teresa, being a mystic, does undoubtedly sometimes have God as the terminus of her prayer. But her emphasis is always either on the external concomitants, or on something sensible (locutions, or 'imaginary' visions, or impressions, or joy), and not on the Divine Union.

St. John of the Cross, on the contrary, cares only for the Divine Union, and rejects everything else. Hence he reduces the really "adequate" means to Union to the 'general' sense of God (in enormously varying degrees, but always indefinable and supra-rational), and Divine touches (again of various degrees, and including such particulars as substantial touches, impressions of the Divine Attributes, etc.). Anything which is *definite* is less than God, and not an adequate means to Union. Though he admits and asserts that visions, etc., 'successive' locutions, etc., are intended by God for our good, when they come from Him, and they will do much good to the soul, provided it is detached from them.

Further, he teaches (being a Christian) that a mystic, outside his prayer, will have to use his senses, imagination, etc., and will rightly occupy them with thoughts of our Lord's Life and Passion.

Contrast St. Teresa. When she speaks of degrees of pure prayer (in her *Life*, in Relation 8 ; in the *Spiritual Castle*), viz. recollection, quiet, union, ecstasy, the degrees are constituted by the effect on the body and lower soul, —they differ solely according to the measure of union of the different powers ; in other words, according to the absence of distraction and the amount of joy ! Of course she explains that these effects are caused by a correspondingly varying amount of contemplation ; but St. John of the Cross would have said the effect depended largely on the weakness of the body, etc., and would have insisted that, the *less perceptible the communications* (the less effect they had on the natural part of the soul), the *purer* and *more powerful* they were. This seems reasonable. It does not contradict St. Teresa, only it changes her " degrees " into a mere description of psychological states, consequent on mystical communications,—but not necessarily comparable with each other as grades of perfection.

But the great contrast (I repeat) is with regard to visions. St. Teresa (in the *Life*) attributes her own progress largely to visions of our Lord with His Cross, or of Hell, or appearances (" intellectual ") when our Lord stayed with her for some time, or spoke. Later, when she reached the seventh MANSION, she still speaks of the immense value of the much higher visions she then had of our Lord's Humanity. She even says that ' imaginary ' visions are *the best*, because they are more proportioned to our nature.

That is to say, she *very frequently* (though not by any means always) regards God's graces as coming through the imagination and emotion UPWARDS to the higher part of the soul; whereas St. John of the Cross contrariwise insists that mystical graces are given to a suprarational use of the intellect, and to a pure and ultra-emotional sphere of the will, whence they come DOWN to the rest of the soul, and purge it. It is a contradiction, therefore, in tendency.

St. Teresa's books contain the most perfect descriptions ever written, and no doubt needed a special grace to pen. St. John of the Cross describes more shortly *all the same phenomena* and more; and pooh-poohs most of them.

Of St. Teresa's own *Life*, I think he would have said that the phenomena were from God, and that she got all the good from them, because she was detached from them; and God took care that she should be thus detached from them by the persecutions she suffered from the good people who declared that they were from the devil. Later on, when she was on the mystical ladder, there was less danger of being attached.

I have no right to make personal remarks. But I may say (with all humility, as I have no right to judge) that I remember, many years ago, you told me " they tell me it is the prayer of quiet"; and I said (naturally) that it was more, presumably, the " prayer of union". Afterwards it seemed to me obvious that the only useful parallel with St. Teresa was the grace she describes in the Supplement she added to her *Life*, of seeing God *in* things. St. John of the Cross would have considered this as due to a " substantial touch", and a very high grace. Now that I have quite given up St. Teresa as a guide to *order*, and to classification of value, I should simply tell you that they were Divine touches. I hope you don't mind my recurring to this point.

It seems to me *quite tenable* that St. John of the Cross is too severe about visions, revelations, locutions, etc. The Church seems to make much of them.

But one's experience is so much against them. Even in this Protestant country, where there are so few nuns, there are so many futile revelations, inside and outside convents. I confess to being prejudiced against them. St. John of the Cross's teaching saves so much trouble :—
" Don't waste time in discovering whether they are from God, or from yourself, or from the devil,—simply detach yourself from them; want God alone, and not His gifts."

Does all this make clear my feeling of the rooted anti-thesis between the two Saints?

A. St. Teresa, with emotional meditation on our Lord's life and Passion, developing into revelations of the same character, and personal intercourse with Him by continually recurring visions. When she was without these for years, she did not know how to pray, and dreaded prayer, and even gave it up. Her advice about meditation in the WAY OF PERFECTION shews that of *dry contemplation* she had no notion. She would certainly have agreed with the usual notion that it is waste of time. She *did* love God, she *did* desire union with God—for she was a real Contemplative, and (especially) no one can sincerely love and serve our Lord without finding that He is the Way to the Father. But this side is not prominent in her books. It is the sensational side—feeling of joy and pain, definite facts, events, knowledge, communication, prodigies— which interests her, and not the incommunicable, indescribable ' general ' knowledge and love.

B. St. John of the Cross, determined to have nothing to do with this world, nor with anything definite or communicable, but only the one thing needful.

Hence St. Teresa pleases all the people (like myself, once upon a time) who prefer Christianity to Buddhism,— who want to use their faculties, and meditate in a warm room, by the fire, instead of going up the mountain into the snow.

I daresay you will say I am simply exaggerating, and that I am all wrong. No doubt I am. But I don't yet see *where* I am wrong.

" The charms of the ' prayer of quiet ', and the human delights of meditations and visions seem more proportioned to our nature." I admit it all. But I distrust it.

And again, " Divine touches are so rare, whereas visions are so ordinary—therefore God must prefer the latter ". But I don't believe it.

It is remarkable how a little course of " arid " prayer transforms people : the results seem so solid. *Dépouille-ment, abandon,*—there is no English for these. I suppose they come just as surely, or more so, by enjoyable prayer —but surely always by *pure* prayer, not so well by all these visions and impressions.

To go back again. Take the titles of chapters of *The Ascent of Mount Carmel*, Book II, e.g. Chapter 8 :—" No creature, no knowledge, comprehensible by the under-standing, can subserve as proximate means of union with God." How very unlike St. Teresa. Yet it seems so very obvious,—and it is the teaching of mystics from the second century, to Dionysius. and onwards.

I am kept from depreciating revelations by my great admiration for St. Gertrude. I admire her more than St. Teresa. (Of course I still *love* St. Teresa personally, as everybody must, and I hate to disagree with her.)

Forgive me for writing all this long rigmarole.

The *mystical faculty* is ATROPHIED by original sin.

1. To know God from creatures in Natural religion is by *natural faculties*, which are impaired (nothing more) by original sin, and reduced to the imperfect state of *pura natura*.

2. To know God as He is by the Beatific Vision, is possible only by a *potentia obedientialis*, not by a natural *potentia*.

3. To know God as Adam knew Him, and as the Angels can (*per sua naturalia*), involves a *potentia* (the mystical faculty) which is not a natural *potentia*, nor a supernatural one (*potentia obedientialis*) as the *lumen gloriae* is, since this provides a communication of God Himself,—but a *preternatural* one ; for it belongs not to *pura natura*, but to *integra natura*, and is atrophied by the disorder caused in our soul by original sin. It is SMOTHERED by the imagina-tion, emotions, composing and dividing intellect ;—we

have to dig away the phantasmata under which it is buried. Solitude and silence make it faintly felt; special grace and diligent exercise of pure prayer develop it. In some persons it is less suffocated than in others. By this Way (especially when it is once dug out and uncovered—but, by almost a miracle, even without this) God can reveal Himself darkly to any extent He pleases, and so transform the will, and purify the rest of the soul. And I feel sure that in souls which have never discovered this trap-door, covered as it is with old luggage, God frequently comes in by it, without their knowing how.[1]

This theory is my present one, for the moment, and is what I have got out of the older scholastics and St. John of the Cross.

It is all *gratia Christi*. Our Lord is always the *End*, but He is also the Way, except in time of prayer; i.e. we must always think of Him except when we *can't*. *Nemo tenetur ad impossibile*. And you can be inside the house and also on the road at the same moment.

Yours affectionately,

H. John Chapman, O.S.B.

P.S. I hope I have made it clear that I distinguish :—

1. Natural faculties   —(Natural religion)
2. Preternatural faculty —(supernatural religion)
3. Supernatural faculty —(in glory).

But that the *communications* which come through the preternatural faculty, are not preternatural but *supernatural*, whenever they are *God Himself*.

But there is nothing to prevent *preternatural* com-

---

[1] The Abbot's ' P.S.' to this letter shows that he was dissatisfied with the above as he had written it, and so added the postscript to guard against possible misunderstanding. In Appendix II, ' What *is* Mysticism ', his considered view of the question is set out fully.

munications (e.g. from angels, or preternatural knowledge of nature) coming in at the same door that God uses; it is not necessary to say of this preternatural trap-door "*haec porta clausa erit, princeps solus intrabit per eam*". But St. John of the Cross wishes us to take no notice of any other comers. But it is possible that a part (at least) of "nature mysticism", and children's dreams of eternity, and Wordsworth's or Tennyson's sensations of the infinite, may be the preternatural use of the mystical faculty. But I agree with St. John of the Cross that curiosity about these things should be mortified as much as (but not more than) curiosity about natural things.

H. J. C.

XCIV.

Palazzo S. Calisto,
Trastevere,
Jan. 29, 1921.   *Roma,* 14.

My dear Father . . . .

I was greatly disappointed to be prevented from coming to see you before I left England. I sent you a long letter, in which I exposed my difficulties about the apparent contradiction between St. John of the Cross and St. Teresa. I wonder what you thought of it. It had bothered me a long while.

But, oddly, this evening, I felt impelled by a certain curiosity to search for, and then read a MS. note or essay on the development of mystical states, which I wrote in the winter of 1912-13. Three-quarters of it were what I expected: but the end of it was quite new to me—I had so completely forgotten my own opinion, as I so often do.

It seemed to make a fairly complete theory, embracing St. Teresa's successive MANSIONS, in complete harmony with St. John of the Cross; so that, for the last half-hour, I have been regretting the criticism of St. Teresa's method, which I wrote in Hastings' *Dictionary*. I am inclined to think that I was wrong (this often happens), and that St. Teresa was right; only that I misunderstood, from looking at the matter from the wrong angle. But it is odd that I should have completely forgotten my own theory !

I am far from saying that this old MS. of mine has removed all my difficulties, and has made everything clear. The subject is very difficult. But I write directly I have seen that I was wrong, to inform you that I retract.

I must think the whole matter out again. The great difficulty about the subject is that all the theologians and mystical-theologians contradict each other, whereas the mystics themselves are often very vague ! And then the enormous differences of temperament in different witnesses have to be taken into consideration.

Then there is a further question, which no one seems able to decide. Is the ' mystic way ' the only road to perfection ? And if so (*dato sed non concesso*) is there only one way of mysticism ? Is it possible to arrive at the same point the other way round ? viz. by mortification and meditation ? Or is there a veiled mystic way, by which certain holy people reach the ' transforming union ' without ever knowing that they are mystics ? I don't see how any attempted philosophy of the subject can avoid answering these questions. I can't : so I can't make a philosophy of the whole subject.

One wants an enormous amount of data. Mere written accounts, however precise and interesting, do not suffice. One wants to interrogate, or even to *experiment* on suitable subjects. It is not a mere question of observation, like (say) Natural History, but of investigation, like Chemistry !

For example,—there are considerable resemblances between all the great mystics, Catholic, Mahometan,

Buddhist,—even Protestant (though much less, of course). But they wrote BECAUSE they had this very emphatic type of Mysticism. Is one to infer that every Saint, who gave no account of his experiences, had necessarily parallel states? Or rather, is it not probable that many gave no account of their states, because they were either less extraordinary, or scarcely extraordinary at all?

I am thinking this out as I write, because I found a page in my old notes, which suggested a possible theory by which a Saint could use discursive meditation and mortification (what is called *agere contra*, in your Society) and active work for perfection (by combating his lower nature, mortifying it, raising up good passions against bad passions, etc., all according to the best ascetical authorities), instead of simply standing aside and letting God do it. In the meanwhile, God would be giving him " mystical " graces in so " impure " a form (i.e. disguised in sugar, or like cod-liver oil in Orange wine) that he would never know he had them. However, this is not really explaining my old theory, which seems to me quite a logical one, though very improbable. But improbable things are so often quite true.

However, this is letting my pen run away with me. I only send this as a recantation.

Ever yours in Domino,

H. JOHN CHAPMAN, O.S.B.

XCV.

Downside Abbey,
Near Bath.

Feb. 28, 1923.

My dear Father . . . .

Many thanks for your interesting review. I quite agree with what you say in general; and I quite admit that the Abbot does look rather as if he took back what he had said at the beginning.[1]

Also what you insist on at the end, is important ; that the thing is *given*, not worked for. It is as a surgeon once said to me about falling in love :—" You don't *do* it ; it simply happens to you." I have not tried either, but I believe it of both. I think I remember that Abbot Butler made it clear that the human activity which *does* undoubtedly prepare for what he calls ' active ' contemplation, is purely negative ; so he would say, *a fortiori*, that higher states could not be the result of activity on man's part.

As to the Dark Night of the Senses, I think Poulain explained it very well in his little pamphlet on the subject, and again in his book. But he puts it in the middle of the book, instead of *before* the " Prayer of Simplicity ". It would (in my view) be *quite wrong and quite useless for anyone to try and practise the Prayer of Simplicity, unless he had manifestly got into the Night of the Senses.*

Poulain, on his pp. 7-8 [of the *Graces of Interior Prayer*], seems to think that meditation naturally develops into affective prayer, and then into the prayer of simplicity. I think, on the contrary that meditation stops, and the prayer of simplicity stops it. You turn over a leaf, you don't continue on the same page. It seems to be a small error, but in practice it is a disastrous one ; all pious people (very nearly), most Religious, and many lay people, need help in this matter ; and, if Poulain's system is followed, they will always be directed wrong. In fact Poulain would come indirectly under all the anathemas which St. John of the Cross directs against bad directors in the *Living Flame*.

[1] The reference is to Abbot Butler's work *Western Mysticism*, Constable, London, 1922.

When Abbot Butler reprinted Poulain's Chapter on the Prayer of Simplicity[1], he had not seen this point; I argued it with him, and apparently he came eventually to the same conclusion. In the note to which you refer, I don't think he meant that Poulain *described* the Night of the Senses incorrectly, but simply that he had got it all wrong, because he had put it in the wrong place. Poulain regards the Prayer of Simplicity as *non*-mystic, and the Night of the Senses as a sort of miraculous entry into the mystic realm. I hold that this division of the two is very wrong, and very dangerous to souls.

However you explain ordinary ' *Simple Prayer* ', you must explain the *Night of the Senses* in the same way. If " Simplicity " is non-mystic, then the Night of the Senses is non-mystic. But you must not separate the two ; the Night is the *only* introduction to the simplicity. Consequently I entirely agree with Abbot Butler's condemnation of Poulain, but I agree with you that it is badly expressed, and might be taken to mean that Poulain had not *described* the Night well ; which would not be altogether true.

But suppose I made an accurate description of Westminster Abbey as being the Cathedral of Timbuctoo, one might say it was a totally incorrect description of Westminster Abbey, since the essence of Westminster Abbey is that it is at Westminster, and I am describing every one of its parts wrongly, if I represent them as being at Timbuctoo !

Thus, the essence of the Night of the Senses is that it is the passage from meditation to simple prayer. It is *that*, and it isn't anything else but that. If you describe the Thames Tunnel as going under the Severn, to join Bristol to Cardiff, you are giving a wholly wrong description of it, even if every other detail as to its origin,

[1] Published by the Catholic Truth Society, London, 1911.

date, disuse, etc., are all correct; for the essence of the Thames Tunnel is that it is under the Thames.

The essence of the Night of the Senses, is that the " senses " get into a night, in which they can't be used. St. John of the Cross means by ' senses ', all that satisfies the sensual and sensitive part of man; i.e. the imagination (by the help of which the intellect works, in this life), and the emotions and feelings which come from it. So long as these can work, a man *can* meditate, and *ought* to; the moment they cease to act (and you can't make them act, and the harder you try, the less you do), you must do without them—there is no other course possible,— and take to ' simple prayer ', which St. John of the Cross defines as a ' loving attention to God '.

There are no other possibilities. Either the imagination works or it doesn't. If it does, you can meditate; if it won't you can't. The stoppage is the Night of the Senses, and the Night of the Senses is *nothing more* than this stoppage, and *nothing else*.

Consequently, unless you put it in its right place, it has no meaning. If you make meditation *normally* evolve itself into " affective prayer ", and then into " the prayer of simplicity ", you are absolutely denying the existence of the " Night of the Senses " as invented (I mean ' discovered ', of course) by St. John of the Cross.

Poulain puts it simply as a rare thing (comparatively) —an introduction to Mysticism. This seems to me absurd. If Mysticism is to have any suitable preparation, you would have thought Poulain's system would be :—

Meditation

Affective Prayer

Prayer of Simplicity

Mystical states

But he can't teach this, simply because St. John of the Cross, the 'inventor' of the 'Nights', makes the 'Night of the Senses' follow immediately upon Meditation. Consequently you get in Poulain :—

(pp. 7-8) Normal Course Meditation	(pp. 200-201) Meditation
Affective Prayer	Night of the Senses
Prayer of Simplicity	

He has to admit that the Night of the Senses is very like his Prayer of Simplicity, " but possessing characters, and two in particular, which constitute it a special kind."[1]

I repeat, this is dangerous doctrine : for Poulain might introduce people into the *Prayer of Simplicity* who have not passed through the *Night of the Senses*. (Of course, more often they will have been in it, without his recognising the fact,—so he won't have helped them.) Consequently, he has given a wrong account of the Prayer of Simplicity itself. The 'extracts' he gives (p. 42 *et seq*.) are mostly very good, but not all on the same level; and there are many things in Chapter II (pp. 7-42), which I wholly disagree with, though it is full of valuable remarks. Especially I disagree with his idea of the *essence* of this prayer, as the Contemplation of a " dominant idea " (p. 7), and that it " differs from meditation merely as from the greater to the less " (*ibid*). He tries, on pp. 8-9, to show that this is possible, because it will not be continuous, uninterrupted contemplation, but the same idea bobbing up again and again.

[1] Poulain, " The Graces of Interior Prayer," p. 201.

I hold that such a prayer is psychologically impossible, and that it does not exist.

Poulain's system comes to this :—as you grow proficient in *meditation*, your *affections* come more and more easily, till a minimum of meditation is wanted,—this is No. 2,—*affective prayer*. Then a mere *thought* is sufficient meditation, it becomes recurrent, and suggests a fervent and recurrent, almost continuous act of the Will,—this is No 3,—" Simplicity ".

I hold that this is not merely inaccurate, but the *exact contrary* of what happens.

1. For beginners, who have had little piety, meditation issues in *affections*, at first, with difficulty, then more easily.

2. Second stage. *Meditation* becomes difficult,—then nauseous or impossible. *Affections*, instead of coming easily, *won't come at all*. Meditation and affective prayer grow together, and decrease together, and cease together.

To this *affective Meditation* succeeds, NECESSARILY, NON-AFFECTIVE NON-MEDITATION ; a prayer wherein neither the imagination (and reason which uses it) nor the affections get any comfort at all (except by accident).

Thus progress in prayer is not (as Poulain would make it)

(1) from troublesome, discursive meditation, to easy contemplation of a beautiful thought : and from weak affections to fervent and strong affections ; but

(2) from easy discursive meditation to the impossibility of meditating at all (except by ceasing to pray) : and from easily warmed affections to no affections at all, —to aridity, that is, and to ' Night '.

A. The *primary* objection to Poulain's system is that it *couldn't happen*, for obviously the more you

meditate on anything, the less effect it has on you ;
and the more you exercise affections, the more
they tend to pall.

B. A *secondary* objection is that it *doesn't* happen,—
simply doesn't !

I meant to write only half a page. But this letter
happened to me. I didn't want to ! Please forgive me.

Ever yours affectionately,

H. JOHN CHAPMAN.

APPENDICES

APPENDICES

APPENDIX I

CONTEMPLATIVE PRAYER

A Few Simple Rules

THE signs which indicate that meditation is to be given up,[1] and a different kind of prayer substituted, are described by St. John of the Cross in three places. First, in the *Ascent of Mount Carmel*, Bk. II., ch. 13 (impossibility of meditating, no pleasure in using the imagination, delight in being alone and waiting lovingly upon God); next, in the *Obscure Night*, Bk. I., ch. 9 (dryness, without comfort either in God or in creatures, painful anxiety as to fervour, inability to meditate); and lastly, more shortly, but with more explicit directions as to conduct in this state, in the long digression in the IIId. Stanza of the *Living Flame of Love*, §§ 34 foll.

But many persons pass long years in this dark night, when they cannot meditate, and yet are afraid to contemplate; and the signs may be less easy to recognize. They have tried methods, one after another, they have tried reading and pondering, and then reading again (a good way of keeping off distractions); alas, perhaps they have almost given up mental prayer in despair. They find it hard to believe that they are in the mystical "obscure night". They do not feel urged by a frequent thought

[1] Under the head of "meditation" I include not only strict and formal meditation according to the method of St. Ignatius or any other regular method but all thinking out of some particular subject, representation of mysteries to the imagination, pious considerations, etc.

of God, nor do they dare to say that they have a disgust of creatures. On the contrary, they have found the spiritual life so dry that they have felt thrown upon creatures for consolation : they have often taken refuge in distractions which are not sinful, because recollectedness seems impossible. They have imagined themselves to be going back, because they have no devotion, no " feelings " ; and perhaps they are really going back, since they have not learnt the right path forward.

But they have the essential marks of the " obscure night ", for they cannot meditate—it is a physical impossibility. (When they attempt it, either they cannot even fix their thoughts on the subject at all, or else they fall into distractions at once, in spite of themselves.) Nor do they wish to meditate. They are as able to think out a subject, to work out a sermon, as anyone else is ; but they feel that such considerations are not prayer. They want to unite themselves with God, not to reason about what He has done for them or what they have to do for Him. This they can do at any time, and all day long. They can examine themselves and make good resolutions, they can think of the mysteries of Christ's Life and Death, of the words of Holy Scripture, or Heaven and Hell ; but when they come to prayer, all this vanishes : they feel that if they think, they put themselves out of prayer ; they do not want thoughts about God, but God.

The rules to be observed by those who find themselves in this state—and it is the ordinary state of most of those who belong to a contemplative order—are extremely simple. St. John of the Cross has explained them in the passages which immediately follow those to which I have referred above. But a few notes, founded on his teaching and also on the experience of a number of people, will possibly be useful.

(1) All those who find it impossible to meditate, not from laziness or lukewarmness, and find they cannot fix their thoughts on a subject, or understand the meaning of the words unless they cease to feel that they are praying, are meant to cease *all thinking*, and only make acts of the will.

(2) There is sometimes a period when meditation is sometimes possible, sometimes not. In this case use meditation whenever it is possible. This state will not last long.

(3) Reading a little, or one minute's consideration of some fresh truth, or a few prayers, may be very useful to help recollection at the beginning of prayer. But they are not necessary.

(4) *Let the acts come.* Do not force them. They ought *not* to be *fervent*, excited, anxious, but calm, simple, unmeaning, unfelt. Otherwise there is danger of our sensitive nature and emotion getting mixed up with the prayer. There are to be no feelings. We are not to know what we mean. To some God may some day give more definite knowledge and love; but I speak to beginners. Let us be thankful if we are like this for no more than twenty years.

(5) The acts will tend to be *always the same*. The first stage is usually (I think):—" I am a miserable sinner: have mercy on me," or something to this effect. But the *principal* stage consists of this: " O God, I want Thee, and I do not want anything else."—This is *the essence of pure contemplative prayer*, until the presence of God becomes vivid. (Then it *may* change, and praise or exultation may be the chief or sole act. But I imagine there is no rule.)

(6) For those who are able to practise this prayer, and who feel this *want of God*, interior mortification becomes as easy as it was before difficult. Any wilful immortification

or imperfection stops prayer at once, until it is repudiated.

(7) The time of prayer is passed in the act of wanting God. It is an idiotic state, and feels like the completest *waste of time*, until it gradually becomes more vivid. The strangest phenomenon is when we begin to wonder whether we mean anything at all, and if we are addressing anyone, or merely repeating mechanically a formula we do not mean. The word *God* seems to mean nothing. If we feel this curious and paradoxical condition, we are starting on the right road, and we must beware of trying to think what God is and what He has done for us, etc.; or what we are before Him, etc., because this takes us out of prayer and spoils God's work, as St. John of the Cross says. Probably this is what St. Anthony meant, when he said that *no one is praying really* if he knows what he is and what God is. The saying is often referred to ecstatic prayer; but this seems to rob the words of all interest. St. Anthony must have meant the lowest kind of contemplative prayer, for he cannot have excluded all forms but ecstasy from true prayer.

(8) Progress may perhaps be seen when the acts are less frequent, and we are conscious of one continued act rather than its repetition.

(9) Distractions are of two kinds: (*a*) the ordinary distractions, such as one has in meditation, which take one right away; and (*b*) the harmless wanderings of the *imagination alone*, while the intellect is (to all appearances) idle and empty, and the will is fixed on God. These are quite harmless.

(10) When these latter distractions remain all the time, the prayer is just as good, often much better. The will remains united; yet we feel utterly dissatisfied and humbled.

(11) But we come away *wanting nothing but God*.

(12) The real value of prayer can be securely estimated by its effect on the rest of the day. It ought to produce very definite results :—

(a) A desire for the *Will of God* exactly corresponding to the irrational and unmeaning craving for God which went on in prayer.

(b) The cessation of multiple resolutions. We used to make and remake our resolutions, never keeping them for long. Now we only make one, to do and suffer God's Will—and we keep all our old ones, or rather, they seem to keep themselves without any trouble on our part.

(c) Hence we have arrived at simplicity : all our spiritual life is unified into the one desire of union with God and His Will. It is for this union that we were made, and we have found a loadstone which draws us.

(13) As to progress in knowledge :—

(i) With some people there is *no* knowledge of God or of His nearness, only a blind certainty that He knows our want. We cannot *think* of His being present, for thinking stops prayer.

(ii) But others have a vague undefinable knowledge that God is there. This should be preserved all day, as far as possible, by those who feel it. It grows more and more definite and yet remains just as indefinite : that is to say, the soul becomes more and more definitely conscious of being in the presence of Something undefinable, yet above all things desirable, without any the more arriving at being able to think about it or speak about it —more and more conscious of its own nothingness before God, without knowing how—more and more convinced of the nothingness of creatures, without reasoning on the subject.

(iii) Again, there are *flashes of the infinite*—(it is difficult to find an expression for this)—when for an instant a conception passes, like lightning, of reality, eternity, etc.

These leave an impression that the world is dust and ashes. The effect must be carefully preserved outside the time of prayer. Some people are more liable to these perceptions than others are. In some people they are habitual, and the less valued for this, and they do not produce the fruit in conduct that they ought.

(iv) In the developed " prayer of quiet " the soul does know that God is there. The pleasurable feelings of which St. Theresa speaks do not seem to be essential to the prayer of quiet. But when they are there, the soul may either be urged by them to more vehement desire, or be satisfied, and rather praise than pray.

(14) It is worth noting that Praise is in itself more perfect than simply " wanting " God ; for the latter is rather hope than charity. Praise is the occupation of heaven, when the desire is fully satisfied. Even on earth, to give glory to God is the whole duty of the creature. But to desire God is right, for man must desire in this world, where he cannot be satisfied with creatures, and where he cannot fully attain to God. This is the virtue of hope—the most practical of virtues in this world, the virtue which most obtains for us an increase of charity. And the " want of God " includes charity ; for God is not only desired as our own good, but as being in Himself infinite goodness ; and this desire of Him is in itself a praise of Him for being what He is.

(15) Outside the time of prayer :—

(a) Meditation must never be dropped. It need not be elaborate consideration, but a mere glance at the mysteries of our Lord, especially of the Passion. Most people will find it very easy and helpful to make the Stations of the Cross in private.

(b) Similarly, examination of conscience becomes automatic so long as contemplative prayer is kept up. Good resolutions make themselves.

(c) Imperfections and even sins are such a help to that humility which is the condition of prayer, that they seem almost a help rather than a hindrance. To feel utterly crushed and annihilated, incapable of any good, wholly dependent on God's undeserved and infinite mercy, is the best and only preparation for prayer. It means an entire confidence, an exultation in being nothing because God is all, which brings the only peace which is true peace.

(d) A little practice makes it possible to meditate a little (or at least to retain the thought of some mystery or some great truth) without losing prayer, i.e. the consciousness of God. But this should not be indulged in during prayer time, as it is a half-and-half state, which produces far less effect in the soul than pure prayer does, in which there is no thought.

(e) Every kind of self-indulgence, or fully wilful imperfection (that is, doing what God asks us not to do, or omitting what we know He wishes us to do), makes prayer impossible until it is disowned. For contemplative prayer implies a state of wanting God and wanting God's Will (which is the same thing) wholly and entirely.

(f) But it does not follow that the beginner is to be expected to show at all a high degree of perfection. God does not show the soul all its faults nor all it has eventually to give up. It gives up something, and in time He will ask more. Meanwhile it has faults which are obvious enough to others, though probably not to itself.

A few hints may be added about the prayer itself.

(i) Beginners want to be alone or in the dark. Practice makes this less necessary. But it is rare that a contemplative is independent of externals. It is easier to be recollected when there is no noise, no distraction. The imagination has to be kept quiet. It is generally easiest to pray before the Blessed Sacrament. The night is a good time. The early morning is perhaps the best of all.

(ii) The simplest way of making an act of attention to God, though without thinking of Him, is by an act of inattention to everything else. This is the same act that one makes when one tries to go to sleep.

(iii) As distractions, when involuntary, do not spoil our prayer, and when merely of the imagination scarcely even disturb it, we ought to be perfectly satisfied to have them. We are not to be resigned to them, but more—to *will* them ; for a contemplative is never to be resigned to God's Will, but to will It. The result of this practice will be to decrease distractions by decreasing worry. If we only want God's Will, there is no room for worry.

(iv) One must accept joyfully and with the whole will exactly the state of prayer which God makes possible for us here and now; we will to have that, and no other. It is just what God wills for us. We should like to be rapt to the third heaven; but we will to be as we are, dry, or distracted, or consoled, as God wills. It is just the same out of prayer. We may *wish* for a great many things—for a good dinner, or for more suffering, or the prayer of quiet—without any imperfection, provided these are involuntary wishes. But we *will* only what we have, what God's providence has arranged for us—only no sin, we repeat, only no imperfection.

A Note upon the leaflet entitled *Contemplative Prayer*.
See Letter XXII, p. 75.

In saying that certain paragraphs of this booklet raised questions in my mind, I had no idea of presuming to criticise the writer's statements, which, so far as my very limited knowledge goes, seem to me marvellously realistic and exact.

I mean only that he does bring out with great clearness certain undoubted features of contemplation of this type, which do seem to lay it open to attack on psychological grounds. E.g. Rules 4 and 5 exhibit with alarming frankness the close likeness of the " prayer of acts " to the practices of auto-suggestion. The " unfelt, unmeaning " character of the acts used in this state is particularly significant ; and so is the tendency to repeat the same act again and again (' Day by day I get better and better '!).

The writer gives one psychological explanation of all this ; but it doesn't, I feel, exclude that which would certainly be put forward by the sort of psychologists I have in view, and will be felt as a difficulty by many spiritual persons who have read some psychology— namely, that what is here described is a deliberately cultivated exercise of the fore-conscious, accompanied by inhibition of discursive thought. I have long felt, personally, that the quasi-automatic character of the acts (often quite outside the control of the will) is a real difficulty ; because it does seem to bring this kind of prayer so very close to fore-conscious cerebration—a sort of enchantment of the mind. There must be a difference ; and the writer is just the person who could tell us where it lies.

All this, of course, leaves untouched the question whether grace does or does not operate in this way. Myself, I should agree that it does : my criticism is merely directed to the point that it seems dangerous to leave the matter so expressed that the sort of explanation suggested above *can* be made to cover all the ground, and thus discredit (for many minds) the supernatural value of this type of prayer. Rule 12, again, does not really exclude the auto-suggestion explanation ; and Hint ii plays even more definitely into the enemy's hands !

It is because I feel the booklet to be so admirable, indeed by far the best thing of its sort that I have seen, and am so grateful for its clear, exact and profound directions, that I do wish they could be safeguarded from hostile criticism at just these points.

I have not dealt with the many other questions which I should like to ask ; chiefly as to the relation of this contemplative prayer to Christo-centric devotion, and the way in which those called to it can combine it with intercession. These problems have no critical interest, and merely arise out of my own ignorance and wish for further knowledge.

APPENDIX II

WHAT *IS* MYSTICISM?

In the above title, the emphasis is on the second word. The third word is hateful, modern and ambiguous. But it will appear in what follows how much I include.

Of late years the variety of answers to the question by Catholic writers has been bewildering. This might seem a strong argument for not complicating matters by yet another theory. But if the truth is to emerge from discussion and mutual criticism, such reasoning is less cogent. In this paper an attempt will be made to suggest a view of mystical phenomena which seems a hopeful starting point for explaining their many paradoxes.

Many theologians will at once protest that no explanations are needed : we know quite well what Mysticism is : it is the working of one of the seven gifts of the Holy Ghost,[1] the first, assisted by the second. And so all is clear.

[1] The 'seven gifts of the Holy Ghost' are derived from the LXX of Isaiah xi. 2, which adds Εὐσεβεία, piety, to the six given by the prophet. They are evidently rhetorical, descriptive and cumulative, not mutually exclusive, and therefore not a logical division, being the inspirations poured by the Spirit of the Lord upon the rod and shoot from the stem of Jesse. (The " seven Spirits of God " in Apoc. iii. 1 and iv. 5 seem to be the angels of the seven Churches, symbolised by the seven stars and the seven lamps, and have nothing to do with Is. xi. 2.) Assuming that what is poured upon the Head, comes down upon His members, the Church has used the list in a prayer for the sacrament of Confirmation ; and theologians have taken 'the seven gifts' (distinguished from supernatural virtues and also actual graces) as revealed facts, to be forced into system and logic out of poetry and mystery. Of course they have done it very well. But when we have said that 'Mysticism' is one of the gifts, we have only said that it comes from God, not even that it is extraordinary ; it is only some of the effects of the gifts which develop into the unusual.

But what we want to know is precisely in what way the abnormal data of mysticism differ from the gifts of the Holy Ghost which are normal and necessary for all Christians. It is not enough to name the Giver: we are asking the nature of the gift.

THE THOMISTIC EPISTEMOLOGY. Catholic philosophers teach us that our intellectual ideas are derived by abstraction (the work of the *intellectus agens*) from the reports of our senses about the material world, so that 'there is nothing in the intellect which was not previously in sense'. Although by this means we do rise up to intellectual truth *aliqualiter*, we cannot 'understand' or 'consider' intellectual truths clearly except by using the imagination (which reproduces and newly combines sensations), that is, by 'comparing them with *phantasmata* or images', such as mental pictures or imagined words. This necessity of 'turning to phantasmata' is based by St. Thomas on our constant experience, as well as upon the authority of 'the Philosopher' who says οὐδέποτε νοεῖ ἄνευ φαντάσματος ἡ ψυχή (*De Anima* III 7).

And as a fact we cannot think without imagined words. Not that our thought is not broader than the words, which only half express it; not that our thought is not immensely swifter than the words, which lag behind; not that we are not vividly conscious of this inadequacy in the case of spoken words, in argument or explanation. But we know equally that thought without some symbols of the imagination is vague and only half conscious, and that it has to be embodied, clothed, coloured by us before we can realise it ourselves. When colourless, pure, naked, it escapes from our grasp, like the shade of Anchises.

But angels, we are told, have no need to compare their knowledge with phantasmata, which they do not possess. They are pure intelligences, having no senses, and no imaginations either. It is their nature to understand and consider intellectual truths without further ado. The matter of their knowledge is supplied to them by pure *species impressae*, which are the medium by which they know God above them and material things below them, whereas our *species* are derived by us from sense. Thus their knowledge works the opposite way to ours : we rise from the material to the intellectual, they descend from the intellectual to the material. We know the material world directly (though not immediately) and the intellectual through it indirectly. They know the intellectual directly (though not immediately) and the material through it indirectly.

The reader will very likely at once object that, though the Aristotelian and scholastic theory of human knowledge is a good analysis or description of our actual experience, this scholastic theory of angelic knowledge is purely in the air, without proof or probability. To this I venture to demur. It is true that we do not know much about angels, and it seems marvellous nowadays that Suarez should have written eleven hundred pages quarto about them. But this theory of cognition is not *a priori* ; it seems to be based on the feeling that we can nearly do the thing ourselves, that our knowledge does not consist of phantasmata, but is helped out by them and goes beyond them. And furthermore I wish to suggest that many of those scholastics and pre-scholastics who have worked out the theory were not without an obscure experience of this angelic method of cognition. For I am about to suggest that it would be well to return to the classical explanation of Mysticism,—that it is cognition by pure species, like that of the angels.

The scholastic theologians also teach us that the human soul after death not only retains its consciousness of the intellectual knowledge it had stored in its memory by abstracting from sensible phenomena during life but, besides this, having no longer any brain, senses, imagination, receives pure species connaturally as the angels do, and has no need to 'turn to phantasmata', which it no longer possesses. It follows that the human soul is radically capable of the angelic cognition. It is, indeed, adapted and in this life joined to a body; and in this condition it naturally works in the way we know by the help of the senses and the imagination. But why not in both ways? St. Thomas explains :—

> 'Man is prevented in his present state from the full and lucid consideration of God's intelligible effects by the fact that he is distracted by sensible things and is occupied with them.' (*Summa*, I. XCIV. 1.)

ADAM'S ANGELIC CONSCIOUSNESS. Adam's nature before the fall was perfect, *integra natura*, and his intellect had both powers, the angelic and the human :—

> 'The rectitude of man as instituted by God consisted in this, that the lower [faculties] were subjected to the higher, and the higher were not impeded by the lower. Hence the first man was not impeded by exterior things from the clear and firm contemplation of intelligible effects which he perceived through the irradiation of the First Truth, *whether by a natural or a supernatural cognition.*' (*Ibid.*)

It was in this way that Adam possessed connaturally a clear and direct knowledge of God, such as the angels have by nature, 'by His intelligible effects', or intellectual truths; for 'God is far more eminently seen by intelligible effects than by sensible and corporeal effects', whereas we, in our fallen state, 'are impeded from the consideration of *intelligibilia* by our occupation with *sensibilia*'. (*Ibid.*)

Now this perfect equilibrium of Adam's nature, by which his senses and imagination and emotions were subject to his higher will and intellect, was preserved in him *by divine help*: for created nature is liable to imperfection and disorder, and it is above nature (preternatural) that perfection should be permanent, or completely regained when once lost. Hence St. Thomas says that 'it was by grace that Adam in the state of innocence had that mode of vision which the angel has by nature' (and, we may add, the disembodied soul has also), 'and therefore he is called a second angel' (*Qu. de Verit.* XVIII, art. 1, *ad* 12).

When Adam by sin lost grace for himself and his posterity, he thereby lost this *integra natura*, and fell into *pura natura*, which we inherit. We find that in our *natura pura* (that is, *lapsa et reparata*), the lower part is constantly impeding the higher part: the will is more or less dominated by the senses, the imagination, the emotions, and resultant passions, whilst the intellect is obscured by all these lower faculties, and is frequently applied by the will to unworthy or idle uses.

But we have fundamentally the same nature as Adam, though imperfect; and grace can so far restore us as to allow us a taste of that intellectual banquet on which *integra natura* could feast, by delivering us at least partially and upon occasion from the tyranny of sense. And this does happen, St. Thomas teaches, in contemplation:—

'In contemplation God is seen by a medium which is the light of wisdom elevating the mind to discern the divine (but not so that the Divine Essence is seen immediately); and thus the divine is seen by the contemplative by grace after the state of sin, though more perfectly in the state of innocence.'[1]

Here St. Thomas seems to assume as a commonplace that God can be seen in contemplation obscurely by the same means as in Adam's clearer vision. He takes for granted the classical explanation of " mystical theology".

CAN WE KNOW ANGELICALLY ? So far we seem to infer that the only impediment to our reception of pure species is the distraction caused by the disorder in our soul :—

'The more the soul is abstracted from the body, the more it receives the influx from spiritual substances [this is from Pseudo-Dionysius]; and hence it is that men know secret things in sleep or in ecstasy.'[2]

In the case of prophecy, St. Thomas considers the infusion of judgment together with an imaginary vision

---

[1] *Qu. de Veritate*, XVIII, 1, 1, *ad* 4. Here St. Thomas has distinctly identified contemplation with the quasi-angelic consciousness by infused species. He says that the medium is the *lumen sapientiae*, apparently signifying the first of the ' gifts of the Holy Ghost'. In his commentary on the Sentence (III, *dist.* 35, *qu.* 2, art. 1, sol. 1) he regards *sapientia* as *quaedam affinitas ad divina*, and says (*ad* 1) that it ' proceeds to a kind of *deiform* and as it were explicit contemplation of the articles which faith holds as it were rolled up ' (implicit). The second gift, *intellectus*, elevates and introduces to the seeing of spiritual things, *ipsa spiritualia aspicienda supra humanum modum*. In the *Summa* St. Thomas is more restrained as to the *donum intellectus* (2, 2, VIII, 1). I doubt whether he is exclusively referring to ' contemplative prayer ' in these places ; for a higher light upon revealed truths is not the same as perception by pure intellectual species, though it may result from the latter. In fact contemplatives do receive (without revelations or visions) a higher light upon revealed doctrines, probably by St. Thomas's *quaedam affinitas*, giving more depth or reality, and especially more breadth and unity (like transforming a mosaic into a picture).

[2] *Comm. in Sent. Bk.* IV, *Dist.* 50, *Qu.* 1, art. 2. Similarly *Qu. unica de anima,* art. XV : ' There is no doubt but that the mind is impeded by bodily motions and by the occupation of the senses from receiving the influx of separate (*i.e.* incorporeal) substances ; wherefore to sleepers and to those who have lost the use of their senses certain revelations occur which do not happen to those who are fully conscious.'

to be its characteristic form, such an imagination taking place in a more or less complete trance. But a higher and less typical kind may be by the infusion of intellectual species (or vision) or intellectual light, and these do not imply any form of trance ;[1] but yet they cannot be understood by the prophet or communicated to others without recourse to phantasmata.

' The knowledge of the truth is infused *with such clearness* into the mind of the prophet, that he does not arrive at the truth by the likeness of any images [as in an imaginary vision], but conversely, out of the truth which he has already perceived, *he can form for himself images* to use on account of the nature of our intellect.' (*Qu. de Verit.* XII, *art.* 12 *in corp.*)

Thus the infused truth is perceived clearly (*clare*) before phantasmata are made *ex veritate iam perspecta.*[2]

Apart from such a supernatural infusion as prophecy, we are impeded from thus apprehending pure truth by the distraction of the unruly lower faculties. But nothing suggests that we are totally and inevitably prevented. If the impeding factors are quieted, some activity of the obscured faculty will not be impossible.

Yet daily life tells us that this seldom takes place ; for men are too much occupied by this world.

And suppose it did happen,—well, it might pass unnoticed. For in the beginnings the gleams would

[1] *Summa* II, 2, *Qu.* 173, *art.* 2.

[2] ' In that prophecy which is said to have only intellectual vision, the whole plenitude of the prophetic revelation is perceived in the intellect ; and thereafter *according to the free will of the prophet* images are suitably formed in the imagination on account of the nature of our intellect, which cannot *understand* without phantasmata ' (*Ibid. ad* 2).

Thus we can receive infused species without alienation from our senses : we can *perceive* a pure truth clearly, and ourselves clothe it with images in order to *understand* it ; otherwise our ' combining and dividing reason ' cannot use it.

surely be but feeble. The faculty is disused and (metaphorically) atrophied : we have forgotten how to employ it. It would feel awkward and uncomfortable. We might perhaps try to smother these X-rays under the material and the accustomed ; and this might prove only too easy.

And if they should be insistent and grow brighter ? Should we recognise them for what they are, or simply take them for a waking illusion ? And if at length we should be convinced, how should we manage to 'understand' this new knowledge by 'comparing it with phantasmata' ? Should we not make the discovery that our faculty of thus clothing it, translating it into human language, was more literally atrophied by want of employment ?

I think these questions describe what does happen.

TRANSLATIONS. It is easy enough to make images to illustrate ideas and truths which have previously been arrived at by abstraction from sense. But to explain pure thought by comparing it with sensible images is to translate it into a foreign language, indeed into a barbarous and inadequate language. For how can pure species, angelic ideas, be represented by phantasmata or by words coined for another use ? Obviously only analogically, in the sense that a sound may be called velvety, or a pain may seem shrill. And the analogy will be stranger than this, and the images or terms will be less descriptive than symbolical. He who clearly apprehends a truth with the angelic consciousness may represent it in his ordinary consciousness by misleading symbols, which when communicated to another may be wholly false. At best these likenesses will be mysterious, and will seem unmeaning nonsense to some and admirably unintelligible to others.

When, therefore, a prophet forms images 'according to his free will' to represent the pure truth which has been infused, he is liable to misrepresent it. Divine truth, says St. Thomas, being of its own nature absolutely simple and universal, needs to be first contracted and specificated into Angelic species, and then ' *by Angels* ' is again translated into suitable phantasmata of the imagination.[1] Thus the translation is from God somehow in a true prophecy. St. Bernard had already suggested that the clothing in images of the pure light received in contemplation was the work of angelic hands, *murenulae aureae et uermiculatae argento* ; his description is from personal experience and very beautiful.[2]

It seems that famous saints have often made very bad translations, insisting afterwards that disbelievers of their words were blasphemers.[3] False Mysticism is not only

---

[1] *Qu. de Verit.* XII, 8. For the ministry of angels in prophecy, see the *Summa*, 2, 2, *qu.* CLXXII, art. 2.

[2] St. Bernard, *Serm. in Cant.* 41, 3 :—' to weave certain spiritual likenesses, and in these to bring the meanings of Divine Wisdom into the sight of the mind which is contemplating, in order that it may perceive, at least "by a mirror and in a riddle " what it cannot as yet look upon face to face. . . . For when something from God has momentarily, and as it were with the swiftness of a flash of light, shed its ray upon the mind in ecstasy of spirit, immediately, whether for the tempering of this too great radiance, or for the sake of imparting it to others, there present themselves certain imaginary likenesses of lower things, suited to the meanings which have been infused from above, by means of which that most pure and brilliant ray is in a manner shaded, and both becomes more bearable to the soul itself, and more capable of being communicated to whomsoever the soul wishes.' Cp. Richard of St. Victor, *Beniamin maior* 4, 11 :— ' Exterius uisum introrsum trahit, quando id quod per excessum uidit, multa retractione uehementique discussione, capabile seu etiam comprehensibile sibi efficit, et *tum rationum attestatione,* tum *similitudinum adaptatione, ad communem intelligentiam deducit.*'

[3] Père Poulain has dealt with these curiosities in his twenty-first chapter, with great effect. I instance his remarks on St. Elizabeth of Schönau (§23) and the great St. Hildegarde (§25). The absurdities of these holy nuns were apparently not mere natural imaginations, but partly due to a mistaken rendering of spiritual lights. Note that it is commonly said that ' substantial locutions', like intellectual visions, are always true and good ; they are not translations. Many visions seem to be natural imaginations, with a gloss or glamour from contemplation on the top. Of course, many are pure delusions. The different grades are psychologically interesting, but for piety they have no importance. St. John of the Cross teaches us that visions are not a proximate means of union

found in heretics and unbelievers and reprobates. It is a delicate art to clutch the inapprehensible. Like the farmer's daughter,

"When you try to approach her, away she skips
Over tables and chairs with apparent ease."

And many clutch nothing at all. They are sure they have had an experience. They cannot say even to themselves what it was.

And I believe that still more numerous are those who, because the experience is untranslatable, are unaware that they have had an experience at all. They do not feel there was an illusion, an illusion is more homely, nearer to flesh and blood. There was only an uncomfortable and disturbing stupidity, accompanied by involuntary distraction. The power of 'translation', the only bridge from the 'angelic' to the 'human' consciousness of the same intellect is atrophied and will not work, so that the left lobe of the intellect does not know what the right lobe is doing. It only notices that it cannot itself act freely, that there is a 'ligature'.

THE PRETERNATURAL. Now the only new point I wish to urge in this paper is this: that granting the classical thesis that 'Mysticism' is perception by pure species after an angelic manner, it follows that this lofty manner of cognition is not 'supernatural' in fallen nature, but merely 'preternatural', since it is a scanty and rare survival of that which was connatural to Adam :—

with God. Therefore it is quite unnecessary to decide their nature in each case : the confessor is to say, ' pay no attention to them '. The patient will thus get no harm if they are diabolical, distorted, misleading, or purely natural ; while if divine, they will produce the effect God wishes, without our worrying about them. This is certainly the most authorised advice to give to good nuns and others who experience these things.

a survival of powers of perception and translation disused and atrophied by neglect; obscured and rendered invisible by our concentration on our natural powers; but yet emerging half consciously in a few and overpoweringly in a very few; but traceable in a good many.

Thus neither the faculty of perceiving pure species nor the act of perceiving them is in itself 'supernatural'; obviously not, in its essence; but not even in the sense of 'miraculous'; nor again, in the sense of a 'gift (special or ordinary) of the Holy Ghost',. conferred in Baptism or Confirmation. But it is beyond the ordinary powers which we expect in a human being; it is not needed for daily human life. It comes as a surprise and it even gets in the way.[1]

NATURAL, PRETERNATURAL AND SUPERNATURAL. We have to remember that actual graces are always *supernaturales quoad modum*, that is to say, they are arranged by God to help our salvation. But they may be external, and merely natural *quoad essentiam*,—such as the good examples we see or read of, or the good advice we are given, or the sudden death of some one, and so forth,— but they act upon our souls by the aid of internal grace. As souls grow in piety, a far larger number of things becomes useful to their souls.[2]

---

[1] It resembles, though on a higher plane, the rare faculty of telepathy, by which a few individuals can feel and even visualise friends or others who are in great troubles or at the point of death, at whatever distance. The facts seem to be proved. But the power is preternatural (some extreme delicacy of perception?) not miraculous.

[2] Gradually they realise that *diligentibus Deum omnia cooperantur in bonum*, so that all things and circumstances and events are seen to be intended as steps to heaven and can be used as such, and all that happens to us is God's supernatural Providence, His touch on our souls, and we can thus live in continual contact with Him. From this point of view there is no event, no feeling, no suffering, no temptation, nothing created, in fact, which is not potentially a grace.

Internal graces, on the other hand, are inspirations in the will, illuminations in the intellect, and also similar assistance in the lower faculties. And if I am right that the intellect of fallen man still radically retains the power of acting 'angelically', then grace will certainly be given upon occasion to this higher use of the intellect, as to all the acts of the soul.

Hence in answer to the question, whether Mysticism is entirely supernatural, and due to the 'gifts of the Holy Ghost', according to my hypothesis the reply is this: Mysticism is essentially only preternatural; but like natural things, it is used by grace.

1. As meditation (to take an example) on good things can be practised without actual grace, so can Mysticism by those who are in the unusual case of being able to employ the mystical faculty.[1]

2. As meditation on God and virtue will not be persevered in fruitfully without some divine help, so Mysticism, in so far as perception of pure truth or of God is good for the soul, will have little fruit without divine help.

3. As meditation cannot have any supernatural fruit without elevating and assisting grace, so the pure intuitions of Mysticism cannot bear supernatural fruit without this supernatural element being added. (But as to 2 and 3, let us remember that God always offers actual grace when it is desirable to have it.)

Beyond this point the parallel with meditation does not go.

4. Mysticism is developed in suitable subjects by silence and loneliness, in so far as they quiet the soul.

[1] When God is perceived by pure species, without grace, this is not a part of Christianity, but it belongs to Natural Religion, or let us say 'Preternatural Religion'. But neither Natural Religion nor Preternatural Religion carry men very far *in natura lapsa*, without the grace of Christ, which belongs to Revealed Religion.

But it is more solidly developed by the production of this quiet by mortification and other Christian virtues, which tend to restore our nature to something of its original integrity. In this way Mysticism is a *result* of grace, being increased by ascetic practices done by grace.

5. Mysticism is more than all this, if it is *the survival of a preternatural way to the supernatural,* that is, to God. When we know God by discursive argument from creatures, we have established thereby no communication. God cannot use our argumentation as a telephone through which to speak to us. But if Mysticism gives a direct knowledge of God by created intellectual species, then, however dim the perception, a connexion has been established with Him, a wire along which God can speak to the soul. The same species which manifest His existence, can be varied to express His action, His will.

Hence Mysticism is not merely a preternatural perception of the Divine, but may also be a means of knowing something about the Divine, just so far as God wills to use the faculty for His gracious purposes. Consequently, though neither the mystical act nor the mystical faculty are supernatural, God can make them the vehicle of supernatural communication, in fact a ' means of grace '. And so it is that saintly mystics find that it is in this way that God gives Himself to them, granting revelations to prophets, inflaming contemplatives with His charity, transforming the perfect by union.

But in the lowest grades, the dimmest, darkest contemplation, even when secret and unconscious, God can give Himself; and beginners in the ' Night of the Senses ' may find a supersensible charity, a practical strength in their will, which tells them of God's supernatural working in a way which is infinitely more convincing by its results than any of the sensible graces they are regretting.

This fifth point is therefore the most important; and it is this kind of Divine influx which is attributed by some theologians to the first 'gift of the Holy Ghost', and to the second. As it is a special way of receiving peculiarly desirable graces, and is in the main concerned with increase of charity in the will, it is evidently right to attribute it to the Holy Ghost.

But I do not regard it as the essence of Mysticism, but only as the highest result of Mysticism. The preternatural faculty and act are not necessarily vehicles of the supernatural to us nor informed by charity, any more than they are so to the souls in hell or to the devils. But from the fact that the exercise of the angelic faculty is impeded in us by passions and worldly cares, it must be only in rare cases that it does not imply some detachment from creatures and unworldliness, if not a state of grace.

NATURAL MYSTICISM. It is extraordinary how often children are conscious from time to time of losing themselves in the infinite. With some this is rare, but vivid. Others can induce it in a mild form by (for example) merely looking up at the sky.[1]

Among grown-up people there are great psychological differences, not only in vivacity of passions or imagination, in power of will or intellect, but in the degree of atrophy in their spiritual sense. The well-known examples of Wordsworth and of Tennyson show us detached per-

[1] The *locus classicus* for this is Wordsworth's famous ode, where the poet tries to make his subject more learned and more fanciful by accounting the phenomena to be Platonic ἀνάμνησις, though he is really talking not of the 'recollections' but of the experiences of childhood. In country children, especially, the mind is not so full of images, the reason is not yet working at full energy, the soul is receptive, therefore, and quiet; the faculty of perceiving pure truth is not yet wholly atrophied. The experience is imperfect, and not in the least understood. In older life it will be perhaps totally forgotten. Yet it seems likely that such a child will never become a convinced materialist (except perhaps in words), but will always *know* (without reasoning or feeling) subconsciously that there is a beyond.

sonalities, inclined to loneliness and to communing with Nature, who now and then would feel carried away by the perception, misty and enigmatical, of another reality by the side of which our material world seems itself but a mist and an enigma. In some persons it is rather that the world itself is transfigured in a preternatural light, and is charged with a new and uplifting meaning beyond any words. Here Richard Jefferies is an eloquent exponent. Others find themselves almost in a trance : the world stops, and eternity or *aevum* seem to be perceived and to endure lastingly in a moment of time. To others comes a shattering experience, sudden as lightning and brighter, with no words to tell it, and yet preceded by an anxious inquiry and succeeded by a strange change in the mind's attitude to the material world.

> "I dimly guess what Time in mists confounds;
> Yet ever and anon a trumpet sounds
> From the hid battlements of Eternity :
> Those shaken mists a space unsettle, then
> Round the half-glimpsèd turrets slowly wash again." [1]

DIVINE MYSTICISM. All I have just spoken about is non-supernatural; but I wish to call it preternatural, as being exceptional and above ordinary human nature. But

[1] I quote the often quoted words, because the poet is better than any prose. And speaking of poetry, I add that I imagine the indescribable glamour over the best poetry and over pictures or music, is due to its suggestion of that spiritual light which to the nature-mystic transfigures the world; and the poets and artists who make the suggestion have, perhaps unknown to themselves, seen some half-conscious, or forgotten glow from that light. I do not mean, of course, that these geniuses do not make their chief appeal to our intellect, our imagination, our feelings; sometimes, as in tragedies, or in Beethoven or Wagner, there is a deliberate appeal to our bodily emotions (so to speak) by violence or jerks or noise, and others appeal to sentimentality or to animal passions. But the highest point seems to be reached by a touch which we cannot analyse or explain except by saying it is unearthly, or *übermenschlich*, too deep for tears or transcendent, or some other meaningless expressions, preposterous were it not that they attempt to convey the inexpressible.

there is another curious phenomenon which needs its explanation. Whereas the scholastics assure us that in this life we cannot perceive God directly, but merely by argument, and that we know His nature only by rising up from creatures, asserting of Him all their primary perfections yet in a super-eminent way above our comprehension, and denying of Him all imperfections that we know in creatures,—and, in fact, most people, whether religious or irreligious, would declare that they have no more knowledge of God's existence or nature than this—yet we may stumble across people who assert that they definitely perceive God. They are probably quite ordinary people. I remember a fellow of some College, a clergyman (I forget his name), calmly declaring that all the proofs of the existence of God are inconclusive and illogical, but that this does not matter, as the one sufficient proof is the consciousness, which each of us possesses, that He is. He spoke with great earnestness, as if every one must certainly have the same consciousness ; and he was listened to with respect, but I think not with conviction.

This made me put the question to a monk of admirable and hard-working life, but not likely to be by nature a mystic : ' if you did not know God's existence by argument or by the teaching of the Church, would you know it by prayer ? ' Like *num*, I expected the answer ' No '. But he said instead :—' I am not quite sure : but the feeling of God is sometimes so overpowering.' I fancy that the majority of those religious of both sexes who practise contemplative prayer would be likely to state that they have no perception whatever of God's Presence or of His Existence, though they are conscious of an intense desire of Him and sometimes of an intense love. Those exceptional souls who are torn by a fierce hunger for God would probably say that they rather want Him than perceive Him, that they are more conscious of His absence than His presence, and would put down their certainty of Him to reason and to faith, more than to perception or consciousness. And even advanced mystics are more eloquent about the darkness in which they embrace God, than about any definite consciousness of Him whom they embrace, or about the divine touches, than about Him who touches.

But the more ordinary souls who say they do know God's existence directly, neither by faith nor argument, are perhaps fairly common; and there is no reason why they should be disbelieved; for the same seems to be true of many who practise contemplative prayer, just as it is true of some of the great mystics,—that their experience is definite though incommunicable. When a layman of high rectitude and accuracy of statement, who is also learned in philosophy, assures me that he perceived the presence of God when he was seventeen, and has never lost it since, I neither disbelieve him nor say it is a case of special supernatural grace. To a man who is religious it becomes, indeed, a means of grace. But it seems to me rational to attribute the phenomenon to nature, and call it preternatural in the sense of unusual.

I suggest that this faculty of perceiving pure truth may be compared to that faculty of grasping numbers, for want of which some highly talented people cannot learn to do more than the simplest sums, while a few individuals have a gift for mathematics which makes all easy. Besides these, an occasional freak is found—a calculating boy—who can multiply instantly in his head seven figures by seven figures. So, I take it, there may be many people, very many (though but a small percentage of the human race), who are by nature less obsessed than others by phantasmata, and hear occasional echoes from another world, even when living rather ordinary lives in this one. But often an unperceived and faint influence draws them out of the business and fuss of affairs, and drives them into greater solitude. Most men who journey in deserts, or are alone on heights (unless they wilfully fill their mind with animal thoughts or business or the world they have left), feel something undefined and alluring, something unearthly and expanding, which is a high and super-sensible enjoyment, and it seems to drive them back again to solitude when they have left it.

SOLITARIES. Surely this is a physical effect of loneliness, —the quiet of soul which enables the still voice of another sphere to be half-consciously perceived though not at all explained. This is what the hermits of the Thebaid and Nitria and the Syrian deserts found to be the best condition for the pure prayer and communion with God for which they strove. The mere flight from men and worldly occupations does not draw ' graces' from God (except in so far as it may be a meritorious action done for Him), but it does appear to be a physical condition of abstraction and peace, and of itself to begin a mystical state.

Now our Lord has given us an example and a precept as to prayer. Prayer in common is a part of natural religion, and family and national sacrifice is laid down in the Old Testament; and so our Lord instituted the Christian sacrifice with Communion. But no words of His about common prayer are recorded; He speaks to us, however, of private prayer:—' Enter into thy closet', and His example is striking. We do not hear of His praying with His disciples; but He makes a ' retreat' of forty days with fasting; He rises early before His disciples and goes to a lonely place to pray (Mk. i. 35); He sends away His disciples in a boat, and goes Himself into the mountains to pray all night; with only three companions He mounts upon Tabor to be in solitude;

with the same three He goes to pray in a garden, but goes on alone leaving them behind, and prays three hours.

We learn, apparently, that communion with God is conditioned by solitude and by length of time. Away from men, from worry, from business, our heart and fancy and reason grow gradually still, but slowly, not quickly. If this is the teaching of Christ, we need not wonder if the effect of abstraction is seen in worldly people and in saints, though in different ways.

To sum up what I have said : it seems that some men and women are *naturally* more disposed to Mysticism than others ;[1] that solitariness also disposes to Mysticism ; and that the effects of pure species are 'translated' in different ways by those who are thus faintly influenced by them : in some they cause a kind of trance ; for some they are a kind of glamour or light upon nature ; for some they cause a perception of God's existence or presence ; in others there is an almost violent reaction to them.

MYSTICISM AND PRAYER. We come to a different and higher category. The surest way towards the partial restoration of *integra natura* is by the practice of the virtues, assisted by the sacraments and by the prayer of petition. The science of Christian ascetics deals with this mortification for the taming of our lower nature and its subjection to reason enlightened by grace. Progress in this work ought to produce a quiet in the soul which will facilitate the perception of pure species. And so it usually does.[2]

---

[1] Father Baker's word is ' propensity '.

[2] Again we have to consider different psychological peculiarities. There are those in whom the mystical sense is naturally smothered, in others it is dormant and easily awakened, but the latter appear to be very few.

But we have also to consider the various temperaments, energetic and sluggish, —emotional, sentimental or hard,—imaginative or intellectual,—combined in

THE LIGATURE. But besides 'translation' there is a second way of recognising 'pure rays'. Just as the natural activities of the soul impede its 'angelic' activity, so the latter impedes the former. Just as the *ligamen sensus* binds the soul to act in accordance with the body, so the mystical impressions draw the soul away from this dependence. The results of this are unexpected and disturbing.

I have already mentioned partial trances, where the material world grows dim. Everyone knows about ecstasies and raptures ; and the ordinary theory of them is that the infused light causes them, through the weakness of the body and of its psychical faculties. It is well known that they occur less in those of stronger mind ; and St. John of the Cross teaches that the bodily faculties and the body itself grow spiritualised and more able to support the impact of these rays as higher states are reached ; though the same phenomena may then recur owing to still stronger rays being sent out of the spiritual world.

But this complete ligature, when all the senses, and the imagination and reason, cease to work, is too like a fainting fit to surprise us, when the symptoms are only those of unconsciousness. And when the symptoms are very nearly those of death, accompanied by insensibility, rigidity, and so forth, they are still paralleled by natural sicknesses.

But the lighter forms of this ligature are curious to hear of, and very bewildering to those who feel them ; and to the theorist they come as a surprise.

---

various degrees in men and in women. Where the emotions or imagination or sentiment are very strong, it is difficult for the mystical sense to emerge ; when it does, it is commonly translated into emotions or images or sentiments, and thus becomes very evident, and (St. John of the Cross would say) very 'impure'. Where, conversely, the upper part of the soul dominates, the mystical species are swamped by the activity of the reason, and easily escape all recognition by remaining totally unclothed, untranslated.

The first symptom—and it is very common indeed—
is in ' the Night of the Senses'. A pious person perceives
that he can meditate on holy things as usual, or better
than has been his custom, *when not praying*; but if he
' puts himself in the presence of God ' (as the meditation
books enjoin—whatever this may mean), and prays,
turning his soul to God (the words are symbolic, not
literal), *he cannot meditate*. There is a physical impossibility. At first it may be now and then; but it becomes
habitual. In the same way *it is impossible to understand
the meaning of a vocal prayer when he tries to say it with
devotion*; but he can understand and taste it with intellectual
pleasure if he reads it as a literary production.[1]

The experience is exactly like that of being unable to
understand what one person is saying, because we are
intently listening to another; only in this case there is the
distraction *without any consciousness of what causes the
distraction*. It is, as St. John of the Cross explains, an
imperceptible contemplation which causes this ' ligature '.
The intellect is tensely engaged in seeing something
invisible, looking at a black night, listening to silence,
speaking to someone who is not there,—these are symbolic
phrases,—and cannot do its ordinary work. That is to
say, the discursive reason ceases to act, because the intellect
is occupied with pure species, and the intellect is unaccustomed to do two things at once. There is considerable evidence that in higher states this becomes easier,
and both actions can be fairly well performed at the same
time.

OBSCURE CONTEMPLATION. But there is a third way
of recognising the pure ray. It is the true nature of the

[1] This phenomenon is extremely distressing to those who experience it, but
are unaware of the reason. St. John of the Cross has dilated upon the subject
in the *Living Flame*, and also in the *Dark Night*, and shortly in the *Ascent of
Carmel*, so no disquisition is needed here. For references *v. supra* p. 59 *n.*

will to follow the intellect. In the case we are considering the emotions are quiet, and it is found that the will is fixed on something unknown, just as the intellect is. The proofs of this are not at first obvious: the will is not felt, for it seems empty of love or feeling, because emotion is wanting. Yet an interruption from outside causes a distinct sense of detaching the will from some unfelt act. Further, the prayer began by a blind turning of the will to God, a dry act of love or service. And there is *at least* a definite determination to keep close to God. But the chief proof is in the result: *after prayer is over*, the dry love exhibits itself in acts, and the soul is conscious of serving God more earnestly than before.[1]

So much for the intellect and the will. As for the emotions, they are quiet; but in some persons they follow the will, and there is a distinct sense of pleasure or peace. When this is vivid, as in St. Teresa, it is what she calls ' the prayer of quiet '; but intense pleasure such as she describes is presumably rare, and the ' quietude ' of earlier writers (from whom she gets the term) did not imply this pleasure, which seems to suggest an ' impure ray '. As a rule the emotions are not noticed, except annoyance at recurrent distractions, or possible boredom; the remedy being to accept such accidents willingly with both hands as God's will.

[1] This explains at once the common experience of mystics of lower and higher degree: that they experience ' more love than knowledge '; that they feel intense super-sensible love to they know not what; a hunger for God without knowing why. [St. Thomas's explanation how *aliquid plus amatur quam cognoscitur*, *Summa*, 1. 2, XXVII, *art.* 2, *ad* 2, amounts to this, that people love something according to what they wrongly imagine they know about it !] The will is following an obscure, untranslated knowledge, and the effects in action are vivid and bright. This is the most noticeable characteristic of the spiritual life of contemplatives: instead of loving God for intelligible reasons, instead of serving Him throughout the day for definite motives, they feel they are carried along by grace. They say they are in ' the passive way ' (they are really very active); their virtue is *abandon*, as the French say; their prayer is *de simple remise, et c'est dans cette remise qu'ils trouvent le carrosse qui les emporte bien vite vers Dieu*. The pun is, like mystic experience, untranslatable.

Lastly, but not least, the imagination has to be considered. It does not suffer from the ligature of the intellect and the will; on the contrary, the occupation of these two powers leaves it free, *just as in a dream*. All sorts of images buzz about, and the will allows them to, and does not want to detach itself from the secret contemplation in order to run after the imagination,—and fetch it back. And what would be the use? This flighty and disobedient handmaid of the natural intellect is perfectly useless in the present circumstance; she can have her free time, if she is harmlessly occupied. Only it is difficult in ordinary cases, when the will is not strongly drawn, not to be attracted by these butterfly images, and the will goes after them, and the intellect thinks them,—and lo, we have an ordinary, commonplace distraction! To avoid this, it is recommended to occupy the imagination with the repetition of certain words which are in conformity with the secret action of the will,—words of desire of God, of giving oneself to God, of resignation, humility (above all), prayer, love, praise, etc. This generally goes a long way towards keeping the imagination still, and supplies a light food to the feelings or emotions,[1] which have to be prevented from attempting 'forced acts'.[2]

. [1] As most people only realise what they are doing by observing their imagination and emotions, they usually suppose their prayer to consist in the saying of these words by the imagination and in the slight feelings which are thus aroused. Then they say it is 'prayer of aspirations', or 'of acts', or 'affective prayer', taking the shadow for the reality; whereas it is a prayer of the pure intellect and the higher will.

[2] This analysis shows that it is the imagination which is the trouble. It appears probable that it is rarely kept empty; perhaps only in moments of complete unconsciousness. For there appears to be a certain 'periodicity' in ecstasies, which reach unconsciousness again and again, with less blank intervals wherein the imagination is not void and inactive. It is, indeed, this imagination, the maker of the phantasmata by which we must needs think, which is the characteristic of our human mode of understanding; so that when the angelic mode begins, its occupation is gone, and it wanders about seeking rest and finding none, and is prone then to get into mischief. This is, as I have said, just what happens in dreams, when images float and combine themselves

THE PARADOXES OF ASCETICS. If the preceding theory of the preternatural element in religion is sound, it is at once apparent why the spiritual life is so full of the unexpected. Grace is not likely to astonish us, for God orders all things *suaviter*, and gives His assistance according to our needs and adapts supernatural *auxilium* to the nature He has given us. Whatever seems irrational is from nature or the preternatural. But 'directors' are always stumbling against surds and absurdities !

How easy for a *Directorium Asceticum* to lay down laws for spiritual progress ! Meditate on revealed truths and on the life of Christ, and grow more and more inflamed with charity; make particular and general examinations of conscience, and root out bad habits by good resolutions; get the virtues by practising them, counting up the increase of the acts until good habits are won; and so forth. And all this works so satisfactorily in the 'purgative way', for 'active livers', and progress is seen and noted.

And then a penitent comes and says he cannot meditate; that all his feelings of love have gone; that he can't examine his conscience, though something automatic happens instead; that he can't make good resolutions, only somehow he wants to keep close to God (only that seems to mean nothing particular); and he is quite sure he has no virtues, and never practises any; and his prayer

---

in our brain without control from the will under the guidance of reason,—and our dreams become unreasonable, yet seem reasonable at the time, because the judgement is asleep. And so sometimes contemplation may be a 'sleep of the soul'.

A curious bodily symptom is the incapability of pronouncing the words of a prayer or of reciting the Divine Office in choir correctly, apparently because the attention cannot be fixed upon it sufficiently. How such phenomena as levitation or incapability of eating are caused, I do not know. They are not natural, and they are not 'graces' to the patient; and they do not look like *gratiae gratis datae* for the sakes of others. So they are possibly best called 'preternatural'.

is only distraction. Only he has no sins to confess, except what the confessor cannot accept as matter.

And another cannot go up to God from creatures, but only down to creatures from God. What does all this nonsense mean? And the director will not read St. Francis de Sales, because he is ladylike, and cannot read Grou or de Caussade, because they are in French; and St. John of the Cross is unintelligible, and meant for saints. And so the poor soul is told not to waste his time in prayer; but if he can't pray, to read some meditations, interspersing some 'forced acts', and to be very faithful to his 'particular examen'.

It would be more practical were it recognised that another element has come in. The old methods are now impossible. A new start has to be made, very uncomfortably; and very humbly. It is the entrance to the 'illuminative way', and the soul has left the preparatory school, and feels very awkward as the new boy in the upper school. Everything is unaccustomed, but perfectly simple; very painful, but easy. The whole spiritual life is lived backwards. There is no visible progress henceforward, no room for self-congratulation; only more and more distrust of self and confidence in God. It is not such an anti-Christian way as some people make out! But it is not natural.

SUPPLEMENT

SUPPLEMENT

THE following Letters have been received by the Editor since the first edition of this work was published. It seemed best, therefore, to print them as a Supplement, and to number them consecutively after the previous series, regardless of date: so as to avoid any change in the numbering of the Letters already published.

XCVI: TO A SECULAR PRIEST.

30th General Hospital,
A.P.O. 4,
B.E.F.

Nov. 19 [1916]

My dear . . .

I am sorry I have left your letter so long un-answered.

I think you can easily get into friendly relations with any Benedictine House you prefer, so as to have a place where you can stay for a day or two at any time, to be quiet and pray, and where you will know you are welcome. The actual rules for Oblates are next to nothing. The spirit is what matters,—to share in the prayers and merits of the Order, and to be in constant relations with the monks, and to get some of the spirit of prayer of the monastery into your secular work.

I think Caldey is rather far off from you. I hope it will develop after the war into a very fervent and fruitful monastery. At present, no doubt, its growth is rather stopped by circumstances.

Farnborough is conveniently near, and the French monks are exceedingly nice. It all depends on your personal attraction. The Office and singing are admirable at Downside, if the liturgical side appeals to you, and you have perfect taste in architecture, vestments, etc.! I have never been to Fort Augustus or to Ampleforth.[1]

If you like the French monks, you will find them admirably regular, and wonderfully edifying. Do you want an introduction to any Abbey? I will willingly write to any you wish.

Sancta Sophia is an extraordinarily fine book. I think it has bits that should be read with caution. I don't agree with Lehodey's *system*: but his details are good. As a practical writer, I think a good deal of Saudreau; especially his *Degrés de la vie Spirituelle* (translated by D. Bede Camm, *The Degrees of the Spiritual Life*). That is a very useful and sensible book.

The one important correction I should wish to make in Saudreau's book is one of names or headings;—viz. he makes contemplation begin in the " Unitive Way," instead of following St. John of the Cross, who makes it characteristic of the " Illuminative Way ". Consequently Saudreau makes contemplation seem too lofty and rare; though he does not mean to do so.

If you happen to read Poulain's *Graces of Interior Prayer*, you should note that " The Prayer of simplicity " IS contemplation, and comes AFTER (or " in ") the Night of the Senses, not before it.

The Anglo-Benedictine Congregation has a good tradition of contemplative prayer, handed down from

[1] It will be remembered that Dom John Chapman did not join the English Benedictine Congregation until 1919.

Fr. Baker's time. The present Abbot of Downside[1] is an exponent of it,—largely by example.

I find it difficult to write letters in war time.

Ever yours sincerely,

H. JOHN CHAPMAN, O.S.B.
C.F.

P.S. First Stages of Mental Prayer.

A. (first kind) MEDITATION.
1. REALISING a truth : directed towards making Faith real.
2. Effect on the Imagination and lower appetite : drawing out ordinary imaginations and pleasures.
3. To make Acts : either resolutions or affections ("colloquy").
   Hence :—

B. (second kind) PRAYER OF "FORCED ACTS".
1. Only a little thinking.
2. Many Acts. } (Father Baker)

(*Note* that B. is not recognised by St. John of the Cross. I don't believe in it, except in the wobbly, transition state.)

C. (third kind) CONTEMPLATIVE PRAYER, in which
1. the Acts are *not* forced, and
2. are *not* the prayer : but only an accompaniment to avoid distractions.

But between B. and C. as above, or as an introductory stage of C. many modern writers place :

[1] Dom Cuthbert Butler.

327

C. The Prayer of Simplicity, i.e. continued acts or
thoughts, with perhaps the thought of some mystery
as a kind of " base ". They put this after, or in " The
Obscure Night ".[1]

30th General Hospital,

July 19, 1917. *Calais.*

My dear . . .

I am so glad to hear that you are to be ordained Priest
on St. James's day. Please accept my congratulations,
and the assurance of my prayers.

Apart from what you rightly say about the " general "
spirit of the monastic order, there is another difference
between " third orders " and Benedictine *confratres* or
oblates. A third order only implies union with the order,
and a desire to exercise its spirit, with the help of a rule
of life. The Benedictine oblate is, further, usually in
close touch with some individual community. In the case
of Franciscans and Dominicans, the *unit* is not the house
or the province, but the Order. In the case of monks,

---

[1] In connection with the above it is interesting to compare the analysis of
the late Abbot Butler who, in his last work, *Ways of Christian Life* (p. 225)
gives the following table of the successive " stages " in mental prayer.
" (*a*) Discursive Meditation.
  (*b*) Affective Prayer.
  (*c*) Prayer of Forced Acts of the Will.
  (*d*) Prayer of Loving Attention, or of Simplicity.
  (*e*) Prayer of Quiet.
  (*f*) Prayer of Union."
It will be observed that he differs from Abbot Chapman in making a definite
stage of " Affective Prayer " between Discursive Meditation and the Prayer
of Forced Acts. Both writers, however, agree with St. John of the Cross and
St. Francis de Sales in placing the Prayer of Simplicity as the first, or lowest
stage of " Contemplative Prayer " which is within the reach of all souls " of
good will ". The two higher stages (*e*) and (*f*) are, of course, recognised by all
authorities as " extraordinary ", and only to be reached by means of a special
grace from God unobtainable by any human efforts.—Ed.

the " Order " is not a real entity, but a fiction derived from the analogy of the thirteenth century orders ; and the unit is not even the Congregation, but the individual Abbey.

Consequently, Parish Priests organise third Orders as parochial confraternities, and large numbers are aggregated to them. Whereas Benedictine oblates have little relation with any common organisation save the Abbey to which they are affiliated.

I suggest this, as it is to be considered when you decide upon belonging to some third order of oblateship.

I did not remember your showing yourself " moody " at Caldey ! I believe *The Christian Platonists of Alexandria* is a good book, but it is some time since I read it. Of course it should be read cautiously,—and that is true of all books.

The best account of the first centuries is (in many ways) Battifol's *L'Église naissante*,—English translation has a slightly different name, which I forget. There is a continuation about the fourth century,—I forget the name! I am sorry to be so inaccurate, but I have no books or memory.

Many thanks for your prayers, which I need very much.

Ever yours in Dīno,

fr. JOHN CHAPMAN, O.S.B.
C.F.

XCVIII: TO THE SAME.

Hôtel Rosat,

SS. Peter & Paul, 1918.   *Château d'Oex.*

My dear . . .

It was very kind of you to write and tell me about the letter in *The Tablet*. The frontier is often closed for a fortnight together, so that letters come very irregularly, and consequently I do not trouble to have any newspapers sent me. I read the Swiss papers only!

I don't see how I can take any notice of the letter, as it is forgotten by this time. I do not know what the controversy was about, so I cannot write fruitfully upon it! And I feel sure that no Catholic who knows me can possibly suppose I think that there is any mean between being inside the Church and outside it.

I wonder if this Mr. N. (I never heard of him) has got hold of a point I have made once or twice : Popes (notably St. Leo I) used to " refuse Communion " to certain bishops without deposing them, as a sign of displeasure—that is to say, they would not deal with them or write to them directly. It was a sort of minor excommunication, as a disgrace : though not strictly an excommunication at all. St. Leo refused to deal with the Eastern bishops who had toyed with Monophysitism, " let them be satisfied with the communion of their own provinces," and be thankful that they are not deposed ;—this was (of course) after they had submitted and begged for pardon. This seems to be exactly the way in which Theophilus of Alexandria was treated by Rome after his persecution of St. Chrysostom and similarly the way in which Flavian of Antioch was treated by Siricius. When St. Chrysostom became bishop of Constantinople, he got the Pope to restore his communion to Flavian ; and Theophilus's nephew and successor, St. Cyril, was given communion by Rome, apparently only after having consented to put St. Chrysostom on his diptychs—(this has been denied, but I forget now where I discovered a proof that St. Cyril *did* accept St. Chrysostom's memory).

I think it quite likely that Mr. N. has got hold of statements of mine about this. But he may have got hold of some other point, and misunderstood it. And I may have expressed myself stupidly, as in the sentence which you quote of mine, about a " schism " being " justified ". Many thanks for so kindly writing.

Ever yours sincerely,

H. JOHN CHAPMAN, O.S.B.
C.F.

XCIX: TO THE SAME.

Commissione per la Revisione della Volgata,
Roma—Palazzo San Calisto,

Nov. 27, 1919.   *Trastevere,* 14.

Dear Fr. . . .

I was demobilised to Rome in March, and was at Downside from July to October. I gave a Retreat at Paris on my way back here. I shall be here, presumably, for Vulgate work every year from October to July—summer at Downside.

I send you a leaflet reprinted from PAX. St. John of the Cross gives the signs of entrance into the " illuminative way " and Contemplative prayer, in the *Obscure Night*, I. 9. It is difficult for most people to practise such prayer, unless they are living an exceedingly quiet and solitary life, or at least an enclosed one. It is easy enough for enclosed Nuns—*almost* all.

Yet from what you say, it sounds as if you are drawn to remain quiet from time to time. If so, by all means do not resist, and think you are doing nothing, but try to keep off all distractions, and remain attentive to God— or to the Incomprehensible. But the whole proof seems to me to be the *effect* of this prayer on a person's life. If the result is that they are more recollected and feel some loss of delight in worldly things, then the prayer was good.

331

Dom Guéranger, founder of the French Congregation, was so enthusiastic about liturgy, that he gave no instructions on contemplative prayer. Benedictines *in general* have just preserved so much of ancient tradition that they recognise that they cannot and need not meditate by strict rule; yet I do not think one can say that any tradition of contemplative prayer, in the strict sense, has been kept anywhere except in the English Congregation—which has been till lately the most "active" of all,—and this simply because Fr. Baker's *Sancta Sophia* has always been an *official* manual, given even to the novices. As a rule, Benedictine monks have practised a sort of half-and-half meditation, i.e. "affective prayer",—a little consideration, a good deal of "affection" (in words), very often ejaculatory prayer repeated (thus being close to the practice of a contemplative),—but *avoiding distraction in the wrong way*, by trying to think, instead of trying not to think. (The result is in many cases extreme boredom in meditation, because distractions naturally increase instead of diminishing.) Hence all sorts of recommendations as to pious thoughts, to act as helps against distractions, and to induce the peace of contemplation. Dom Guéranger and his followers always recommended the words of the liturgy, as next best to Holy Scripture. You will find many pious monks trying a sort of see-saw of half-consideration, half-affection (=contemplation), with varied success. I don't condemn this. It is unsatisfactory—but then so many have arrived just inside the Dark Night so that they cannot get anything out of meditation, yet are not sufficiently solitary, recollected or (perhaps) earnest, to get any definite "contemplative prayer"—and it is so easy to lose it after getting it,—and it is so *absolutely necessary* to refuse nothing that God asks in order to keep it,—and it is so impossible to give God all that He asks except by the help of this prayer,—that it is very usual for those

on the threshold to remain in a wobbling state for years
and years. It is the " way " of those who have " left the
world ",—and how few leave the world. But some have
a slight, or a great, or an enormous " propensity " to this
prayer,—and for all these it is easier to begin it. (Just
as some people are naturally charitable, or unselfish, or
chaste, or good-tempered.)

But I am sure a vast number of people would practise
it, if they only knew about it.

As to " attainable by all ", as to which you ask,—I
should say : *Yes:*—in the sense that all are radically capable
of it. *No:*—in the sense that in ordinary circumstances
it is impossible for most people. For a few people (of
strange psychological composition) it is possible under
ordinary conditions of life. For a few it is almost impossible
even in an enclosed community, and the desert would be
wanted! For *most*, it is unlikely, except in a quiet life,
with much time for God.

I shall like to hear how you get on. I promise you a
memento at Mass. Heart-felt thanks for your prayers.

Ever yours in D̅n̅o̅,

H. JOHN CHAPMAN, O.S.B.

C: TO A YOUNG RELIGIOUS.

Downside Abbey,
Near Bath.

[1933]

Dear Brother . . .

It is plain that, in making solemn vows in a Religious
Order, we throw ourselves in darkness into the arms of
God, believing that henceforth our life will be directed
by obedience to our Superiors, without any of that prudent
consideration and provision for the future which is proper

and necessary for those who have to govern their own lives in the world. This is what is meant by the Fathers when they speak of " blind " obedience, and it is the great consolation and the peculiar privilege of the Religious State.

As Religious we hold by Faith that, in an Order approved by the Church under Superiors whose jurisdiction is derived from the Sovereign Pontiff, who is the supreme Superior of all Religious, we have a right to believe that every detail of our life of obedience is not merely pleasing to God, but is exactly what God wants of us. The perfection which God intends for us by this subjection is worked out in us by the very imperfection of the Order or house to which we belong, and the faults of our human Superiors ; and our obedience is due absolutely in every conceivable case, except where there is manifest sin.

We have, therefore, to live in the darkness of Faith, which unites us to God, and not in the light of our own judgement. If our will goes after ideas or ideals or illuminations of our own, however admirable these may be in themselves, we are acting directly against our vows and the essence of the Religious Life, as laid down by the Saints, and most of all by the Holy Rule of St. Benedict : we throw ourselves out of God's arms, who is carrying us straight in the darkness, and follow our own human lights—excellent, perhaps, were we in the secular state, but incompatible with the abandonment which, by God's special grace, we have chosen and embraced by our profession.

Yours very sincerely in $\overline{Xpo}$,

H. JOHN CHAPMAN, O.S.B.